AF763007

LAW AND IMPERIALISM: CRIMINALITY AND CONSTITUTION IN COLONIAL INDIA AND VICTORIAN ENGLAND

Empires in Perspective

Series Editors: *Tony Ballantyne*
Duncan Bell
Francisco Bethencourt
Caroline Elkins
Durba Ghosh
Advisory Editor: *Masaie Matsumura*

Titles in this Series

1 Between Empire and Revolution: A Life of Sidney Bunting, 1873–1936
Allison Drew

2 A Wider Patriotism: Alfred Milner and the British Empire
J. Lee Thompson

3 Missionary Education and Empire in Late Colonial India, 1860–1920
Hayden J. A. Bellenoit

4 Transoceanic Radical, William Duane: National Identity and Empire, 1760–1835
Nigel Little

5 Natural Science and the Origins of the British Empire
Sarah Irving

6 Empire of Political Thought: Indigenous Australians and the Language of Colonial Government
Bruce Buchan

7 The English Empire in America, 1602–1658: Beyond Jamestown
L. H. Roper

8 India in the French Imagination: Peripheral Voices, 1754–1815
Kate Marsh

9 British Narratives of Exploration: Case Studies on the Self and Other
Frederic Regard (ed.)

Forthcoming Titles

Slaveholders in Jamaica: Colonial Society and Culture during the Era of Abolition
Christer Petley

Royal Patronage, Power and Aesthetics in Princely India
Angma Dey Jhala

LAW AND IMPERIALISM: CRIMINALITY AND CONSTITUTION IN COLONIAL INDIA AND VICTORIAN ENGLAND

BY

Preeti Nijhar

Routledge
Taylor & Francis Group
LONDON AND NEW YORK

First published 2009 by Pickering & Chatto (Publishers) Limited

Published 2016 by Routledge
2 Park Square, Milton Park, Abingdon, Oxfordshire OX14 4RN
711 Third Avenue, New York, NY 10017, USA

First issued in paperback 2015

Routledge is an imprint of the Taylor & Francis Group, an informa business

© Taylor & Francis 2009

© Preeti Nijhar 2009

All rights reserved, including those of translation into foreign languages. No part of this book may be reprinted or reproduced or utilised in any form or by any electronic, mechanical, or other means, now known or hereafter invented, including photocopying and recording, or in any information storage or retrieval system, without permission in writing from the publishers.

Notice:
Product or corporate names may be trademarks or registered trademarks, and are used only for identification and explanation without intent to infringe.

British Library Cataloguing in Publication Data

Nijhar, Preeti
Law and imperialism : criminality and constitution in colonial India and Victoria England. – (Empires in perspective) 1. Criminal law – India – History – 19th century 2. Criminal law – Great Britain – History – 19th century 3. Criminal justice, Administration of – Social aspects – India – History – 19th century 4. Criminal justice Administration of – Social aspects – Great Britain – History – 19th century 5. Constitutional law – Great Britain – Colonies 6. India – History – British occupation, 1765–1947 I. Title
364.9'54'09034

ISBN-13: 978-1-138-66512-5 (pbk)
ISBN-13: 978-1-8519-6639-4 (hbk)

Typeset by Pickering & Chatto (Publishers) Limited

CONTENTS

1 IMPERIAL MIASMA

> Man is human only to the extent to which he tries to impose his existence on another man in order to be recognized by him. As long as he has not been effectively recognized by the other, that other will remain the theme of his actions. It is on that other being, on recognition by that other being, that his own human worth and reality depend. It is in that other being in whom the meaning of his life is condensed.[1]

Introduction: From Fragments to an Empire

The literature on the relationship between Victorian England and imperial India is growing with a welcome contribution from Subaltern Study scholars. The latter increasingly emphasize the dynamics, the bilateral relationship between the two societies. Previous assumptions of the passive role of indigenous peoples in those processes have been overturned by varied empirical studies.[2] Scholars are increasingly turning their gaze to questions of empire, colonialism and post-colonialism, in order to provide an understanding of imperialism, and to the dynamics of imperialist technologies to the colonial project.[3] This book adds to that body of literature by examining the intimate relationship between law and imperialism, in which two case studies of legal similarity and difference, are offered here.

In *Law and Imperialism,* we consider the marked reduction of the legal status of the non-Western, by examining the active contribution of both the colonials and the colonizers, to changes at the imperial centre. The growth of Empire was not a one-way process in which British agencies constructed Indian society in their own image. Rarely has there been serious discussion about the role of India itself, which made its own significant impact on British structures, culture, discourses and behaviours, than a previous generation of historians acknowledged.

The trigger for the development of such a historical view has not been a sudden revelation, a paradigmatic breakthrough, but the accumulation of apparently significant insights. This approach aims to fill a particular lacuna in critical legal studies:

'law has been to the forefront of that very relation. Yet the lack is also understandable because the engagement between law and postcolonialism would drastically disrupt legal academic renditions of the relation – disrupt not just the persistent orthodoxy of law and development, but also the newly settled consensus around law.[4]

My purpose, then, in *Law and Imperialism,* is to disrupt this main mode of engagement between law, empire and the colony. We offer, and indicate, from such minor details, a set of analytic and conceptual tools that are adequate to understand the enactment and function of similar legislation governing the lives of lower social strata in both societies. Such a concurrence appears in the wording of the Habitual Criminals Act of 1869 in Victorian England, and the Criminal Tribes Act of 1871 in imperial India. Simple questions arise from that legal congruence. Was the similarity of legal discourse simply a matter of exigent duplication? Alternatively, did it represent the way the governing executives perceived social collectivities in an identical way – to which a near-identical legal prescription was the solution? Asking these questions in turn raises further issues; why was this legislation (focused on lower social strata in England and India) characterized by inquisitorial assumptions of guilt prior to any evident infringement? Contrary to the new adversarial Victorian practices of legal codification, these measures appeared to be a remnant of an earlier age, when classes of persons, rather than classes of actions, were the object of legal penalty.

From these initial questions arise larger enquiries of history, of law and of imperial relations. Legal fragments, when linked with the structure of knowledge in which they are embedded, contribute to a mosaic about the rationales for the embodiment of inequality in criminal law reform in Victorian England and in imperial India. Newly assigned socio-legal statuses of criminality reified the categories of 'dangerousness' in both jurisdictions. The so-called 'criminal' tribes and castes of India,[5] were legally and socially constructed contiguously to the identification of 'dangerous' classes[6] in Victorian England. Concepts of 'race', emblematic of a demeaning social Darwinian status, played a key significant role in this process. Such 'racial' discourses enabled political elites to sanitize, to segregate through a legal prophylactic, the social contagion of a lower order species, which might undermine social stability.[7] Victorian law, both in the metropolis and in colonial India, aimed to contain these emerging threats and to affirm unequal statuses. Here the operative role of the law is to preserve those identities. Hence, the legal judicial reasonings and its processes had a structural function in stabilising the relationships between social unequals in the metropolis and in imperial India. It was also affected by particular contingent agencies.[8] The new mosaic assists in the creation of a postcolonial paradigm in which the empire did not just exist 'out there' but also 'at home' where, as an imperial social formation, it makes its presence felt in institutions and values at the heart of British society.[9]

Discourse and the Assemblage of Empire

Empire (that hugger-mugger of a term, as we now belatedly understand) was not a process of intentional growth. Indeed the very term itself is essentially a weasel-word that fails to reflect the nuances, the subtleties of imperialism. It is a euphemism, a hubris that conveniently summarizes a variety of projects, of national designs and of subjectivities. Though this book focuses narrowly on the relationships between England and India in developing a dialectical understanding of both entities, those national signifiers may be misleading. 'England' in the late Enlightenment was a term used generically to cover the practices of the nascent nation-state of England, Wales, Scotland, and to a lesser extent, Ireland. The India of Warren Hastings, with its myriad of minor domains and jurisdictions – some principalities in their own right, other vassal dependencies, often owing more to accidents of territory and nominal history – was not that of the post-'Mutiny' period, when the British Empire annexed de facto what it had already achieved de jure in replacing the East India Company (EIC, 1600–1858). However, while those and similar reservations arise throughout the literature, we will continue to use that shorthand terminology while recognizing their subordination to more eclectic and larger notions of the East and of the West, of the Orient and of the Occident, as well as indicating more complex local entities.

The colonial and postcolonial realities have been obscured and misunderstood as a consequence of persistent and ingrained ideas that have structured traditional scholarship on the history and theory of criminal law. Processes of colonialism and later of the more substantive imperialism, have been open to varied historical interpretation. Several of the polarities of latter accounts latter are perversely pertinent, and have an enduring effect on this study. For instance, the early materialism of Marx's view on India has matured into a notion of cultural imperialism. Here, ideology underpinned the interests of the original international robber barons, who by accident or by design, carved out stepping stones in the construction of a globe coloured pink in Victorian Atlases, 'where the sun never sets'. From that angle, colonies were there to be exploited, furnishing cheap labour, valuable materials and in George Bernard Shaw's words a market for 'adulterated Manchester goods'.[10] Conversely, at the other polarity, institutional histories have been important. Such Whiggish discourses of moral progress constitute a major theme, of varying but continuing importance through the period. Pioneering evangelism did not fade during the nineteenth century as illustrated by the efforts of the Salvation Army in India and the colonial training in the

Christian public schools (hallmarked by a Spartan manliness, self-control and discipline, and an absence of emotional expression[11]) to which many early and later administrators owed their provence. The direct appeal of those adventure stories where the white Englishman always triumphed and behaved impeccably, instilled middle-class values in countless public schoolboys, who would always 'play the white man.'

For others, the colonies were a site of experimentation – the later paternalistic socialist New Lanark could be developed in virgin territory. They were 'laboratories of modernity',[12] where the new sciences could inter alia create ethnological human zoos in which to experiment on primitive character. The Enlightenment commitment to modernity, reason and free will, had given birth to a bastard child, that of positivism. There are other versions of imperial history, some more important than others, lying between these extremities of interpretation. Some approaches have coexisted or have been discarded. Others have often been more opaque in their contribution. Whatever the connections between the colonial and postcolonial interpretations, the explicitly and unquestionable European character of law has been characteristically asserted by historians. That view consists of a series of doctrines and principles that were developed in Europe, ideas which emerged out of European history, experience and values systems that were extended to the non-Western world. But one difference does stand out legitimately in the most recent postcolonial interpretations. The colony, however circumscribed by competing definitions, and its inhabitants, contributed as an agency rather than simply as a victim. The unilinealism of colonial export has largely been dismantled. Colony was not simply an empty space to be filled and incorporated by imperial authority. Its own dynamic processes, history and subjectivity, ensured a different project and identity. From that perspective, as in Cooper and Stoler's exposition of a cultural Marxism,[13] the major failure of histories of empire have been the insensitivity, to the dialectical relationship between the colonizer and the colonized. Law, criminal and civil, was one major instrument in this process of colonial reconstruction. Law was a hybrid creature, and far from being peripheral to imperialism, was central to its formation. However, law had to be seen to be responsive to a variety of situations, including those involving non-Westerns in both the metropolis and in colonial India, for its own integrity and identity.

A Word on Discourses

This book extends the aphorism of 'watching St Giles to guard St. James'[14] – surveying the rookeries of London's St Giles parish to prevent its dangerous inhabitants threatening the Palace of Westminster – in several ways. Firstly, it uses the term 'policing' in a Foucauldian sense,[15] to include not only the direct agents of the state entrusted with implementing the new forms of control but also, more importantly, different legal regulations and doctrines. Secondly, the term 'scientific racism' is shorthand for the pathological measurements – scientific theories of racial difference, imbued with the mythology (such as that surrounding the uprising of 1857 in Cawnpur, especially of British heroism and native barbarism, confirming notions of inferiority and superiority). Such sentiments and attitudes were given further credence through the Victorian genetic and anthropometric sciences – as part of the process of governance. The St Giles dictum was conventionally applied to Victorian London, and less specifically to other British urban milieu, it was also applied generically to Britain's colonial territories; in this case, to parts of India during the replacement of EIC rule by imperial suzerainty. Further, the key term utilized throughout is the notion of 'dangerousness'. This imperial logic of the dangerous type associated in the presence of home rule in India with 'racial characteristics' mirrored the broader currents of understanding in Victorian England. Often used by Victorians as a synonym for the criminal classes, dangerousness with its evocative imagery is the key to appreciating the importance for understanding the imperial conception of the criminal tribes of nineteenth-century India. Finally, the text borrows from the language of postcolonial theory, Edward Said's imagery of the Occident and the Orient, with its insistence on the binary divisions between the Western and the non-Western, and also Homi Bhabha's ambivalence, in which the problem of identity is one of proximity to, rather than distance from, the Other.

Within the postcolonial theoretical framework, the self can be dehumanized by practices of othering. However, without the examination of these exclusionary practices, based on essentialist concepts and scientific logic which were central to the imperial project, this book would be at a loss. Central to understanding the key theoretical concerns of the book are academic discourses, such as a revisionist criminal justice history; the contribution to that eclectic body of studies from the developing body of postcolonial theory, from critical legal studies and from criminological social constructionism. These insights are relevant, not only in examining the key concerns of this book, but necessary also to uncover the ambivalent and contested sites of identity formation. Further, the book draws upon a range of published works, as well as raw empirical data from colonial legal archives, to break down binaries of imperial discourses, in order to disrupt and challenge the orthodoxy that sustained the practices of law and imperialism. It is the intimate relations between the Europeans and its racial Others which lies at the heart of this study. An introduction to theory and methodology is now in order.

A Hybrid Approach to Understanding: Identity and Subjectivity

In this book, three key elements of methodological inquiry are adopted. The first is a comparative method; the second a critical historiographical reading of primary and secondary sources; and thirdly, a case study approach to provide an analysis of the 'dangerous' groups in Victorian England and their equivalent form in imperial India.

A few words first, on my methodological concerns. Comparative methodology requires establishing certain features common to disparate groups or societies as well as a range of factors which are different and which need to be explained in the linking of the commonalities. This book focuses on two comparable situations and collectivities: the 'criminal' classes of Victorian London and the 'criminal' castes and tribes of imperial India. While there are clear differences between the two situations, there are similarities of image, of space, of social status and of social structure. One represents an internal colony (with its ethnic component), the other an external colony (India). In essence, each collectivity was subject to a variety of 'scientific' descriptions. Each was spatially confined to a particular 'here be dragons' space. Varied techniques and doctrines structured their social and physical locality. Each collectivity lay at the base of its respective social pyramid. Indeed, each could be said to be marginal to the larger stratification system – a kind of underclass. During a period of rapid social and economic change, whatever their past practices, the groups labelled as 'dangerous', were forced to adopt new survival techniques.

Whilst there are similarities between the two instances, there are also differences – superficially: the urban context of one, being adjacent to the structures of England's emergent industrial economy, contrasts with the other being confined to the periphery of Empire. Using the case study approach, this book argues that particular features of similarity between the two societies are more important in explaining their contiguous experience of discretionary legislation.

The understanding of imperial law is enhanced by a historical consciousness of what constitutes the legal process in different societies, and how different types of offensive behaviour are identified in colonial and postcolonial societies. Concepts of dangerousness and of the criminal type provide unifying themes and the basis for research strategies, highlighting the importance of the historical perspectives through a postmodern understanding of crime, law and social change. This historical sensitivity furnishes a link between the present to an understanding of the past, in the continuity of attitudes that have been regularly employed by indigenous postcolonial elites and Western states in their suppression of the lower strata and the non-Western. Critically examining past narratives, especially the British Parliamentary Papers, EIC legal records and related primary and secondary archival materials, allows a reinterpretation of official sources, adding to our understanding of how narrative traditions were situated, and who they were designed to persuade. Through a history enriched by competing narratives, however fragmentary, these accounts invite us to look beyond objectivity and see a wide range of subjective possibilities and new actors. This study affirms an alternative legitimate non-Western discourse by examining the topology of dangerousness and its statuses and social history in both the colonial and Orientalist histories of India. It transcends the master narratives, in which the history of India was constructed from Western categories, to a social history of India, which has been reinvented in recent times outside the nationalist framework of the state, especially in the highly influential series of Subaltern Studies. The colonized criminal subjects do not remain in these pages as passive victims of colonialism. In this text, these subjects became participants in a moral and cognitive venture against their oppression. In doing so, we aim to broaden our understanding of the intimate relation between the non-Western and Western, and between agency and power. Readings of various cases and illustrations from the archives reveal the extent to which the 'natives' make (albeit limited) choices. Only a new theoretically informed historiography can make sense of their experience.

Given this insistence, it may be productive to adopt an analysis based on a case study approach. Case studies permit a deeper qualitative reading of experience, which quantitative studies often fail to document. The main technique of case-study research has been to isolate populations in similar situations with the intention of discerning some more generally applicable features. The methodology in this text has been informed by Yin's (1994) model of case-study research,[16] which prioritizes the role of theory in the design and selection of cases, and provides a framework for their analysis. For example, concepts such as race, in any given period, cannot be isolated from their specific context. Racial classifications and scientific taxonomies are always contingent and never pre-fixed. Such a stance draws upon prevailing historical discourses, and shapes narratives in highly ambiguous ways, especially in relation to the use of myths and stereotypes. Further, these themes are articulated with other problematic questions of modernity and progress, which inform ideas about law, order and dangerousness. By moving away from conventional methodologies that conceptualize British imperial history in terms of a discrete separation between the metropole and India, and by engaging the histories of Britain, we can reconceptualize the processes through which imperial identities were formed, sustained and challenged.

By locating the case studies within a comparative methodology, the relationship between the metropolis and the colony, especially with its dangerous groups, can be uncovered in order to expand and enrich our understanding of imperial relations of domination and of subordination within the legal context. The formation of identities and the debates about law and order in both settings, coupled with the ideas about race, provide for a more comprehensive understanding of how relations of inequality were constructed, maintained and eventually challenged. To explain this tension, we draw on two instances, the discussion of the constitution of dangerous types in colonial India, and their equivalent form in Victorian England, to offer insights and provide a piece of the jigsaw in the continuing debate on modernity, of criminal law, and of postcolonialism.

The Beginnings: Chapters and Mapping the Territory

In order to understand the dynamics of colonial and imperial identities, Chapter 2 lays out the theoretical contributions in assembling the mosaic of imperial identities. Sequentially, the chapter provides a summary of the inputs from critical criminal justice history, from postcolonial theory, from critical legal studies and from social constructionism. Importantly, criminal justice history underpins the study, furnishing several key tenets. The latter provide an understanding of the processes of criminal justice, which is central in analysing larger social relationships and social structure, especially in relation to hierarchies of inequality. In such conceptions, certain forms of deviant behaviour defined as criminal may simply reflect a process of social conflict between unequals. However, and as later chapters reveal, lower social strata historically have had their survival practices defined as criminal in order to justify and maintain their inferior status. Most importantly, the survivors' own story is often missing from the institutional histories. Therefore, crime may be better understood as an active component in the struggles against their assumed betters.

Postcolonial theory, in its different guises, is essentially about understanding the identity of the different parties in colonial relations. Identities of the opposing parties are unstable and frequently derived from labels assigned to them, rather than a result of specific proclivities. The modernism assumed of the imperial state, and in its categorization of dangerous types on an evolutionary scale, may simply be a statement of difference. The labels serve to unravel the imperial state's anxiety over its own status, which is managed by applying definitions of the 'criminal,' and the 'savage' to exclude its colonial subjects. Identities, far from being stable in their construction, are inherently unstable, and remain forever in an ambivalent relationship to the thing being constructed and those doing the construction.

Critical legal studies furnish three central insights. In the context of the modernization of the common and criminal law of Westminster, and essentially its core assumption on an adversarial process and technique, certain groups remain within an essentially inquisitorial and unequal status. Legal equality does not equate to social equality but merely camouflages the latter. More pointedly, law in relation to the designated social outcast is permissive, allowing legal advantage to be taken against the socially and economically weak. Finally, social constructionists emphasize that the key focus in understanding crime and deviance, should be on the processes of definition, rather than on the actions of the assumed offenders. Criminality is a label created by colonial legal authorities for their own purposes, and reveals the anxieties inherent in those who engage in defining and labelling the Other, and tell us less about those defined as part of the criminal class or caste.

Chapter 3 and 4 engage with the two major discourses that structured racist views of subordination in Empire: law and science. Under the mantle of superiority, the West constructed legal and scientific discourses to label the non-Western population as inherently dangerous, in both imperial India and in Victorian England, in order to alleviate its own fears and anxieties. The analysis of this legal discourse distinguishes not just between form and substance, but also within form itself. Statutory principles were one thing. Practice was another. The Benthamite adversarial reforms promised equality of all citizens, and delivered otherwise. Inequality was a product of the exigencies of practice. But inequality was also intrinsic to the nature of law itself. Inquisitorial powers such as the vagrancy legislation weighed, by definition, most heavily upon the lower strata. The habitual offender was a legal construct, not a specific object. Similarly, civil statutes such as the Poor Law emphaized the presumption of guilt of those in need, unless they could establish otherwise. Appeal under the array of policing, criminal and civil, was rarely an option. Policing systems operated to confine the poor and the ethnic, to curtail their 'nomadic' habits. As Chapter 3 demonstrates, generic legislation and functionaries confined the lower strata of the metropolis and of the Empire within a punitive straitjacket, despite protestation of legal citizenship, in the construction of hierarchical identities.

More pointedly, Robert Young's comment that academics invented racism may be hyperbole.[17] But in the history of the subordinates of Empire, it has considerable truth. Chapter 4 considers the discourse and debates of scientific racism and how it reached its apogee, as a key informer of policy, in mid-nineteenth century England. Contrasting monogenetic and polygenetic accounts of origins, ethnographic and anthropological academic disciplines, and their offshoots, such as craniology and anthropometry, were in conflict throughout the process of colonization. Competing initially with religious accounts of difference, through much contortion, scientific racism came to complement evangelical Christianity in underpinning inequality in Empire. The latter was a laboratory within which specimens could be drawn and experiments conducted, as a key legitimation for imperial policy of tutelage. Travellers, administrators and missionaries furnished their experiences to amplify the scientific record, though like academics, they conflicted over nature versus nurture in the product of the savage. During the critical period of legal incorporation, inheritance theories dominated. Social Darwinism (already nascent before the birth of that author) was reconstructed to legitimize a ladder of evolution which comprehended the imperial world as perceived by England's elites. Science, especially later in its criminological guise, justified prejudice in converging with legal discourse to construct imperial identities.

Chapter 5 uses, *inter alia*, the example of the Vagrancy Act of 1824,[18] with its origins in early industrial England, to demonstrate how collectivities were socially excluded and labelled as dangerous. Through the lenses of social constructionism, the chapter demonstrates how the West, obsessed with the clarification of its identity, seized upon such labels to determine their separate status. In applying the insights from the previous chapters, Chapter 5 concentrates on analyzing the construction of the traditional notion of the *white* Victorian 'dangerous' class, consisting of the indigenous English labouring classes, and/or the social residuum[19] of the Victorian rookeries, the migrant Irish and other dislocated groups. It describes how criminal justice policy in England absorbed a new disciplinary discourse.[20]

The criminal classes were created through the conflation of law, of crime and of new racial sciences. Facilitated by a Utilitarian philosophy, the aim was to create a rational bureaucratic regime, embodying both legal practices and spatial divisions.[21] This new configuration was directed at containing the emerging dangerous classes, which included the vagabonds, the petty thieves, the habitual criminals, prostitutes, and more generally, workers in the secondary economy of the street, and inhabitants of the urban rookeries – against the backcloth of the transformation of England as a mercantile capitalist society. Significantly, these recalcitrant Others were defined and signified not in terms of their offences, but rather in terms of their propensity to commit crimes, by the nature of their characters, their appearance, their physical location and their associations. The continuing socio-economic changes had produced a residuum, no longer easily disposable by transportation. In short, as a result of expansion overseas (to India and the colonies) and the perceived internal threat from the urban 'dangerous' types, much of criminal policy was shaped into a system of scrutiny, control and discipline, and the penal system, as reconstructed in the wave of reform from the 1830s onwards, to deal with this social mass. Suspected individuals frequently defined as guilty on the sole basis of no fixed abode, or of no stable occupation, were sentenced under the Vagrancy Acts, later came under the direct gaze of the Habitual Criminals Act of 1869.[22] In essence, we explore the legal production of the subject through the modes of its articulation, through various operative legal discourses, of criminal justice institutions in which the non-Western subject is formed. In particular, the book reveals the transformative potential of these subjects as they are revealed as subjects to, and disruptive of, these formations. The non-Western was located deeply within, yet excluded from, the grounds within which they were significantly constituted: the legal system.

More importantly, in Chapter 5, the new processes of law and enforced social segregation were a response to territorial and social aggrandizements, and resolutions of problems of social control as England extended its domain beyond the Irish Sea through the ventures of its mercantile capitalists.[23] This incremental imperialism created a diaspora in which various ethnic groups were transported as migrant labour to England, contributing to the diversity of the threatening masses. These ethnic minorities disrupted existent Victorian identities. As a result of imperial tensions and anxieties overseas, the new ethnic minorities came to share similarities in image and in ascribed status with the metropolitan 'dangerous' groups. For example, from an early part of the mid-nineteenth century, the specter of habitual 'criminals' waging war on society loomed large in the minds of those who enforced the law, and created criminal policy.[24] The criminal types were portrayed as a 'race' of outcasts (*sic*) addicted to crime, not simply as an economic necessity, but as self-reproducing – as a way of life. Criminological positivism, especially the figure of the monster, the criminal type, sits prominently in the process of racial thinking and identity formation and became an ingredient of the new human sciences, committed to racial notions of difference. It was this differentiation process which was appropriated to label groups as dangerous and irredeemable in both the metropolis and in colonial India. Imperial trade had constructed a transient group of Asian and African sailors, the lascars,[25] as well as a more permanent population of domestics, the ayahs.[26] The chapter argues that the West Africans,[27] Afro-Caribbeans and various destitute Asians[28] were now confined ethnically in Victorian England under the label of the 'dangerous' classes. Legally discriminatory practices, used initially against both the Irish[29] and the so-called Atlantic residuum,[30] were now applied to the non-Western, both socially and spatially. In short, as their contractual relationship was terminated, many ayahs and lascars found themselves on the streets of London, Cardiff and Liverpool.[31] The new discourses of surveillance, control and punishment were extended from the indigenous lower classes to include a complex ethnic component as a 'criminal' class, resulting in the enforced removal of individuals to workhouses and poorhouses, and to destitution and death on the streets of the metropolis.[32] The constitution of the ethnic component amongst the criminal types functions to uncover the mediated links between the metropolitan and the colonial situation. The South Asian population in Victorian England was more extensive and heterogeneous than is evidenced by the orthodox emphasis on indigenous and Irish components. Visible minorities among the metropole's newcomers, as well as the earlier Irish, were fragmented.

Chapters 6 and 7 draw upon the previous analyses to assess the social and legal denigration of the lower strata in colonial India. Similar to the presence of the non-Western in the metropolis, which was portrayed popularly in scientific racist terms, a similar set of terms of inclusion and exclusion were used for the 'criminal' tribes and castes of colonial India. In parallel developments, the Indian 'dangerous' castes and tribes were treated within a similar legal form, while differing significantly only in spatial location. Like the Habitual Criminals Act of 1869 in Victorian England, the Criminal Tribes Act of 1871[33] in colonial India was articulated and reified to contain many itinerant tribes and castes that posed a threat to Western identity. Dangerousness, nomadism and vagrancy were the defining features.

The criminal types in India expand the construction and reveal the similarities in legal reification, in containment, exclusion and imagery. The metropolitan experience of its dangerous classes was integral to the Indian developments. More importantly, in colonial India, a remarkably similar criminal and legal discourse was apparent. Criminal law excluded many colonial subjects by portraying them as pathological and irredeemable, while simultaneously including them as subjects of the evolutionary process, imposing an Anglo-Saxon legal mode of incorporation. Western ideological construction extended the same mode of comprehension to its own indigenous population, when constructing an Indian social hierarchy of those who could be included – the 'martial races',[34] and the Brahmin castes, and those who were excluded – including the innately and irredeemably 'criminal' tribes and castes. Colonial technologies employed to manage this fear and tension, aimed to subordinate or co-opt within the system, some figures, by singling them out as 'martial', noble and warrior like.

Chapter 6 draws upon the work developed by the Subaltern School of Indian historiography. It links colonialism and law with the subordination of indigenous social strata. European presuppositions were the standard against which the criminalities of the dangerous castes and tribes of colonial India came to be understood. These modes of assessment,[35] of measurement, and the subsequent marginalization of the 'dangerous', were key methods appropriated to criminalize the subalterns. Transfer of English criminal procedure and practices to India involved two linked stages, both influenced, if not fully determined, by Benthamite and Utilitarian modes of thought. The first stage required familiarization with the laws of India – both Muslim and Hindu. The second involved the construction of particular criminal laws for imperial India. For example, the key institutions of justice, especially the police,[36] drew heavily not only upon British and Irish precedents, but also incorporated and subordinated many of the combined functions performed by indigenous policing agencies.[37] The result was not so much a totally new modern criminal justice system in India, as the incorporation of indigenous laws into an inchoate Western model. The effects of the new structure of criminal laws, of penality, of the establishment of criminal tribe settlements under the Foucauldian[38] supervision of evangelical agencies such as the Salvation Army[39] and of penal reformatories, are evaluated in Chapters 6 and 7. The Indian system of caste provided a neat recognizable system, through English eyes already familiarized in part to the division between the 'respectable' and the 'dangerous' classes of the metropolis, to gradations grounded in a racial dichotomy between purity and impurity in India. These racial differences, with clearly defined distinctions between the Aryans[40] and the non-Aryans, the 'pure' versus the 'polluted', furnished the colonial project with racialized stereotypes of 'natives,' the barbaric savages, to facilitate the legally sanctioned hierarchical regimes of discipline which were deemed necessary for the 'orderly progress' of imperial destiny and identity.

The constitution and the surveillance of the Sansi as a criminal group and their proclamation under the Criminal Tribes Act of 1871 is the focus of Chapter 7. This limited[41] case study of the Sansi furnishes an example of the social and legal construction of a particular caste as 'criminal' in the North West Province of Punjab. The Sansi are important but relatively undocumented in colonial criminal justice history.[42] The Sansi[43] were the largest tribe to come under the direct measure of designated[44] gangs and dacoit tribes as a group of 'nomads'. Few historians of criminality and criminal justice in India[45] have acknowledged the suppression and the criminalization of the Punjab Sansi population. The Sansi, labelled criminal, in contrast to the alternative positive stereotyping of the Punjabi, as a 'martial race' (in English parlance – the contrast between the 'roughs and the respectables' of Victorian England). Disciplinary legislation and procedures were used to remould the recalcitrant unproductive Sansi communities into 'useful' participants in modernity and towards some sense of civility. In essence, the Criminal Tribes Act of 1871 was also used against many other smaller communities, the wandering tribes, the nomadic petty traders and pastoralists, the gypsies and the tribals. The 1871 Act was applied to a wide variety of marginals who did not conform to a pattern of settled labour.[46] The 'criminalization' of various castes and tribes often stemmed from changes associated with imperial economic policies which led to episodic famines[47] across imperial India.[48] Criminalization frequently resulted in many tribes and castes being confined to criminal settlements. In many cases, where moral panics related to the colonialists' own crimes and punishments,[49] the reaction was to transport those so defined across kala-pani[50] (black water) to the imperial penal colony of the Andaman Islands.

However, and as it will be shown throughout the succeeding chapters, although often subordinated within dominant discourses, the criminal type is not utterly subjugated there. The subjugated, whether it is the lascars or the ayahs of Victorian England, or the Sansis in colonial India, through the discourses of power, often resisted and even reframed them in empowering terms, and did achieve access to the very resources and spheres of power from which they were intended to be excluded. Exclusion was not absolute, and law had to be seen to be responsive to alternative voices and resistance.

More pointedly, the tensions in the two case studies presented here illustrate the ambivalent relationship of the law with its criminal types. The revelation of the non-Western in these two instances challenges the theoretical trajectories that dominate so much literature on law, empire and colonialism. A crucial argument is that the formation of these criminal types and subjects, and in particular the way in which they stand as agents, is neglected in typical accounts asserting the existence of colonial law and order.

To return to our original position, the concluding Chapter 8 conflates the comparative, historical and case-study material through the heuristic vehicle of the Indian Census of 1872, to answer the original questions regarding the similarity in the constitution of dangerous groups in Victorian England and in imperial India. Drawing on the body of overlapping critical legal theory, from revisionist criminal justice history, from postcolonial theory and from social constructionism, the similarities between the two domains can be explained in a comparable way. Imperial tensions found a voice through the law, and these efforts at containment of the non-Western in both settings, are especially telling, for ultimately they reveal the identities of both entities. Those so constructed as innate criminals and beyond redemption, were criminal types that threatened the social hierarchy, and by its very presence, endangered social identities. Stereotypes used by the Western to categorize and 'criminalize' the recalcitrant in the metropolis and in the colony, were not just coincidental, but a direct result of the same problem, however modified by local exigencies. Imperial identity was created, sustained and challenged, in a constant reference to the non-Western population it feared. The savage heathens who were readily classified as 'outside', especially in imperial India, were also 'inside' the walls of the 'enlightened world' – the West. The proximity of the Other in both settings reveals the similarities in the methods deployed to alleviate Western fears. Certain aspects of criminal law and various symbols were abstracted from the metropolis and given a new meaning in the colonial setting, just as social categories and caricatures had been abstracted from colonial India to be applied to the 'dangerous' classes of Victorian England.

What is significant here is that neither identity nor difference, as is suggested throughout the book, could have been complete, or indeed been possible, without the Other. The encounter between the colonized and the colonizer was real. The reactions to this 'dangerous' encounter along the boundary of 'savagery' revealed the divisions and instabilities inherent in imperial identity. As a result, Western identities were managed through the imposition of the law. Western law, through the construction of the non-Western as 'backward', 'dangerous' and 'criminal', resolved that anxious predicament. The repeated attempts to preserve Western identity cannot be separated from the image of non-Western identity. The Western identity is, in fact, derived from its actual association with the non-Western. In that resolution, what is significant is that the metropolis's judicial structures not only helped shape colonial India's judicial system but preconceptions about the latter also framed the judicial structures in the metropolis. The constitution of 'dangerous' groups in colonial India was influenced by parallel developments within Victorian England. The colonial construction of 'dangerous' groups, which gave rise to the Criminal Tribes Act of 1871 in India, reflected similar tensions and anxieties which gave rise to the Habitual Criminals Act of 1869 in the metropolis. In sum, the insistent and contrary presence of the criminal types in both settings makes explicit the connection between racial and cultural conditions and forms of governance in general, and in doing so, as we shall see throughout the book, also makes explicit the relation between the dangerous and normal types, a relation that is as intimate as it is fraught and anxious.

2 THEORY AND THE CONSTITUTION OF DIFFERENCE

> 'Criminal tribes – er – I don't quite understand' said Paget.
>
> We have in India many tribes of people who in the slack anti-British days became robbers, in various kind, and prayed on the people. They are being trained and reclaimed little by little, and in time will become useful citizens, but they still treasure their hereditary traditions of crime, and are a difficult lot to deal with. By the way, what about the political rights of these people under your schemes? The country people call them vermin, but I suppose they will be electors like the rest.[1]

Introduction: Contributions from Criminal Justice History

To answer the questions outlined in Chapter 1, this text relies principally on an array of scholarship and insights from a critical social history of criminal justice. Such ideas have their origins within the Warwick[2] contributors of the 1970s and 1980s, as well as in later feminist work. The older approach from Hay et al.,[3] E. P. Thompson and the more recent Subaltern studies, interpret the specificity of crime and punishment practices from a particular reading of the data on criminal justice history in England and Wales, and also in colonial India. Social conflict and social relations can, in effect, be 'read off' from the history of criminal law and of its application. Integral to that work is an emphasis on the biases in the rule of law, criminal stereotyping of lower strata and partisan crime control, together with symbolic public punishments, which were the social cement of class relations of Georgian and Hanoverian England.

The paramount lesson drawn from the earlier works is a critical stance on the normative presumptions that structure both 'criminalization' of the dangerous classes and subsequent historical readings. For such critics, crime and criminality are a microcosm of larger social conflicts. The perpetration of crime, its legal construction as an offence, and the policing of that criminality, signifies covert conflicts between different social formations. Criminal justice processes should be understood as the essentialism of divisions over political and economic resources and – to an arguably lesser extent – over gender roles. Larger structural forces are at work within the minutiae of local and central criminal justice practices.

Amongst other relevant examples of such work is the justly famous reference for any study of the operation of law and its limitations is Chambliss's seminal study of English vagrancy legislation, *Analysis of the Law of Vagrancy (1964).* As the interests of the dominant social classes changed in England between the sixteenth and the eighteenth centuries, so did the focus of legislation on those who were to be criminalized. Fluctuation in definitions of vagrants, related to changes in the material problems facing the social order.[4] Shortages of labour resulting from the Black Death culminated in vagrancy statutes to retain peasant workforces.[5] In the late seventeenth and early eighteenth century, with the rise of a new mercantile class, original vagrancy statutes were now extended to cover the 'vagabonds' and the 'gypsies', who threatened mercantile trade on the King's Highways. In the early nineteenth century, the same legislation was used against a new class of offenders, the 'idle beggars' and 'hawkers', whose means of livelihood undermined the economic prospects of the new class of urban shopkeepers.[6] Accordingly, the meaning of crime and vagrancy changed according to economic imperatives.

Methodologically, the Warwick School was committed to a 'history from below'. The Subaltern Studies group adopted a similar approach, concerned with 'recovering' the experiences of those who have been hitherto 'hidden from history'. A central issue for the Subaltern Studies group is the representation of the experience of colonization from the perspective of the colonized. The Subaltern historians argue that the colonized were not, as is overly represented, passive victims of colonialism. They were actors, representing themselves, in an uneven contest. They produced their own history.

These historical insights were later modified. The grand designs of criminal law as postulated by the Warwick historians did not always function as planned.[7] Agency and context impacted. The major objectives of criminal justice in both India and England were relatively clear-cut, aiming to stabilize class relations as a prerequisite for imperial trade and local tax collection. In India, the emblematic Collector occupied a more dominant role than that of Magistrate, though often combined in the same functionary. In reality, as Skuy illustrates, legal practice did not always follow the directly defining discourse.[8] Much of what was actually implanted in imperial India owed more to pragmatic resolutions, to limited sources of knowledge, and to the contingent role of particular individuals. Agency by the latter ensured that the process of criminalization was two-way – the locals fought back either directly or indirectly, and modified outcomes. Hence, the process of criminalization was unilinear. There is an interplay between those defined as criminal and those enforcing criminal law. In other words, those subject to the criminal law sometimes affect the identity of the definers. Agency modifies structure. On the anvil between two competing forms of legalism – on the one hand, a dominant class seeking to impose the 'rule of law' over the locality, on the other, local peasantry committed to the preservation of their own cultural practices and normative order – agency found a space (as in Hay's classic essay on poaching[9]) demonstrates. Cultural practices were uneasily maintained, independently of external coercion through law.

Similar to the postcolonial theorists, the later Warwick historians maintain a commitment to the relative autonomy of agents, while conceding the restriction at externalities imposed by structure. Their work illustrates the way in which various survival techniques, commonly referred to as social crime, were appropriated by the lower strata to combat their impoverishment – for example through poaching, wrecking, rioting and machine-breaking.[10] In colonial India, collecting the 'fruits' of the forest from restricted locations was a necessary everyday occurrence. Agency was maintained, not just as a riposte to the power of the external forces, but also through autonomously derived indigenous practices and cultures. In this text, postcolonial studies and critical criminal justice accounts converge in this discourse, articulating the experiences of those defined as subordinate strata, to further our understanding of the historical emergence of criminal laws, the conditions of its operation and limits. This is an interdisciplinary project that takes the form of bringing criminal justice history back into the history of colonial law and order in India. This practice illuminates one of the most telling instances with which this book grapples – the tensions between the Western and the non-Western, law and empire.

Discourses of Postcolonialism, of Law, and of Social Constructionism

This chapter pursues three discourses, which furnish the meat within this criminal justice sandwich – postcolonial studies, critical legal scholarship and criminological social constructionism. Postcolonial theory makes three important contributions to explicating the initial legal conundrum. It recognizes that culture, has a life partly autonomous of the material base of the colonial relationship. Secondly, (as above) it recognizes the power of agency, appreciating that the subordinates have a limited freedom to affect their own destiny. Postcolonial theory gives expression to 'voices from below' – the discourse of the subaltern in expressing those histories and desires. Thirdly, postcolonial studies demonstrate the power of cultural definitions, as embodied in the authority of legal discourse, as a means of structuring power relations. Identities, on both sides, are constructed in that process. These themes link directly with the epistemology of critical criminal justice history.

In this chapter I draw on two related arguments from recent critical legal studies. First, I take issue with the orthodox view that English law was drastically reformed between the eighteenth and nineteenth centuries with equality of trial procedures extended to the common people. The evidence in this text suggests that the opposite was true for castes and criminal tribes in India and for the labouring and criminal classes in England. Indeed, it is the unequal exchange between castes and classes that provides a telling instance. Secondly, I claim – counter-intuitively – that the extension of English criminal law and citizenship throughout the imperial domain reinforced social inequality rather than creating equal citizens before the law. In particular, rights embodied inequality of status. The modern law, the law of the bourgeois white male, operated with its constitutive negatives – of equivalence, of modernity and civilization which are posited in contrast to custom, savagery and the irredeemable heathens. Our concern here lies with an understanding of the way the tensions of empire, both at home and abroad, were managed through law. Finally, this chapter outlines the criminological discourse of social constructionism. Here heuristic insights directly link historical and postcolonial critiques. Social constructionism is primarily concerned with the application of demeaning labels to subject groups and the conditions under which such designations adhere. Unlike its earlier manifestation as labelling theory, social constructionists argue that stereotyping is neither a one-way process nor simply a function of interpersonal relations. Rather, the identities of both parties are contested, curtailed and managed. Master statuses as deviant and criminal are frequently sourced structurally, rather than interpersonally. Defining labels result from a power struggle between unequals which have a self-fulfilling effect. The defined collectivities come to assume the characteristics imputed, subject to agency and resistance.

The First Wave of Postcolonial Theory: Edward Said

The discourse of postcolonialism arises in the interstices between a reductive Marxism and structuralist accounts of imperial relations.[11] This book takes its place in a larger movement of intellectual inquiry that started, for better or worse, with the pioneering work of Edward Said's *Orientalism,*[12] representing the first wave of postcolonial theory, and the new orthodoxy on colonialism and the construction of identities. It locates the discussion of law and colonialism in its social and political context. Said innovated by demonstrating how Oriental identity is constructed in relation to its apparent opposite, the stability of a European identity.[13]

Said's text provided a relief from the traditional Eurocentric character of scholarship on modernism and post-modernism. It relied heavily on Foucault's formulation of the structures of power and knowledge. However, Saidean discourse, while appearing progressive, seemed to maintain the integrity of the models of Orient and of the Occident. It treated the different identities as separate rather than as reflective, the Orient as unstable and shifting, the Occident as stable and unquestioned. Saidean discourses represented non-Western value systems as defective and artificial, in which 'European culture gained in strength and identity by setting itself off against the Orient'.[14] The West's past was systematically represented as the present of the non-Western world. What the modern West had once been, during its pre-modern incarnations, now characterized the colonized, which remained rooted in the trough of the non-modern.[15] As such the Orient was labelled as backward, superstitious and traditional. Through its own claims to reason and to modernity, the West became the measure of everything valuable, culturally and psychologically. It was the professional expert to the Orient in diagnosing the latter's sickness. Indeed, the Occident understood the latter's predicament as being incapable of appreciating itself, because the Orient lived in its present (the Occident's past), having no conception of an alternative future. Thus, the West knew and knows the Orient's future better than the Orient itself. Its shortcoming, however, is that the latter still has to approach modernism, for it remains attached to a past that is devoid of any reason and modernity, whereas the West has already achieved its goal. At work here is a powerful subtext of universal morality, an inherent human understanding that emanates from Europe.

Without any denials, this reductive mode of reasoning and thinking is still prevalent in both historical narratives and evident in the ongoing subjugation of the non-Western. This logic of difference, as between the colonizer and the colonized, the modern and the subhuman, is assumed to be the primary driving force. Non-Western forms were deemed chaotic, uncontrollable, disorganized, irrational and morally inept – at a different point in the evolutionary chain to the West. For example this reading of the undisciplined, the insensitive, the savage Other permeated many aspects of the West's dealings with the non-Western. That orthodoxy was a hallmark in the fabrication of the Orient. Non-Western values and normative structures were represented in stark contrast to those of the West, as traditional, primitive and lacking the contours of modernity.

There are fundamental flaws in this Saidean construction of binary opposites, which have often been overlooked, oversimplified and may be reductive in nature. Given that this binary constitution was so central to Said's work, he declined to provide us with a clear definition of the constitution of the Occident. More pointedly, although Said's theoretical position at one level is informative in its position on the essentializing project, it is especially insightful to the technologies of violence and typologies of racial types which were used by Europeans in colonial India and Victorian England. However, on the other hand, while it is clear that pertinent functionaries, Warren Hastings, Colonel Sleeman and J. S. Mill, among others, might be seen in such terms as Said describes, to speak for the Orient, and thus to create it in the minds of their readers, theirs are not the only representations of the Orient that exist. The myriad forms of violence unleashed and perpetrated by the colonials, was resisted and reframed, when the 'natives', especially the criminal castes and tribes, fought back against their oppression and articulated opposition. Similarly, in Victorian England, there are instances in which both the lascars and the ayahs resorted to acts of violence, in order to survive the menace in the metropolis. The very fact of the existence of such historical accounts disputes the point Said makes about the Orient as only being spoken for, from outside, by Europeans. There exist representations of this Other, which are presented through his/her eyes in Victorian England too. Given the importance of these alterative voices to the imperial project, Said's binary logic is fractured by the silence with which it operated to further silence this Other, in both the metropolis and in the colonies. Divisions are no longer credible. It is these tensions, as ambivalent as they are fractured, inherent in the identity of both the Western and the non-Western, that we shall trace out in colonial India and their equivalent form in Victorian England, which ultimately represent the limits of law, modernity and imperialism.

The Second Wave of Postcolonial Theory: Homi Bhabha and the Subaltern School

The later critique of postcolonial draws upon the work of Bhabha[16] and of the Subaltern Studies group. In those conflated studies, the Western state created an imperial domain, both 'within' and 'outside' institutions, which allowed it to reinforce its own identity and self-confidence. The constitution of criminal tribes and castes in India (like that of the criminal classes of nineteenth-century England) had been given by Said an uncritical identity, located within a problematic notion of modernism. This second wave of postcolonialism shows how the identities of both the colonizers and the colonized were continually renegotiated.

These postcolonial scholars argue that Said was confused over the status of the Orient,[17] especially as he had generalized about the progressive nature of Western identity by creating an opposite, composite stereotype known as Orientalism.[18] The main mode of postcolonial engagement lies in the study of the West's relation to its Others. The second wave took issue with the assumption that Occidental and Oriental identities are unstable, in an unfixed relationship. The former self is not a given. Its identity is as open to change and instability as that of the Orient.[19] Central to that process is the necessity of projecting an image of the Orient as resembling the West at an earlier stage of history so that the different trajectories of the two, and their relative position on the evolutionary ladder, can be justified. Assumptions of colonial social and legal progress were based on a myth of modernity informed by the notions of superiority, of progress and of civility inherent within Western identity in that process. Modernity, as the embodiment of progress, is a façade. In its essentialism, it is unstable, displaced from evolutionary history – not modern at all. The modern state should logically be able to accommodate a plurality of cultures. This acceptance of differences is possible, however, only if it excludes the particular and the contingent, to which a modern rationality is opposed. The contradiction, contained within modernity, reveals its insufficiency as it fails to accommodate the non-Western. This ambivalent relationship poses a difficulty for Western consciousness. The proximity of non-Western peoples threatens to reveal that the lack of modernity attributed within the imperial identity,[20] is a mirage, and ultimately based on myth. In this respect, Bhabha has pointed out:

> Orientalism betrays the desperate activity of a 'Western consciousness' which may, more productively, be regarded as less concerned with the assertion of a constant superiority and more with the anxious attempt to conceal its own fissility.[21]

More pointedly, identity is constantly open to negotiation and reconstruction within the interstices of power relations. 'Otherness' is not a fixed domain. Said's text reified a social construct, a chimera of the Orient, an image created by the Occident. What the Western discourse reveals, in its celebration of the Oriental Other and in its difference from the non-West, derives from its own status uncertainty and instability in its own origins.[22] Further, the repeated assertions of difference by the West reveal its own inner demons – its fears, anxieties and disowned self. The repeated assertions of difference shift the arena of conflict away from a confrontation between the Self and the Other imagined as separate entities. In sum, there is no pure origin in the identity of the West.

As Fitzpatrick notes 'Western identity was formed obliquely by excluding non-European peoples who were accorded characteristics ostensibly opposed to that identity',[23] – the 'savages' and the 'barbaric races'. However, Occidentalist discourse was not absolute in determining its own image. Conversely, the Orient was less passive in affecting that composition.[24] The creation of identities is not a unilateral process (defining and measuring the Orient through an Occident calculus). Both identities are subject to (unequal) negotiation, reflecting uncertainty in status ascription.

Thus law plays a crucial role in determining those identities. However, within the imperial project, law was restricted by the assumption of modernity to which it remained tied. The implementation of the tenets of English law ensured incorporation, but that inclusion reinforced difference, not similarity. In constructing those new legal identities, the West succeeded in retaining a referential distance, institutionalizing a new social hierarchy between those above and those below, both in England and in India. The West's strategy of difference further resulted in constructing a sub-strata of the dangerous and criminal class from the ethnic minorities within that class. Internal processes were extended externally to colonial India, and internally to England, with the same objectives.

Difference: Ethnicity and Identities

The debates surrounding the criticism of Said raise new questions about ethnic and racial issues, especially with regard to the construction of racial others as dangerous and irredeemable. This opening provides the space to explore the work of the later postcolonial scholars, to the problematized concept of the racial other in the discourses of crime – as here with images of dangerous classes in nineteenth century England, and of criminal tribes in imperial India. The Western face of modernity and superiority concealed uncertainty over different racial statuses. The identity of the West in respect of its own position toward non-Western peoples, in and from imperial India, involved counterposed identities.

For most of the nineteenth century, Western anxiety reflected widespread fear of the degeneration of the European 'race' into a racial condition akin to that of savages, the state of grace which the indigenous peoples of the colonies, were thought to inhabit. The paradigm of European superiority constructed the primitive as the irrational savage, on the lower stages of evolution. In both imperial India and in Victorian England, this evolutionary differentiation produced itemized individuals and collectivities that required social control to prevent contamination. Various measures of difference were established to contain the proximity of the savage other. Sanitation by legal devices, by cultural imagery, and by spatial designation were necessary safeguards.

For example, anxiety about the allegedly increasing population of inferior 'races' on the English streets was alleviated by the discourse of otherness. Imported moral panics propagated by imperial accounts of the thugs,[25] of the practice of suttee,[26] (widow-burning), of the killing of girls by upper-caste Brahmins,[27] (especially infanticide) and of criminal tribes unreformable by virtue of their inherited criminality, prompted and justified imperial fears of contamination both in India and at home,[28] in the metropolis. In colonial India, appropriate differentiation was measured on an assumed continuum of progress. Imperial stability through the assignation of inferior labels was framed by the emergent 'social scientisms' of the Victorian period. The official knowledges of positivism, with its attendant typological, anthropometric, legal-administrative and eugenicist measurements determined location.[29] This quantifiable inferiority could be overcome by extending Western moral and legal culture, scales of difference assessed by a rational calculus, which in turn would stabilize Western imperial identity and superiority. The imperial powers relied on an elementary scale for measurement. Standards and values of the native culture were deemed to be at an earlier stage of a graded evolutionary path to that of the Western. The civilizing process depended on the implementation of categories via the medium of Western legislation – the measurements of modernity. Such evolutionary tutelage would eventually result in a rational social order, especially in the new Utilitarian principles. Reason would make sense of, and categorize the disordered and allow them to progress. Replacing the paternalism of the EIC, British Colonial Office relied on the mental security of a legal-structured regime to classify the ethnics.[30] The colonizers established a comprehensive framework which could secure the distance between the Western and non-Western people. A series of inclusionary gradations and statuses was constructed intended to contain both imperial identity and the identity of the subordinate Indian. Such categories had to be constantly reinforced, to avoid active challenge. Once remoulded, some – a better class – of the natives were to be partly incorporated – 'imaginary' Europeans in their manners, in their habits of mind and in their impulses. In Macaulay's words, this entailed the creation of:

> a class of interpreters between us and millions whom we govern – a class of persons, Indian in blood and colour, but English in taste, in opinions, in morals and in intellect.[31]

The proximity of the incorporated, however, threatened Western identity. Difference had constantly to be asserted. Increasing proximity was a problem (as in the discussion of the lascars and ayahs in Chapter 5), the internal challenge of an apparently ever-growing 'dangerous' class. While subjectively located outside, their physical proximity prompted tension over Western identity within Victorian England. Outcast (*sic*) London could only be normalized to a limited extent.

Law and Empire

Law is fundamental to postcolonial analysis. It defines social status, legitimates authority and appropriates behaviour. Critical legal studies contribute three heuristic elements to this analysis: firstly, a critique of the history and rationales for the imposition of Modern English law on imperial society; secondly, the proposition that English common law as developed and conducted in Victorian England (becoming known later as adversarial or due process) despite formal appearances, actually embedded discretionary procedures and principles that allowed advantage to be taken by the state against lower order individuals and collectivities.

The terms of that debate have become redundant but the outcome remains instructive. That supposed position is located within the determining structure and society, whether in Victorian England or imperial India. Thus, with

Pashukanis, the terms of equivalence are a product of commodity exchange, and therefore the legal process, counter-intuitively, enshrined inequality not equality in relation to such collectivities.[32] In its very failure, it reveals the ambivalent nature of law, especially with regards to the criminal classes and criminal tribes. Finally, that same body of law, again apparently adversarial, contained within its totality a quite different – essentially inquisitorial – mandate in the legal construction of the non-Western. Most crimes of the common people remained within the structure of an older system of justice. Yet the integrity of law depends on the very recalcitrant it opposes. All this is not simply a matter of theoretical clarity. It was massively confirmed in the experience of law and imperialism.

The traditional understanding of law regards colonialism as the cutting edge of the civilizing process, in which it was the inalienable right and duty of the white man to educate the native, to guide him on the path away from his own barbarity. Such powerful evocations of the barbaric and the savage confirmed the difference between Europe and the colonies. These marked differences are most evident in the development and export of English modern law to the colonies in the eighteenth and nineteenth centuries, which was not an extension of equality, but rather of inequalities. It is now widely acknowledged that law, contrary to the principle of universality, is based on differences – of ascribed status and of 'race'.[33] Modern adjudicative standards and processes are not ideal creations, they are responsive to, and draw upon, wider structural rationalities operating beyond adjudication and law. Rather, modern law is a reinforcement to the legal straitjacketing of social inequalities. The explicity and unquestionable European character of law has been powerfully exposed. In constructing non-Western people as citizens of Empire and conferring on them, as imperial subjects, the benefits of a notionally reformed criminal justice system: the colonial state simultaneously reified them as social underclasses. This systematic application of an equal scale to socially unequal individuals served to reinforce structural inequalities,[34] while at the same time ideologically constraining those newly recognized legal equals within the absorbent apparatuses of the imperial state. Criminal justice systems were used in both the metropolis and India to select 'criminals'. Processes of legal reform took place not only within the metropolis and with regards to its own internal 'dangerous' types, but extended externally to cover the various castes and tribal groups with which the imperial state was confronted in India.

The traditional view of colonial law is that it consists of a series of doctrines and principles that were developed by the West, that emerged out of European thought and experience and that were eventually extended to the non-Western world which had existed outside the realm of European law. The legal-rational Utilitarian writers, John Stuart Mill and Jeremy Bentham, wished to deal with 'real natives' as if they came from a static, inflexible tradition, a tradition which had no autonomous impulse to change. Legal tutelage and control was required.

Intervention, according to the Western modernizing project, was necessary to assist the colonized in divesting themselves of their own 'barbarity'. Criminal justice policy reflected, and was part of imperial incorporation. This process was triumphantly completed by Thomas Babington Macaulay,[35] who adopted, if in haphazard fashion, the principles of codification and drafting techniques of Bentham and John Stuart Mill,[36] and the inherent inequalities, in applying them to a criminal code for imperial India.[37]

Seen in this way, legislatures enacted legal labels, based on presuppositions of inferiority and superiority (the Social Darwinism of imperial social relations), and stereotypes (adapted historical wisdom). The imperial state administered and interacted with its colonial 'others' as if they were nothing but what was perceived through Western eyes, especially within concepts enshrined within Victorian society's constitution of its own 'dangerous' classes. Modernity required that the perceived incommensurability with its recalcitrant 'others'[38] be resolved within terms and concepts which 'made sense' – which were, in effect, legally rational.

Faced with the contradictions between ideals of Enlightenment and liberalism on the one hand, and the material interests of colonialism on the other, the colonialists, as increasingly influenced by Utilitarianism,[39] asserted modern notions of citizenship, of representation and of the rule of law. The imperial state initiated a grand redeeming project, bringing the marginalized into the body corporate. The Enlightenment legacy required that those beyond the liberal equation had to be qualitatively different from those within it.[40] The uncivilized were to be civilized by juridical techniques and institutions necessary for the enterprise of incorporation. The West presented its own systems of law as rational and appropriate to rule. The prevailing Indian judicial system was deemed to rest on statuses and practices in severe need of modernization[41] and of reform towards civilized standards. Western values were embodied in the procedures enacted by imperial civil servants such as James Mill. The rights of the modern citizen, in England and in imperial India, were constructed as evolving naturally from the history of Western progress.

Inevitably, this construction collided with Indian notions of rights. Those rights (see Chapter 6) stemmed from 'Hinduvata', in which an individual was born according to the values of the system of 'caste'.[42] Individual rights were submerged under the collectivity of caste. To Europeans, such collective caste rights arose from a lack of civilization. Hinduvata enshrined practices including *inter alia:* a failure to observe the principles of natural justice; an inability to appreciate the rationale of punishment; a lack of individualism in identity and responsibility; and a failure to follow legal procedure and precedent. These failures and weaknesses were identified as a pathology,[43] which arose from the 'nature' of Indian ideas, practices and beliefs. In Said's notion of a 'sovereign Western consciousness',[44] the native was inscribed as 'equal' by the writ of imperial law. The discourse of equal rights became complicit in practical subordination through its insistence that everyone had a right to equal treatment. Only the colonial form of 'being' was licensed – legal as belonging but unequal in terms of the caste system. Legal equality confirmed and obfuscated social inequality.

However, rights are cultural constructs. They are relativistic.[45] Rights imbued with Western legal ideologies are difficult to relate to Indian traditions and social hierarchies. Tribes and castes were defined in relation to 'Varna'.[46] The notion of equal rights involving equal practice appears more than a little problematic when faced with these alternative categories. Rights were determined according to a calculus, a set of values derived from, and beneficial to, a minority in the West. These colonial rights were formulated within, not separate from, the imperial mission of civilizing, a standard of civility assessed in opposition to those supposed to be uncivilized. To civilize meant that the identity of the rulers of Empire could no longer be challenged. This civilizing process gave the non-Western the illusion of becoming the same by the legal artifact of conferring citizenship under the guise of the rule of law.[47] Non-Western people played an insignificant role within these schemes. Illusions of becoming the same entail conforming to the grand redeeming project of bringing the uncivilized into the fold, into the realm of civilization and its attendant values. In short then, these mechanisms of exclusion and inclusion are as essential part of the imperial state, as are the strategies of incorporation and transformation.

As a result, Indian people, like the non-Western in the metropolis, were neither fully excluded nor fully included. In essence, law, as the central moral imperative, ought to have assured stability and the ultimacy of determination. However, for the law to rule, especially in the imperial setting, it had to embrace the opposite attributes. The non-Western, with their ascribed status of caste and of 'race', were considered distinct. The characteristics and repetition of these distinctive qualities, in terms of 'savagery' and of its attendant dangers, assigned 'caste' a place outside modernity but encompassed within the assertion of the continuum of evolution of modernity and progress. The law extended to include the non-Western, in terms of legal equality, but drew back and reasserted itself by ensuring the affirmation of social inequality. As Balbus argues, the imperial law had a clear hegemonic mission to perform. The task was the imposition of 'repression through formal rationality', which served to depoliticize collective violence and militate against the growth of consciousness and solidarity of the participants.[48]

The imperial state required the non-Western to participate in the discourse of its own civility and progress. The implementation of the Criminal Tribes Act of 1871 in India, as with the Habitual Criminal Act of 1869 in England, symbolized a deliberate limitation to the ascription of equal rights. Specific legal artifacts created a 'dangerous' class, and at the same time the law ensured their place in its principles of 'equivalence'. Home-grown statutes were extended to cover the various castes and tribal groups with which the imperial state was confronted in India.[49] Those legal extensions shaped the form and content of the Indian judicial structures, as well as those of the metropolis. It was a simultaneous engagement. Imperial law was a hybrid. Local practices were incorporated into imperial law. The legal process in India took original historical experiences, such as peasant rebellion, and transformed them:

> ...into a matrix of abstract legality, so that the will of the state could be made to penetrate, reorganise part by part and eventually control the will of a subject population.[50]

The distinction between the civilized and the uncivilized: the atavistic and the barbarian is crucial to the formation of imperial doctrine and to the exclusion of others. This basic reasoning finds expression in different vocabularies and doctrines throughout the British Empire. And further, legal reforms, with all the distinctive styles of judicial reasonings and outcomes, suggest its profoundly enduring character. This dynamics of difference, as well as the civilizing mission, continues below in Benthamite reforms.

Benthamite Reforms and Social Inequality

Three principles are among the key inheritances of nineteenth century legal reform in England. The reforms of that period assumed as axiomatic that the primary characteristic of English law, especially in relation to criminal process, was its commitment to judicial process as a contest between equals. In essence common law guaranteed the rights of the accused: innocence was presumed; a trial by one's peers would be a right; and imprisonment without trial would be prohibited. Secondly, the imperial formulation of identities proceeded principally through the realm of these doctrines and rights, the recognition of legal citizenship. As citizens of Empire, formally, the non-Western was also assumed to be 'equal'. Once before the courts, legal citizens, whether rich or poor ensured that they enjoyed equal rights. From that *de jure* principal, *de facto* social equality is assumed. A unitary system of law was formally intended to cover all as legally equal citizens of society.

Until recently, (as developed in the succeeding chapter) criticisms of the Benthamite legal reforms have been mute. The well-established dictum that all defendants are 'innocent until proven guilty',[51] and the axiom that it is better for ten guilty men to go free, rather than one innocent man be convicted, remain the cornerstones of legal ideology. Justice is intended to be administered rationally as well as effectively. The methods employed in safeguarding the suspect population are crucial. These principles are embodied within the administrative directions governing police questioning and interrogations, which enable the detection, apprehension and processing of the offender population. Legal rationality guides the processing of defendants, regardless of ethnicity or social status. Impartial resolution guides the relationship between the prosecution and the police on the one hand, and the individual accused on the other. Standard procedures and rules operate independently of political considerations and regardless of who is standing in the dock.[52]

The Benthamite tradition[53] assumes that the relationship between the individual and the state enshrines the values of equality of individualism. Thus, objective value-free mechanisms are incorporated in official legal discourse. The fundamental legal cultural basics, which arise from the 'rule of law' for the protection of the individual suspect, are systematically underpinned, reflected and reinforced in institutions of criminal justice. Where occasional inequalities in this process are acknowledged, these are considered less important than the general good, which law achieves for society.

These assumptions have, however, been subject to much critique,[54] which has taken two forms. Liberal, 'aberrational' accounts insist that the evident inequalities experienced by the non-Western in the criminal justice process are primarily due to mechanical failings of the system. 'Law-in-the-books' represents an ideal but 'law-in-practice', often fails to live up to that ideal, resulting in justice being miscarried for some suspects and other defendants. On the ground, despite the form of law, in the Justices' courts of Victorian England, the vast majority of the population was relegated to a legal territory in which untrained magistrates often dispensed justice largely as they felt appropriate, given also local exigencies of resources such as incarceration and policing manpower.[55]

Other critics[56] have argued that these failings are structural.[57] It has been argued in a variety of recent studies[58] in relation both to lower-class suspects and to members of minority ethnic communities that legal process, in its failings, relates primarily to innate defects in English law. It is 'law-in-the-books' that is the problem, not its occasional malfunctions, as is evident from recent miscarriages of justice in England. Central to the latter was a presumption of guilt rather than of innocence. This imputation framed the suspects from the beginning of the trials to eventual imprisonment. Criminal justice personnel, from the police to the judiciary, treated the defendants as ethnic (Irish) unequals rather than as equals, and used the machinery of the state to conclude guilt independently of procedural safeguards.[59] Extra-legal factors (dress, appearance and language) and behaviour (location and activity) of the accused were assembled within a paradigm, which assumed guilt through a particular ethnic identity. Similarly, identical exclusionary practices were most evident in the case of colonial subjects in imperial India (see Chapters 6 and 7), and also of Asian and Afro-Caribbeans in Victorian England (see Chapter 5), in which, while the law decreed rights and equality of treatment, practice determined otherwise.[60]

As evident in the succeeding chapters, the savage state of being provides law with a credibility that is necessary for its self-image. More pointedly, principles of equality and universality, which stand opposed to racist inequalities, actually reinforce them.[61] This compounding of inequality derives from the very nature of legal processes. The applications of criminal procedure transcend the bounds of the rule of law. For example, in selective investigation[62] and the pressure exerted upon the defendants within plea-bargaining,[63] and the structure of magistrates' justice,[64] exist to work systematically against the defendant. More importantly, the existing criminal justice system works in the way it does because of these features, not despite them. Legal discretion is a key component of the system. It allows the criminalization of the lower social orders in public space, as most apparent in the imperial vagrancy legislation. Discretion is formally required by due process, and judgements and the criminal law provide the space, legally and metaphorically, through which partisanship enters. Structural injustice results in part from the exercise of partisan discretion conveyed to the court by cultural assumptions and structural imperatives. Injustice is linked to the law itself, not only to the people who operate it. It is the nature of the 'law itself', which facilitates the reproduction of inequality.[65]

Law's insidious practices against the non-Western is carried out by its key functionary, the police. Policing discretion is especially important. The police are the gatekeepers of the due process system.[66] The police may act entrepreneurially to define criminality, where legislation is permissive, within their own occupational cultural terms. In colonial India, it was frequently police officers (especially Colonel Sleeman) who promoted the legal classification of the criminal tribes.[67] The police legally participate in the creative construction of evidence.[68]

Central to policing is 'reasonable suspicion', which operates within social, cultural and economic parameters as part of the police public order mandate.[69] Police occupational culture[70] evokes law enforcement decisions within the boundaries of the law, not outside the law. Formal guidance on the use of discretion reinforces that mandate.[71] Equal treatment for suspects belonging to the lower social order is scarcely enshrined in law at all.[72] The formal structure of legal rules and procedures allow and even facilitate the erosion or violation of the rights of defendants.[73] The official rules, which characterize the enforcement of the law and the policies adopted to sanction police malpractice, actually provide a licence to ignore them.[74] Police deviations from legality are institutionalized in the judicial process.[75] How police officers behave, and how they should behave, is rarely checked,[76] within the wider legal parameters of practices and legislation, which bear most heavily on the lower social orders.

Adversarial Process for Respectables, Inquisition for Savages

In Victorian England and in imperial India, criminal justifications and codifications were implemented. Legal constructs of identity, both of those subject to the process and, conversely, of those doing the construction, were manifest. This represented the Enlightenment reaction to the previous era.[77] The notion of equality in law is a key context in which relations between the West and the non-Western become explicit. Legal reform represented a future based on equality, progress and individual rights. It allowed the West to identify and proclaim itself as the embodiment of truth and progress. However, the standards the West proclaimed in this move were used to subordinate the uncivilized whom were characterized as having to learn, and conform to, civilized standards of modernity. Due process of law acted in this way to bind the Orient within the Enlightenment. Hidden inequalities served in practice to solidify, not to decrease, social inequalities. Under Utilitarian legislation, respectable citizens were conferred individual rights, with equal consideration in the criminal justice process. In the courts, they appeared as individual bearers of rights, and cases were determined on merit not character. Conversely, those determined as unequal, the criminal classes of Victorian society and the criminal tribes of India were regarded essentially as collectivities, composed of artificially conflated individuals. In the legal process, they were tried as members belonging to the stigmatized groups. Collectivities were labelled in a relationship at odds with the dominant assumption of rights-bearing individuals under criminal law. Enabling clauses and categories of offences under Victorian legislation allowed those groups to be treated in discriminatory ways by the same body of laws. They were suspect, indeed, guilty, until proven innocent – the reverse of the formal assumption. They were found guilty by their associations and by their characters rather than by their actions.

In essence, impartial legal procedures, legal equality and the notion of a legal subject, can be located in a modernity which has its genesis in the Enlightenment. Equivalence of legal subjects was created by an Enlightenment modernity, which constructed all men as equally reasonable and equally liable for their action. This rational calculus created a notional equivalence in the legal setting. Whilst contrived in late eighteenth- and early nineteenth-century Western Europe in the writings of the legal theorist Beccaria,[78] the concept of legal equality was also an important mechanism used as a means of controlling the non-Western subjects.

These developments in criminal justice process were fundamentally embedded in fear for the social order and of new risk groups: the mob of the late eighteenth century now appeared in the identification of, and anxiety about, the dangerous classes (what was later to be called Outcast London[79]) and later the identification of and anxiety about the evolutionary racially inferior. Undercurrents of anxiety and insecurity guided criminal justice policy in new directions.[80]

The reconfigurations in theories of the criminal appeared to demonstrate the importance of culture and the persistence of the savage instincts and the 'primitive' within the civilized. The discourse of social constructionism finds its justification for colonialism as colonial subjects continued to be portrayed as childlike and driven by impulse and instincts and therefore in need of moral guidance from the civilized Europeans.

The Discourse of Social Constructionism

Criminological social constructionism (labelling theory) has described how social collectivities can be constructed as a threat to the social order. Occasionally, agency intervenes, and practice is skewed. Ideas of race became a powerful tool of stereotyping and stigmatization, which lent itself formidably to a particular strata within a society, in search of its own social, moral and political empowerment. The previous sections outlined the way in which law can make a major contribution to the dynamics of statuses, both equal and unequal. Postcolonial theory shows how this occurs through the process of interaction between the colonized and the colonizers. The structural critique of adversarial law shows how a legal system, which appears to embody the principle of equality, may actually enshrine inequalities. The West used social constructionist processes in significant ways, in both Victorian England and in imperial India, to categorize several groups as dangerous. Imperial labelling of the non-Western as dangerous and uncivilized, worked to give the West a context in which identities were sustained in both settings. In particular the role in the invention of dangerousness, justified and disseminated ideas of racial hierarchies as part of the imperial project. Arguably, this witnesses the unraveling of the project of the civilizing mission and the universal spread of Western scientific knowledge (see Chapter 4).

Social constructionism, in its interface with postcolonialism and critical legal studies, offers further directions in explaining the development of colonial regulation in Imperial Britain and in colonial India. The novel aspects of constructionism are its insights into the formation of master statuses such as criminality, the key censure, as a category imposed upon social inferiors by powerful others. Constructionism[81] transcends the notion of deviant behaviour as inherently abnormal and pathological. Deviance and crime are social constructs. The focus is on the social and legal processes by which individuals and groups are criminalized. From this perspective, the stigmatization of lower strata as criminal classes in Victorian England, and the subsequent criminalization of castes and tribes in imperial India, owed more to the perceptions of the definers than to those defined. The subsequent processes of stereotyping by the Europeans, coupled with the concepts of danger emanating from the savage heathens and the primitive natives were an expression of Imperial anxieties and fears of the non-Western.

What is important here is the identities of both the governing and the governed. Two related themes are illustrated. First, identities are a consequence of the imposition of labels by others, and partly by a process of negotiation of the two parties. Power is often a major feature of this relationship, in which new identities are constructed on both sides and new social hierarchies affirmed through law. Second, history is important to this conundrum. The constitution of identities is commonly a product of historical assumptions and experiences. Crime control is not a static imposition of law but rather a dynamic struggle over the negotiation and imposition of statuses and identities. This insistence between the definer and the defined links postcolonial debates and the critique of adversarial law within the practice of legal proscription in the metropolis and in imperial India.

The study of definitions imposed by respectable Victorians on the criminal classes, and by Westerners (locals and incorporated) on the non-Western, when informed by constructionism furnishes considerable insights. It provides an interpretation as it shifts the object of criminal enquiry, from explanations of why a pathological few break the criminal codes, towards an analysis that focuses on how a historical struggle between colonial social formations is central not only to the construction of the crime problem, but also to new identities and hierarchies. Similarly, just as criminal law is constructed within society, criminal and normative identities are also social constructs. The subject, rather than the object, rules. Thus, social phenomena are created, and not pre-given.[82]

Reformers saw themselves as the saviours of the natives, as guardians of evolution, and segregated the fit from the unfit who needed to be isolated and eliminated. Rather than focusing on the defined offender, then, in imperial India, criminal castes and tribes were not innately deviant. Their status was imposed upon them by powerful others who located them as criminal subjects within the context of the class and racial configuration process of Empire. By framing the debate within this constructionist perspective,[83] there is a broader scope for understanding how criminal identification engages with postcolonial theory and imperial law. Identities were determined and managed, by regulation of the perceived threat to the social order from the supposedly criminal, as in the legal labelling of the criminal classes of Victorian England, and the criminal tribes and castes in colonial India.

The central tenet of social constructionism is that statuses, such as that of the 'criminal' are manufactured. These statuses are not given but labels applied by human reaction and subsequent action.[84] In this context, statuses are negotiated between different, unequal, ethnic parties. Official statuses are created in the interplay of deviant style, of legal authority and of social divisions based on 'race'. Those definitions reflect the interactional anxieties and uncertainties over statuses felt by the more powerful. They locate individuals and collectivities in a special social status and play a significant role in the demand for greater legal (and scientific) classification and regulation.

In the early nineteenth century, Western reaction, and the reality it constructed, determined who was criminalized. Colonial legal discourse eventually resulted in the bestowal upon certain groups of a criminal identity. The status of the West was sustained by the conferment of the label on the Other. However, assigning a status on the lower order could not have happened without an adjustment in the identity of the dominant party. Not merely were criminal classes, the criminal tribes and castes, given a new constructed identity but, in the same process, the definers were elevated to a new and clearer status in the social hierarchy.

Further, constructionism demands that it is necessary to understand, both how statuses are conferred, and also the dynamics of the legal culture. The latter may consist of the imageries which inform the deviant definition, as in the phantasmagoric discourse regarding the savage heathens, of the criminal class, and of the criminal tribe. It also involves analysing the law-making processes, from vagrancy legislation to the Habitual Criminals Act of 1869, and of the Criminal Tribes Act of 1871. The actions of status enforcers, from the New Police of Peel to the entrepreneurial practices of Colonel Sleeman and his fellow officers of the colonial police, are also problematized.

Applying criminal labels to those less powerful can serve several functions, principally in relation to the construction of new identities. Firstly, it enables the deviant to be excluded from normal society into a fixed social and territorial space – the criminal reservation. Such new locations symbolically marked out moral boundaries by dramatizing the deviant image as outside and below, while still included as a reference point for the new social hierarchy.[85] The out-groups may be isolated through degradation ceremonies,[86] from judicial denunciations to the designation of the children of the criminal tribes as innate criminals from birth, and therefore subject to paternalistic colonial tutelage.[87] Secondly, defining groups as inferior has the effect of increasing the status of those not so defined. The respectable working class of Victorian England colluded in the social construction of the criminal classes. It enhanced its own, higher, identity. In turn, the indigenous criminal class could feel it was morally superior to the increasing presence of lascars and other ethnic itinerants on the London streets. It stabilized the social hierarchy – in effect, elevating that status of the definer.[88] The deviant identities become a form of hierarchical ordering. In India, as Cannadine argues, the West absorbed the existing social hierarchy of castes in a way which was recognizable within its domestic hierarchical ordering, and as a consequence criminal classes equalled criminal tribes in that structure.[89]

Thirdly, castigation of a group as inferior or criminal allows it to become the scapegoat for larger social ills. In imperial India, it was easy to blame the Sansi, a nomadic ethnic tribe, for the problems of starvation in the Punjab rather than the vicissitudes of the market economy forced on the indigenous people,[90] in a similar way that a different imperial ethnic group, the 'feckless' Irish, had been held responsible for the potato famine. Further, in a period of rapid social change, social norms and values become problematic.[91] New symbolic boundaries are constructed by creating new rule-breaking. Colonization could only be successfully implanted in India, and given new moral boundaries as in the emblematic notion of dangerousness.

Separately, constructing a group as deviant serves to construct solidarity between previously alien groups. In the Indian context, indigenous Brahmin elite could feel more integrated with the homeland of the Queen Empress[92] when they shared similar views about the identity of the criminals. Judicial decisions, and the social reactions which accompanying them, created a new homogeneity of interest. One Indian visitor wrote to *The Times* in order to complain about the presence of Indian beggars who were 'great annoyance to the Public, but more to the Indian gentlemen who visit 'England'.[93]

Denunciation of the criminal caste of 'thugs' resonated for both Westminster and indigenous elite groups.[94] Criminalization served to create an artificial emblem of morality. By treating those who shared a common identity as deviants, by segregating and isolating them from the community of respectable castes, the powerful denigrate as unequal those who do not share that common identity. This designation of deviance extends well beyond publicly proscribed and formally processed wrongdoing. In colonial India, the rules laid down by the powerful were internalized as the basis for contact with the designated inferiors. Daily interaction between imperial police officers and the lower castes and tribes of India depended upon prescribed formal and informal rules.

Finally, identities can be reinforced by the moral panics, sudden outrages at the apparent increase in a particular form of deviance. Moral panics and the assertion of identity have a long imperial pedigree. In imperial Britain, garrotting epidemics played that role.[95] In imperial India, similar panics in relation to the non-Western have a long historical history. 'Thuggee' again constitutes the example (see Chapter 6), an emblematic remnant from Victorian panic over garrotters transcribed into contemporary discourse as thugs.[96] Moral panics in the nineteenth century induced a series of legal measures in which the non-Western was reaffirmed as inferior. Imperial society could displace its internal anxiety and related fears by projecting them on the non-Western. Imperial identity was sustained by constructing the non-Western as 'evil', 'pathological', 'barbaric' and degenerate.

Negotiated Identities and Stereotypes

Central to the construction of identities are the social psychological processes of stereotyping, retrospective interpretation and negotiation. Stereotyping in particular is based on selective perception and information, and consequently results in the biased assessment of others. In the colonial setting, Bhabha suggests that the stereotype

> is the major discursive strategy of colonial discourse, it is a form of knowledge that oscillates between what is already known and what is always in place, and something which must be constantly and anxiously repeated in order to sustain its credibility.[97]

All social interaction occurs through an initial negotiation in which facilitative identities are constructed. Colonial discourse is marked by the recognition and amplification of racial and cultural differences in this process.[98] Stereotypes, retrospective interpersonal constructions, reinforce the assembly of the offender's master status. The 'imaginary' knowledge of the deviant negatively informs public sentiment. Subsequent collation of information on the offender reinforces the unsavoury aspects of life history.

This process of negotiating roles and identities is most apparent between unequal parties. In caste relations, prescriptive definitions of the lower groups require compliance with the new role. For example, in the colonial context, the labelling of an out-group by the imperial state was only effective when the former came to accept its secondary status and to act in appropriate supplicant fashion to the colonial masters. Through retrospective interpretation, the interactional process substitutes a new and debased conception of the person's essential character. Only those aspects of the evidence consistent with the imputed deviance are given emphasis. A self-reinforcing subculture develops, reinforcing deviant identity, a rationalization of that identity and a barrier to denial.[99] The cost of rejecting caste definition, degrading though it may be, is greater than that of maintaining the deviant status.[100] The outcast comes to reinforce the official view of the new identity and learns to conduct the assigned deviant role with a minimum of trouble, in order to avoid further labelling and stigmata. Hence, habitual criminals learn the new rules.[101] Victorian offenders, like mental patients and the inferior stock of imperial India (as in the 'criminal' tribes settlements), once defined, were subjected by law to institutional and spatial segregation, surveillance, and control and confined to their own company.[102] Yet, (as in the following chapter), it is through this process of exclusion based on popular imagery of the phantasmorphic types that the European takes its identity and asserts itself as an entity. But this process of identity formation in the marginalization of the other, through various scientific racial formations, fails to fully or finally exclude the non-Western, as the separation from that dangerous type reveals a relation to it. So, the constitution of identity is a process which emanates from a tension between the relation to and from the separation from a declared outside. The process of separation and coming together is based on an active exclusion at the promise of inclusion. Thus, the acts of exclusion, based on definitions of the criminal types, monsters and the barbarians, marked through the new emerging sciences, reveal an instability and ambivalence within identity formation. In order to conceal this truth, the West obsessively engages in this act of exclusion, based on scientific racism and stereotypes, which is continually repeated, as is evidenced in Chapter 4.

Synthesis

This chapter has laid out the jigsaw parameters of which Victorian legislation contributed the initial pieces. The devil, as they say, is in the detail – in the evidence from the following chapters. A revisionist criminal justice history furnishes one side of the jigsaw. Crime and the process of criminalization are a microcosm of structural conflicts – in this case the concern by imperial Britain to rule and to incorporate its colonial subjects. Postcolonial theory recognizes that the identity of the subjects, indeed of the rulers, is subjective, unstable and based on an unequal power relationship. Critical legal studies introduce several themes. The codification of law in nineteenth-century England maintained a systemic inequality for the lower social orders. The opportunity for social groups to influence the formulation of the law, and hence possess the power of social censure, is related to their relative power – there is little parity between the powers of the Victorian state and those of the under-class, or of the imperial order in relation to the 'criminal' castes and tribes. Social constructionist perspectives suggest that it is through an historical narrative, the structural sources of the negotiation of identity by which criminal labels are determined and sustained. Law is the critical social censure. The legal process reflects powerful interests[103] which become reflected in public policy, rather than an instrument which functions outside of those pressures. Though law may control interests, interests in the first place create law. Criminal law may work to the detriment of others.[104] Law enforcement, as a crucial part of the legal process, primarily serves the interests of the key decision-makers.[105] Police work, for example, is ordering work in which partisan conceptions of social order may be imposed.[106]

One concern of this book is to consider the way in which a particular social formation, the criminal tribe of the Sansi, was historically constructed through the criminal justice processes as an official 'criminal' group. Their criminal identity illustrates how such constructed statuses may be a product of historical and material relations. The disciplinary themes in this chapter demonstrate how that combined mode of analysis informs the construction of criminality in Victorian

England and its equivalent form in imperial India. Although the West sought to define the non-West as pathological, weak and deviant, it simultaneously viewed the latter as a grave threat capable of destroying the very core of the West's own self-image. While the West was spurred by moral imperative to 'improve' the non-West in the West's own image, it also evinced an intense desire to preserve its identity in the face of the non-West. That signification process does not mean simply a change in the identity of the deviant groups. It also has implications for the status and identity of the definers. In late eighteenth- and nineteenth-century, images of race, class and dangerousness, acted in congruence, generating a repressive imperial ideology that was to be reflected in all aspects of Western legal and administrative treatment of the non-West.

3 IMAGERY AND LAW IN THE CREATION OF IDENTITIES

...The criminals are like 'criminal' tribes who are likened to gypsies, when in need, resorting to plunder rather than submitting to the discipline of steady work.[1]

Victorian Imagery: Creating Identities

Institutionalist histories of crime and punishment in eighteenth- and nineteenth-century England are narrated through changes in categories of criminal legislation, in policing, and in penal structures. More critical perspectives focus on the object of that legal reaction, arguing that such controls were designed to deal with a generalized dangerousness, covering fears of both crime and social disorder, rather than specific criminality. Form rather than substance characterized Whig histories. Far from criminal justice form being progressive, it simply perpetuated in different guises the summary justice meted out to the poor.[2] The process of criminalizing the lower strata in the early nineteenth century drew upon key images of morality and of pathology, revealing the ambivalence that pervades the creation of identities in law. Law was aimed as much at the social, cultural and epidemiological attributes of the lower classes as at the physical threat they presented. Consequently, legislation focused on the assumed collective attributes, rather than directly on individual actions. The crime problem was not one of deed but of vicarious character.[3] Reforms of criminal law aimed to contain this notion of threatening character and dispel by intervention its associated criminal images. Criminal classes were defined in terms of their communal propensity to undermine social harmony. Such a stratum, as in the parallel process in India amongst the criminal tribes, was anxiously understood through a proliferation of stereotypes and labels imbued with this threatening menace. The production of images in Western discourse of the non-Western of the Orient was expressed through the latter's sickness and criminal tendencies, being more corrupt and licentious than the Europeans. The dangerous and threatening required control and regulation.

Colonial officials shared information with their counterparts in the imperial centre, especially over the need to deploy harsh regulation and regimes against the natives in response to their wayward habits in relation imperial discipline. British functionaries in nineteenth-century India and England promoted legislation that would respond to the unruly heathens. Specifically, it was the anxiety stemming from the proximity of the non-Western which demanded such strict legislative intervention. The non-Western also appeared threatening within England, The ethnic labour of imperial trade enhanced the diversity of the fearsome masses in the British metropolis.[4] The new ethnic minorities of Victorian England's empire – including Africans, Caribbeans, Chinese, Malays and Indians – contributed to the kaleidoscope of anxiety-inducing images. Both European and Occidentals lower strata were imbued with fashionable images of savagery and degeneracy.[5]

This unfathomable fluidity of oriental Others was echoed when internal missionaries adopted the language of Empire in that denunciation. Typically, Reverend Greatbatch denounced the Lancashire lower strata as 'heathen races' in the early 1800s.[6] The New Police became known as 'urban missionaries'.[7] Later in the century, Booth enumerated the class as consisting of 50,000[8] 'outcasts' (sic!), including street hawkers, beggars, thieves, the pathologically violent, those fallen from higher status, foreigners and exiles. He continued with collective condemnation:

> These outcasts of London who live and gain their livelihood in the streets and lanes of the metropolis, some are more guilty and ignorant than others, but all speaking of them as a class, savages in the middle of civilisation, heathens in the heart of Christendom and potentially, at least, enemies to their fellow-men.[9]

The Times wrote of a 'caste apart that is idle, unprincipled and dissolute amongst us',[10] comparing it with the Indian Thuggee cult. They were an unregenerate mass. Mayhew (again using Oriental imagery, imbued with moral and biological concepts) saw it as a cancerous growth on the upright, and distinct from, the urban working class:

> born to the street ... felt to share a particular cult predisposition, imbibing the habits and the morals of the gutters. The child without moral training goes back to its parent stock – the vagabond savage.[11]

He claimed that such lawbreakers were quite distinct from native stock, especially in physique.[12] They included the Irish, the first tangible ethnic outsiders (though the New Police itself had enrolled many Scots, Irish and rural English – strangers policing strangers – Miller)[13], but mainly the casually employed locals, surviving as day labourers, on the street economy of the rookeries and their environs.[14] The migrant Irish,[15] furnished a stereotypical predecessor of the later imperial migrants, incorrigibly criminal, beyond redemption.[16] In 1844, Fredrick Engels recounted a description of one such Irish rookery in Manchester:

> The race that lives in these ruinous cottages, behind broken windows, mended with oilskin, sprung doors, and rotten doorposts, or in dark, wet cellars, in measureless filth and stench, in this atmosphere penned in as if with a purpose, this race must really have reached the lowest stage of humanity ... in each of these pens, containing at most two rooms, a garret, perhaps a cellar, on the average twenty human beings live; that in the whole region, for each one hundred and twenty persons, one usually inaccessible privy is provided; and in spite of all the preaching of the physicians, in spite of the excitement into which the cholera epidemic plunged the sanitary police by reason of the condition of Little Ireland, in spite of everything, coming the year of grace.[17]

Within the master colonial language, the urban poor became known as the savages of the metropolis. Like denizens of empire, they were objects of fear and consequently targets of social and administrative experimentation. Imperial discourse of Empire was further invoked to describe their locations, metaphors of the Orient informing the Occidental – *The East is West.*[18] Later accounts by W. H. Stead[19] writing about the East End criminal classes, drew heavily on views of darkest Africa and the divisions between the pygmies of the jungle, where there is:

> The commingling of the worst vices of East and West. While Christian heroism was being so conspicuously exhibited in penetrating the jungles of India or the darkest forests of Africa, so little has been done to explore the haunts of the heathenish in the very heart of the great Christian city.[20]

On the later period, Emsley observed:

> During the 1850s to 1870s, a succession of intrepid explorers picked up their notebooks, as often as not, found trusty guides among the stout-hearted, blue-uniformed helmeted, guardians of law and order, and penetrated the dark and teeming recesses of poor working class districts. They then wrote up their exploits for the vicarious delight of the reading public as journeys into criminal districts, where the inhabitants were best compared with Red Indians or varieties of black savages.[21]

Later still, Jack London was to further these essentialized images of empire and savagery, by applying them to the Victorian 'criminal' classes in the metropolitan centre. In central London, he described the

> menagerie of garmented bipods that looked something like human and more like beasts, and .... brass-buttoned keepers kept order among ... these males looked at me sharply, hungrily, gutter wolves that they were, and I was afraid of the paws of a gorilla. They reminded me of gorillas. Their bodies were small, ill-shaped, and squat ... They exhibited, rather, an elemental economy of nature, such as the cavemen must have exhibited. But there was strength in those meager bodies, the ferocious primordial strength to clutch and tear and rend. When they spring upon their human prey, they know even to bend their victim backward and double its body until the back is

> broken. They possess neither conscience nor sentiment, and they will kill for a half-sovereign, without fear or favour, if they are given but half a chance. They are a new species, a breed of city savages. The streets and houses are their hunting grounds. As valley and mountain are to the natural savage, streets and buildings are valley and mountain to them, the slum is their jungle and they live and prey in the jungle.[22]

Popular conceptions of crime relegated criminal acts to the urban lower classes in the rookeries, specifically to the criminal classes living in the squalor and abject poverty of London's East End.[23] Many Victorians were obsessed with notions of purity and the drive to eradicate sin[24] in the metropolis. Contagion was feared from the ghettoes. Sweeping urbanization fuelled these concerns, influenced in part by the new media and fiction.[25] Broadsheets, as the first popularly accessible forum, ensured that the London populace was able to imbibe the latest gruesome details of the city's crimes.[26] Sensational criminal fiction, tales of immoral women, of venereal disease and 'true-life' crime and punishment narratives fed the Victorian imagination, its audience, with a regular diet of salacious tales, which would not only have shocked genteel folk, but also reinforced the sanctimoniousness of the respectables. For example, in the 1840s, the Chartist, G. W. M. Reynolds, published the fictional *The Mysteries of London* that gave his readers a vivid portrait of a brutalized savage poor, and depiction of the truly fallen dangerous type.

Crime was perceived to be increasing. There was some truth in that assumption. Many displaced, low-paid and unemployed workers of both genders had turned to crimes of survival under the impact of urbanization and industrialization.[27] Social and clinical problems accompanied such increases in crime. The rookeries, bereft of facilities, were perceived not merely to be the source of crime and immorality but also of disease.[28] The consequences of the rapid growth resulted in inadequate habitations and lack of access to clean water, refuse and sanitation facilities, which made the urban slums resemble early concentration camps. Devastating cholera, typhus and yellow fever epidemics had affected urban life. Venereal disease was emblematically regarded as rampant and could potentially affect respectable families and eventually threaten the security and stability of the British Empire at home and abroad. Crime and disease were conflated.

The *Report of the Royal Commission on the Rural Constabulary* 1839 described criminality as rooted in the poorer classes. Poverty and indigence did not lead to crime, the Report insisted. Criminals suffered from two vices: *indolence or the pursuit of easy excitement and were* drawn to commit crimes by *the temptation of profit of a career of depredation, as compared with the profits of honest and even well paid industry'*. Criminals made an irrational decision to live by crime rather than by labour. While vagrancy (nomadism in imperial discourse) was a common feature of the criminals, the 1834 Select Commission on Drunkenness identified a criminal class as possessing the worst habits of all. Inexorable alcoholism was partly at fault for their impulsive behaviour.[29] The problems were the interlinked features of inebriation and the poor's lack of morality. Continuity over the century in this view was maintained with an 1870s feature article in the *The Times* which informed readers that these men:

> Are more alien from the rest of the community than a hostile army, for they have no idea of joining the ranks of industrious labour either here or elsewhere. The civilised world is simply a carcass on which they prey, and London above all, is to them a place to sack.[30]

Criminals were perceived as overwhelmingly male. Female membership of that class was perceived as minor and largely due to prostitution (not itself a criminal offence). But such women were feared not because of their habits but more because they were regarded as carrying infectious diseases: hence the introduction of the inquisitorial and permissive Contagious Diseases Act of 1864.

Utilitarianism, Enlightenment and Crime: Imagery informing Regulation

In early nineteenth-century England, a central concern of governance was consequently the condition of the life of the emerging underclass. With the growth in mercantile capitalism, the prevention of crime and the imposition of social discipline became key concerns of the London propertied classes where the imagined crime problem threatened the health of the social order and required proactive measures of obedience and control. *Inter alia*, colonial disturbances had made politicians and moral entrepreneurs anxious of the ways in which unaddressed social, governmental and economic situations could suddenly explode – as typically manifested in the urban rookeries 'bursting forth' into the respectable streets.[31] A blind eye could be turned for the most part. In Hobsbawm's words:

> The period which culminated about the middle of the century was therefore one of unexampled callousness not because of the poverty which surrounded middle class respectability was so shocking that the native rich learned not to see it, leaving its horrors to make their full impact only on vesting foreigners, but because the poor, like outer barbarians, were talked of as though they were not properly humans at all.[32]

But the danger was ever-present. Degenerate behaviour had to receive a clear response. Post-Enlightenment, it could be subjected to paternalist moral improvement, prospects that informed Utilitarian discourse and criminal and civil regulation, rather than overt coercion. Crime and criminality were emblematic of a collective and perceived unprecedented breakdown in individual civility. These anxieties on moral degeneracy encompassed a heterogeneous non-labouring poor. Imaginative imagery, reflecting the moral anxieties of the social audience of the urban elites was central to the new regulation and classification of the poor and criminal deviants

Emerging Victorian bureaucracies of law, morality and disease focused on *imagined criminalities* in shaping criminal policy,[33] and the practice of enforcement agencies. This anxiety contributed to the Utilitarian impetus to reconstruct criminal and civil law. Regulations were enacted and new punishments of body and mind devised to ameliorate the urban crime problem. An external discipline (the enclosure of the body in the new carceral archipelago, from prison hulks to new purpose-built prisons replacing the generic Houses of Correction and the decaying holding institution of Newgate) and internally of the mind (the mental isolation and uniformity of the Panopticon) were conceptualized to establish new forms of discipline capable of restraining the social detritus of the *laissez faire* policies of the market, an urban lumpen mass.[34] The policing strategy was therefore logically selective, not directed at controlling industrial labourers of the nascent manufacturing class, but instead on clearly identifiable maleficent groups. While later, commentators, recognizing that the level of crime might be overstated, also believed that an irredeemable residuum had to be disciplined by new evolving methods. This residue, the criminal class, was varyingly referred to by Mayhew as 'professional' and by the legislators as 'habitual' criminals. The notion of a criminal class was a convenient one for the governing classes, especially in their insistence that most crime was something committed on law-abiding citizens by an alien group, as respectable commentators informed the audience of their peers. It was accessible to rational (often spatial) control. (In fact, most crimes were opportunistic and petty, with acts of violence largely involving intimates and not strangers.)

However, contagion was a powerful metaphor, because of the fears associated with newly popularized racial theories. Specifically, there were concerns about the Asiatic dockside neighbourhoods, as they were associated with breeding grounds for epidemics, which might infect not only the metropolis but also the colony. These categorizations of the pathological different and idle type, with similar metaphors of the non-Western constructing the reality of the Occident, concealed larger material sources of urban malaise – dislocation of communities, destruction of traditional rural productive processes, and the growth of industrial production, with boundaries that must be policed. For the governing classes, it was necessary to contain this threat, both legally and spatially.

Nineteenth-century legal reforms aimed to replace the omnibus crime and penal control processes of the previous century in response to the new images of the criminal class. Dissatisfaction with the Hanoverian and Georgian crime measures (from the scaffold to transportation)[35] as being too absolute, too inefficient and too capricious, led to new proposals for reform of the system of crime and punishment. Reliance on the repository of transportation overseas (predating later Indian experience in relation to the Andaman Isles), and almost unique to British penal culture, in which minor criminals or those reprieved from the death sentence were banished to foreign lands as indentured labour, was a fallible solution.[36] The development of the New Policing system (formally from 1829 but in practice pioneered much earlier)[37] was conceived as a *cordon sanitaire* to contain that residuum. The police would not only observe note and prevented deviations. Their regular presence would symbolically provide models of virtuous conduct to those they policed.

Codification and individualization of law from the 1820s[38] was a key part of the reform process. The Enlightenment influence of Beccaria[39] and the Utilitarianism of Bentham had inspired, in principle, the creation of a new judicial and moral philosophy, which focused on providing a reformative, rather than retributive, measure of punishment.[40] Modernity was to be guided by the fundamental reference point of a science of ethics founded upon nature's command, as assessed in England by Bentham's mathematical concept of the rational calculus.[41] The influence of these Utilitarian writers helped to initiate a broad shift in the focus of inquiry and level of explanation, based on the principle of humanitarianism.[42] Influenced later by adaptations of Social Darwinism, this notional sensitivity represented the creation of a new form of knowledge, with the extension from repression to rehabilitation through the imposition of a medical model.[43] This mode of analysis marked a radical departure from the dominant contemporary understanding of crime, of law, and of justice. More importantly, if criminality was determined by factors of pathology rather than the rational choice of Classical Theory, then offenders would be punished by spatial and mental segregation from the rest of the population while their abnormal condition would be subjected to programmes of treatment.[44] By employing methods of graduated penality, criminality came to be seen as a legally remediable condition. Key officers of the nineteenth-century criminal justice system embraced these new forms of knowledge. Controlling criminal tendencies intertwined legal changes with developments in the human sciences (see Chapter 4).

The new penal policy was warmly embraced by state officials and the respectable classes in England.[45] It was hailed as modern and objective in its advance on the detection of the criminal types. The prototypical mechanisms of legal changes regarded that crime should be seen as a function of irrationality, which in turn arose from individual and collective pathologies. In turn, this could facilitate the rapid detection of would-be offenders,[46] which in turn would prompt the offenders' progress towards a designated, reformative location on the evolutionary scale. Intertwined with this scheme of detection was a new form of segregation of offenders. Of these, isolation, in its various guises, from penal isolation to surveillance of the rookeries, became the main technique to deal with criminal collectivities. This modernized conception of the criminal type required a differential array of sanctions and dispositions to curtail further criminality in accordance with the nature of the offender and not the criminal act. Apart from those whose deviance was regarded as inherited, there were others who were excluded as potentially open to redemption.[47] Through a system of controlled discipline and punishment, the West demonstrated that the central purpose of incarceration and segregation was the return of the criminals to legal reasoning,[48] an attempt to bring them within the fold of civilization. These views became embodied in the new penological emphasis upon individual and collective rehabilitation programmes.[49]

This perspective was represented in the emerging discourse of social policy – what to do with the 'criminal' classes?[50] In legal discourse, it had emerged in representative form with Jeremy Bentham's idealized model of the Panopticon.[51] The Panopticon structure, with its physical and symbolic characteristics, provided for an accessible classificatory system to inform the evolving legal discourse. Later, calculated measures (most clearly detailed in the omnibus Town Police Clauses Act of 1848 in England) signified the increasing translation of moral and scientific imperatives into legal maxims. The other major change occurred with the professional and specialist state authorities who dealt directly with 'experts', giving them the executive power to supervise and control the criminal types and deal with potential deviants. Hence, deviant identities were analysed and separately classified. Belonging, or rather being designated to a criminal identity would eventually lead to rational responses by the state. Specialists in the various categories of deviance would direct those so defined into eventual appropriate segregation in asylums, penitentiaries, reformatories, workhouses and settlements.[52] (These measures are now better understood within Foucault's conception of the carceral society). Criminal justice procedures were inextricably linked to the practices of domination and the establishment of disciplinary regimes required by industrializing society.[53] The instrument of incarceration was about the power of 'normalization' which operated to isolate the criminal lower classes from the Victorian labouring classes, and from the emerging bourgeois society, and the rough from the respectable poor. The differentiation exclusionary process was incremental from the vagrancy legislation of the 1820s, to the ultimate definitions of the habitual offender in the 1890s, ensuring the continuity in the construction of social identities through law and through the medical, psychological and anthropometric sciences. The impetus for dangerous and immoral acts had became gradually less susceptible to economic explanation, and associated more with the poverty and irrationality of the heathens. For example, the pauper (or more generally, the criminal class) remained threatening, but was singled out to be confined within a restrictive system of criminal and civil tutelage. Unlike the itinerant poor, the urban problem populations could be contained by a system of close educational and penal surveillance. This categorization did not only determine the identities of the lower indigenous classes – and by reflection that of their masters – but also the migrant Irish and the minority groups cast on British shores by the labour requirements of a maritime Empire (see Chapter 5). The authority provided by legal innovations determined the parameters of social status and of identity, legally uplifting the majority and legally denigrating the Victorian criminal classes.

The Formal Structure of Legal Reforms

Institutionally, the period from 1750s to the 1850s constituted a major conjuncture in the English legal system. The early nineteenth century encompassed a haphazard, but considered, overhaul of penal and social policy, and more specifically of the criminal justice process.[54] The focus of the Enlightenment critique centred on traditional penal policy, its harsh sentencing policies, its collective concepts of crime, and especially its ineffectiveness in the legal control of the urban residuum.[55] The transition from Classical legal principles in which crime control was characterized mainly by its deterrent function, and in which judicial discretion was paramount in utilizing public displays of capital and lesser forms of punishment to maintain sovereign rule was to be drastically altered. For the vast majority of lesser crimes, character rather than infraction was to determine judicial process.

Formally, at least, the new system drew upon utilitarian modes of thought. It featured a process of individuation in which the quality of the offence rather than of the offender determined punishment. New citizen rights of due process were ascribed to the accused. Courts were to become a trial, impartially balancing out the equal rights of state and accused. Private responsibilities for apprehension and prosecution were to be replaced by state responsibilities. A new enlightened system, emphasizing innocence until proven guilty, formally took root. Whereas Hanoverian law had relied on the deterrent effect of legal authority, such as the scaffold, Victorian criminal law shifted attention to the criminal's personal responsibility for his behaviour. As Weiner argues, Victorian punishment was restricted so that its discretionary, public and violent character yielded to forms more calculated to promote the development of inner behavioural controls. At all levels, prosecution was made easier, punishment more certain, and penalties more predictable, impersonal and uniform'.[56] Changes in criminal process mirrored and helped to underpin the emergence of the responsible, contractual individual. Reformers Jeremy Bentham and, later, John Howard, through their redefinition of crimes as symptoms of a decaying lower class, as informed by positivistic science, advocated the control of these dangerous impulses through a plethora of criminal statutes.

A new principle of rationality informed criminal legislation. For Bentham, this was dependent on the logical mediation of individual thought and reflection. Within the mental process, however limited, one would be able to locate the necessary polarities of *wrong* and *right*. Applying this principle to the offender it was possible to calculate the benefit or the harm inflicted on society through the individual act. Gratification could be deferred by mental foresight concern about the intensity of pain or pleasure relating indirectly to the cause of an offence, being mediated by factors of gender, age, physique, mental state, moral sensibility, and financial circumstances – and by inference – racial proclivities. Government's function was to stimulate individuals to develop their character and moral worthiness.[57] Individual context would contribute but collective responsibility would not. Those subject to the disciplinary regime of the moral reformers became popularly constructed as the 'dangerous' classes (as above).[58]

Given the tensions between deterrence and moral progress, the Utilitarians advocated drastic reform, notably in the penal domain. Prison would not just incarcerate (deter). It would also educate (reform). Bentham, who had effectively rendered the emblematic public execution redundant, also provided a detailed blueprint for the introduction of criminal justice institutions based on the model of the Panopticon and procedures both in England and abroad, in colonial jurisdictions (as later in the Andaman Islands). Thus, the penitentiary, the new police and the co-terminous changes in criminal jurisdiction, reflected the needs of the propertied classes to suppress imagined criminalities and to instill new forms of civility and discipline on an emerging class of urban criminals.[59]

At the apex of this construction lay the physical Panopticon of the prison aimed to reconstruct the recalcitrants into useful members of society.[60] At the periphery lay the variety of criminal and civil legislation, and social regulation. By 1858, the main features of the Panopticon discourse on penal policy had been firmly established. Although utilitarian philosophy was grounded in a discourse of discipline, it had also developed a sophisticated interpretation of the perceived needs of lower-class society.[61] This was a process of the regulation of the lower orders through individuated criminal and civil legislation. The constructions of the criminal Other validated the transformation of penality, in which categories of disruptive and unruly poor were identified and classified under criminal legislation. This new perspective on penality was imbued with the idea of, on one hand the minority of irredeemable born criminals, lacking in intelligence and 'moral instinct', who would intergenerational transmit the worst of these defects, and on the other, of the majority who could be reformed.

Most early Victorian penal policy conceived of the criminal as mentally deficient with a discourse of inferior character. Moral reform therefore pinpointed the need to ameliorate such waywardness by controlling their passions, firstly external controls and then by self-discipline. This penal reformers' agenda of 'character-building' derived from utilitarian tenets. Crime was signalled as not only a social disorder but also one linked to defective social engineering. From the mid-eighteenth century, a debate on devising an efficient system for categorizing 'criminals' had been vigorously pursued. Reform of the individual criminal soul was sought through what Beccaria had earlier detailed as the replacement of severity or flexibility of penalty with the certainty of punishment. All punishments should be immediate and proportionate to the crime as determined by law.[62]

Thus the principle of rationality advocated by the Utilitarians was effected by a series of efforts to contain and master personal impulsiveness deriving from criminal characteristics. The ultimate goal of the action of any individual or group ought to be the principle of achieving utility, which for Bentham was an innate characteristic of man .[63] Approval or disapproval of every action ought to be measured or assessed according to its tendency to augment or diminish personal happiness.[64] This principle not only applied to the actions of individuals, but also to every measure of government. Consequently, in officialdom, any act of authority of one man over another, for which there was not a necessity, was considered tyrannical. The sovereign's right to punish crimes was founded upon the necessity of defending the liberty of all entrusted to its care, which was preserved as inviolate.[65] Rules were amended, regulations enacted, and new punishments devised as part of a gradual transformation into laws built on perceptions about criminal character.

The discursive component of the reform process in criminal matters was constructed around two distinct modes: a distinctive portrayal of the inhumane, irrationality of the past criminal judicial system, and specificities of the new calculative framework of criminal justice. Bentham's proposals and those of his followers such as Edwin Chadwick, required an entire transformation of the law, based on conclusions drawn from 'indisputable' facts revealed by an inductive scientific approach. Scientific applications would test both morals and law, both intended to promote the rational calculus, which could lead to the perfectibility of man. Utilitarian pursuit of happiness regarded ideals of equality as a secondary matter. C*onsequentialism* was not simply to transform the existing moral basis of society, but also the means to establish and maintain a rationally-ordered society. Imprisonment and more generic careful punishments should be contrived to 'grind rogues',[66] by way of deterrence and of retribution.

Violation of the legal codes, as far as the criminal justice functionaries were concerned, was linked to individual pathology.[67] The consequent shift from punishment aimed at the body to systems of incarceration aimed at the mind was necessary to facilitate self-change, a way of building character, of reshaping the mind of the inferior.[68] The objective of punishment would be to prevent the offender from doing further injury to society, and deter others from committing the same offence. Punishments, therefore, and the mode of inflicting them, ought to be selected for their deterrent capacity on the minds of others, with the least torment to the body of the offender.[69]

This preoccupation with the criminal population culminated in attempts to distinguish between the 'deserving' and the 'undeserving' poor.[70] Official knowledge about pauperism was grounded in the humanism of the Enlightenment. The criminal and the poor were required to participate in the discourse of their own civility and progress, because the Other resided at a lower stage of evolution. Evolutionary tutelage could advance progress and modernity. Notional equivalence of character could be achieved by engineering the less-evolved groups into a modernity based on the principle of eventual equivalence and civility. The criminal, the pauper and the pathological Other, were required to reconstitute themselves in order to be included as subordinates on the path of progress. In this way, the Utilitarians subjected three major components of the legal system – criminal law, policing and penality – to interwoven changes and reforms. From Peel's police reforms in the 1820s, this procedure gradually led to the reconstruction, in its entirety, of the criminal justice system. The several Commissions on law reform and policing in the 1820s and 1830s and, later, in mid-century, the medley of prison and prevention of crime legislation, embodied classifications on pauperism, criminal classes, habitual offenders, suspected persons and more generalized social disorder, seeking to implement the principle of rationality with regard to social control of such categories.[71]

Incarceration gradually came to symbolize the entire criminal justice system. Processes of isolation, segregation and observation (incrementally developed as the 'separate' system under which isolated inmates worked, ate and meditated in their cells) ensured that offenders were removed the malaise of their fellows.[72] This penal system of discipline and of control was reflected in congruent reforms – the regulation of the rookeries by the New Police patrol, to the affirmation of the criminal and civil law to enable surveillance of all suspect groups, in the interests of social discipline.[73]

Typically, the Royal Commission on Criminal Justice in 1834 proposed major changes in sentencing (replicated later in Macaulay's Indian Penal Code of 1860). It replaced the generic (capricious and arbitrary) reliance on capital punishment with a wide range of secondary punishments. The latter, like transportation, imprisonment and fines, were (unlike the death sentence) graduated, in order to precisely deter crime and reform criminal behaviour. Similarly, penal control was extended to ensure that offenders were discharged in regulated probationary status where experts, the doctors and police officers, would be able to treat these offenders[74] for their own good. While this extension of the Panopticon ideal remained at the level of principle rather than of practice, however, it set the standard for Empire in which criminal classes like the criminal tribes and castes of imperial India were dealt with rationally in order to relocate their identity within the evolutionary process.

The New Police: Pre-Emptive Patrols

Gradual reorganization of criminal justice affected the modes of detection, prosecution and punishment, leading to a decline (sometimes by accident rather than design, as with the police) in non-state control. (In parallel terms then, the EIC had attempted to privatize the policing of lascars as early as 1815 'the impossibility in this free country of confining those persons within the prescribed limits, and of thereby preventing their intercourse with the dregs of society, which gives the Lascars of vicious dispositions facility in selling their bedding and clothing, and of contracting loathsome disorders').[75]

Once outside the formal domains of the penal regime, individuals remained under the surveillance of the state's new local police.[76] Part of the reason for this external control was (as above) the threat to the local political economy by disturbances from the criminal areas – memories were long of the Gordon and Caroline outbreaks in the late eighteenth and early nineteenth centuries. New policing powers were asserted. Control of public space was imperative. In the name of prevention, the constabulary was primarily committed to regulating survival patterns in criminal neighbourhoods. Under the Metropolitan Police Act of 1829,[77] waged beat patrollers were to contain the urban criminal class. The police colonized the ghettoes according to a systematic formula. The New Police patrolled the rookery boundaries, occasionally invading that increasingly alien territory, and establishing new stations of control and regular patrols into a disciplinary system of carceral control.[78] Discretionary legislation endowed the new policing agencies with ubiquitous powers for use against those presumed guilty by virtue of character rather than of action. Police surveillance of suspicious characters was intensified. Like the prison, the proactive constable was a cog in the larger machine directing those designated immoral to the discipline of labour, to identify them at an appropriate moral status[79] on the evolutionary ladder.[80] Preventive tutelage rather than coercive reaction was the key – reconstructing the Other within the civilizing process. Policing legislation expanded the scope of the criminal law. The state, local and central, through legislation and discretionary beat surveillance, intended that criminal potential was discovered and checked at birth. Policing supervised the construction of the deviancy label, and collated the characteristics upon which a conviction, a master status, could be founded.

In its development of the professional police, Westminster had created a convenient and effective agent for extending first to the provinces, and later to Empire, its social and crime control policies.[81] A penetrating and constant surveillance was created over the centre of Empire.[82] In policing methods, within discretionary law, a new bureaucracy apprehended criminals and reconstructed immoral and disorderly behaviour. The police were a prophylactic against contagious disease, both moral and criminal.[83] Reforms in policing and punishment were closely linked, as with ticket-of-leave system for habitual criminals. A rational system of criminal justice required both calculated gradation in penalties and proactive policing. More significantly, the reorganization of criminal justice, affecting the spheres of detection, of prosecution and of punishment, led to a significant increase in the scale and scope of legal authority.

Criminal and Civil Laws: the Construction of the Criminal Class[84]

Reading of the legal archives, debates and commentary, reveals not only the speed with which codification of both the criminal and civil codes took place, but also the broad consensus in favour of the legislation. The remarkable widespread concerns as to the nature of criminality, related diseases and the general health of the nation, in both the metropolis and the colony, coupled with the imagery of the savages and the primitive, are most revealing. Three intertwined criminal justice policies of the 1860s were directed at habitual criminals[85] and were central to both Victorian English and imperial Indian legislation. Firstly, prison discipline was tightened; secondly, cumulative sentencing was increasingly employed; thirdly, police supervision of repeat offenders and suspected habituals was increased. Similarly, release from custody was in part dependent upon the prison authorities certifying a person as 'cured'. The duration of punishment would depend on the qualities of the remorse and character reconstruction:

> Incarcerate them all indefinitely and consider returning them to society when we judge their reclamation to be genuine and complete, when we have regenerated their will.[86]

As the social constructionist approach demonstrates, there was not an innate criminogenic population, but one that was redefined, as regulation, control, and discipline became the bedrock of the new structures of the Industrial Revolution. New identities were constructed through a range of criminal and civil legislation. Bentham advocated that the legislation could be used both directly (as in the Vagrancy Act) and indirectly (though the Poor Laws) to establish social discipline of the labouring and non-labouring classes. Law reinforced social control. However, the legal system also unified social interests by realizing the principle of utility.[87] *Social therapeutics* aimed to condition human behaviour on the model of respectable society through social legislation and the creation of institutions ancillary to the prison – the poor houses, the schools, and the mental institutions. Law reform encouraged and enforced the growth of a more self-restrained character type in the general populace and especially in the criminal classes, modelling them on the popular ideas of morality, of values, and of respectability characterizing the propertied classes.[88] Law, criminal and civil, was intended to create a new identity not just of the criminal classes but also of their *alter egos*, the respectables. As Said notes '...the development and maintenance of every culture requires the existence of another different and competing *alter ego* ... the construction of identity involves establishing opposites and Others whose actuality is all subject to continuous interpretation and reinterpretation of their differences from 'us'.[89]

In this text, the construction of the penal Other throws more light on the thinking and perception of the respectable classes than it does on the observed. The bourgeois construction of a criminal class in the Victorian media gave the respectables a sense of superiority over the so-called criminals and also alleviated some fears and uncertainties about crime.[90] New subjectivities and categories evolved, with identities for the criminal and the non-criminal, the unemployed and the habitual vagrant, the immigrant and the criminal alien, the first offender and the habitual criminal, and ultimately a moral distinction was made between the respectable poor and the incorrigibles.[91]

To repeat then, the construction of social categories was based on stereotypical assumptions and essentialized. For example, under the several Vagrancy Acts of 1824, 1829 and 1862, suspicion was legally based on lack of occupation and of abode.[92] Once formally suspected of vagrancy, incarceration and public denunciation of the offender would follow expeditiously.[93] The vagrants were determined by legal reaction rather than by actual behaviour. The centrality of fault in vagrancy reinforced the norm of personal responsibility; if individuals were suspected of vagrancy and failed in normal livelihood, they were deemed responsible for their own misfortune. Variations on the same theme applied to the related misdemeanours of begging and hawking. The survival practices of the poor, not just their more evident recidivist criminality, were subject to criminal control. Legislation redefined social crime,[94] and the struggle of the poor (indigenous and the new imperial minorities) to survive was met by the governing classes criminalizing traditional common law practices. Enforcing the wage economy on the new urbanized masses led to the criminalization of traditional rights of the non-waged on the street.[95] A new exclusionary zone was set up for those who were judged to be parasites.[96]

Criminal Law: Habitual Offenders and Police Powers

The history of codification of criminal law in England was one clear signifier in the construction of demeaning identities. From the mid-1850s, the moral reformers demanded statutory habitual offender control. Inveterate, inherited criminals had to be distinguished from their less intransigent brethren

> The public should no longer confound the honest, independent men with the vagrant beggars and pilferers of the country and that they should see that the one class is as respectable and worthy as the other is degraded.[97]

The Habitual Criminals Act of 1869 was the first system of preventative custody, determined to curtail the supply of potential criminals.[98] The legislation included key clauses expanding police supervision of released prisoners, and gave magistrates new powers to imprison summarily former offenders and vagrants on suspicion alone. The 1869 Act incorporated into statute the notions of a criminal class. The Act constructed a category of incorrigibles, criminals irrevocably addicted to that way of life.[99] Habitual criminals, argued Mayhew, were hedonistic persons who felt labour to be more irksome than others, owing to their inability to apply themselves. As a consequence, habitual criminals were given harsher sentences on suspicion alone, sanctions more severe than provided under the Vagrancy Act of 1824. Experts, whether police constables, prison officials or the judiciary, marginalized habitual criminals as a self-contained and organized criminal class who lived exclusively by crime.[100] Habituals were released on license under a 'pass' system but were subject to surveillance by police officers. If the former inmate could not prove he was conducting honest labour – the onus was on him – he was subjected to a potential further seven years imprisonment.[101] (The practice also appears to have encouraged both police arbitrariness and police corruption.) Enhanced police discretion, as in the assumption of prosecution roles,[102] later led to further prevention by targeting criminal areas.[103] Criminal areas were clearly recognizable as a breeding ground for crime and immorality, and a threat to the political and social order.[104] Repeated warnings to the respectable classes amplified fears of the category of habitual criminals and this class was reminded that they were not to be confounded with labouring classes.[105] As the most prominent psychologist of the Victorian period, Henry Maudsley claimed:

> The evil propensities of habitual criminal as veritable instincts ...We may take it then that there is a class of criminals formed of beings of defective physical and mental organisation; one result of the defect, which really determined their destiny in life, is a deficiency of moral senses.[106]

Legislation consequently extended supervisory and penal powers beyond the walls of the prison.[107] Categorization and classification became widely employed in state institutions like the workhouses, prisons, mental hospitals and schools. Once subjected to normalization, correction and surveillance, suspected persons were deemed capable of entering into civil society, or else they were segregated from public space to minimize any damage they could inflict.[108]

Civil Law: Vagrancy and the Workhouse

Demarcation between types of offence and the 'criminal' was conflated with social legislation based on the work ethic and social need. In the diversionary process, minority groups and especially the Irish (to be succeeded by the other ethnic minorities) were labelled with the imagery of the sturdy beggar, unwilling but able to work. The criminal and civil legal mix was morally underpinned.[109] For example, Bentham's examination of the poor, and his resulting evidence of the relationship between poverty and indigence, had led him to the proposition that poverty was essential to the creation of wealth '...As labour is the source of wealth so is poverty of labour. Banish poverty and you will banish wealth'.[110]

In particular, the non-labouring recipient of poor relief was to be less eligible than that of the industrious poor; otherwise the incentive to work would be removed. These principles had been incorporated in Edwin Chadwick's New Poor Law of 1834.[111] The workhouse was introduced to provide care for the elderly and infirm, and work for the able-bodied. However, the conditions in those institutions deliberately deterred all but the most desperate from entering. Pauperism was seen, by implication, as a wilful choice of the idle, who were denied community membership, not just by physical removal to the workhouse, but also by moral condemnation. The new arrangements for poor relief were based on the notion of the 'idle' individual. These arrangements reflected the intention of the policymakers to discourage pauperism with the workhouse as the deterrent, which also gave the parish effective control over the 'vagrants'. The vagrants were then separated from others. Pauperism received moral condemnation from the 'respectable' poor who saw these social menaces as arising from idle individuals. The 1834 Act was instrumental in its disciplinary mechanisms as it came to be based on the principles of 'less eligibility' in order to encourage workers to make provision for themselves.

In essence, aims of the Poor Law were to regulate the poor, not only to combat the condition of pauperism but of vice in which most of the vagrants found themselves.[112] The new Poor Laws embodied the principle of eligibility: 'The situation of the individual relieved, must not be made really or apparently so eligible as the situation of the independent labourer of the lowest class'.[113] It was believed that the state of dependency would reproduce itself 'Callous to its own degradation and the failure to work was a moral failure and dependency, the cause of moral degeneration'.[114]

Interestingly, the Poor Law legislation mirrored criminal legislation. It was imbued with the belief that persistent indulgence in immoral acts and behaviour threatened to destroy social institutions, especially the foundations of life, namely the family, and threatened values of self-discipline and respect, for the property and persons of others, upon which social stability and national survival supposedly depended. Conversely, severe penal sanctions were imposed on vagrants who rejected the Workhouse.

Bentham's proposals for pauper management were based on the application of the penal Panopticon model to Industry Houses. The latter would be built on the principle of central inspection, and relief based upon the principle (not dissimilar to Charles Booth's plans for the rural settlements)[115] of entering productive labour. Those considered vagrants were to be apprehended and forced to work for their keep in the workhouse. Their children were to be indentured as apprentices, bonded to the workhouse until reaching adulthood. The principles of the factory system would determine the management of paupers, but also the time and work disciplines of capitalist production would transform them into productive labour, assisted by moral education.

While vagrancy, like habitual offender status, became a major signifier in constructing the meaning of criminality universally, the Poor Laws had a more local mandate. Controlling paupers was the direct economic responsibility of parish councils. The workhouses were emblematic of the treatment of the poor by the law which was established both as a means of discipline and of relief.[116] The Vagrancy Statute of 1862 enhanced punishments for idle and disorderly persons. Incorrigible rogues were sentenced to hard labour. Categories of vagrant were reinforced. Incarceration processes differentiated between the 'idle' and the 'able', between the 'deserving' and the 'undeserving' poor.[117] Vagrancy was blamed both for causing crime directly and also for creating the poverty, that led to crime. The process of poor relief was a mechanism of assessing the needy as a means of control. Relief was dependent upon coercing and training the impotent poor, the able-bodied, and the residuum to work; there were penal sanctions for those who absconded.[118] The divisive Poor Law statutes were later strengthened by ancillary civil legislation such as the Contagious Diseases Act of 1864, conflating notions of illness, immorality and crime.

Essentialism in the Modernizing Project of Law

In reality, much of the legal reform was ephemeral. For example, new rights in trial only related to felony crimes. The more serious offences, some 10 per cent of the whole, were dealt with by the Assizes. For misdemeanours, mainly crimes against property, household crime and so-called 'victimless' crimes, the formal view (as enunciated much later in the Gladstone Committee of 1895)[119] is deeply suspect. The offenders were dealt with in the inferior courts, where the contractual individual was only ephemerally present. Lay Justices of the Peace became much more important. Their previous allotment of so-called victimless crimes of vagrancy, drunkenness and disorder, was now vastly enlarged with those discarded by the higher courts. For the vast majority of minor offences, offending meant trial (often a euphemism for arbitrary processing) by the justices. Criminal justice was indeed fundamentally transformed in this period but not as traditionally assumed. Magistrates' justice was summary justice. Justices were typically laypeople incapable of adhering to the letter of the law in imposing supposedly well-defined individuated penalties on convicted offenders. They persistently exercised the older judicial discretion in dealing with the common people who formed their primary constituency, often being ignorant of (and at times, breaking) the letter of the law in their legal decisions. Penalties were subject to local exigencies such as the costs of incarceration. Local prisons, for example, were poorly funded and subject to rapid turnover. Individuated experience of law, from arrest to incarceration, may have been the form of law but it was not the substance.[120] Inquisition rather than accusation was the norm.

The identification of a criminal class and related social categories owed more to those involved in that defining process than those who became subject to it. Legal labelling was an apparently arbitrary but actually rational device. Most common and habitual criminals were a creation of legal and social discourse. So-called habituals were only criminal by virtue of their need to survive during periods of unemployment and public denunciation of their characters.[121] The construction of a criminal class owed more to the imagination and anxieties of lawmakers. Social reaction created homogeneity out of heterogeneity. Law violation through economic circumstances had many versions.[122]

In the following chapters, these issues are pursued. The relevance for the central questions raised at the outset lies in Freitag's assertion, in 1991, that the debate behind the Habitual Criminals Act of 1869 was well known by administrators deliberating the enactment of the Criminal Tribes Act of 1871 in imperial India. She quotes one official:

> Even the English law has recently introduced exceptional powers against the habitual criminals, [because] when prospective criminals become a dread to the community, then it is necessary to impose laws of exceptional rigour, and to accept some amount of evil to evildoers against a large number of the general public.[123]

The Criminal Tribes Act of 1871 for India had been passed by the same legislative assembly that was instrumental in constructing the almost identical powers in the Habitual Criminals Act of 1869. Images of the dangerous strata were near identical in the construction of new identifies. Broad swathes of criminal legislation had demarcated the criminal classes in Victorian England. Such legal innovations in the identification and control of the dangerous strata occurred not because of substantive alteration in the characters, motivations and composition of the 'criminal' classes but rather because of ideological perceptions of that social formation. What changed in early nineteenth-century England was not so much the rise of the new urban mass, but rather the development of a coercive criminal justice apparatus, built on scientific identities. Subsequent chapters argue that through the vehicle of a legal rationalism, the West reconstructed the subordination of the non-Western. However, a distinction was made between the minority ethnic groups judged irredeemable and an indigenous criminal class which could be reformed – made modern. Criminal judicial functionaries engaged in an exercise of separating the indigenous lower classes from the new ethnic minority groups. The social construction and subordination of the non-Western was reflected in the way in which the discourses of race and civility converged. Definitions and categories, like identities, are social constructions and necessarily operate to exclude the Other. In temporality, the violence of that construction functions to conceal and transform its exclusions into fact.

4 SCIENTIFIC RACISM AND THE CONSTITUTION OF DIFFERENCE

'The British, or rather the East India Company, are the masters of India because it is the fatal destiny of Asian empires to subject themselves to the Europeans'.[1]

In 1875, Thomas Carlyle asked Darwin whether 'there was a possibility of men turning into apes again'.[2]

Introduction: Difference

The previous chapter focused on the functions of law in the criminalization of an indigenous white class in Victorian England. Under new legal regimes, identities assumed new meanings. The main aim of this chapter is to illustrate the contribution of the new human sciences, and especially of criminological positivism, to the construction of the status of crime and criminals for both the indigenous poor and those deemed racially inferior and irredeemable. The language of science lent itself formidably to the structures of authority based on models of rationality, which seemed to provide the most potent explanations of the modern world. In the nineteenth century, scientific taxonomies and popular fiction shaped narratives in highly contested ways, fitting newly discovered forms within classificatory systems complemented by legal ascription. The history of criminal and scientific discourse illustrates how racialized constructions were enhanced during a key moment in which Western identity strove for a new assignation. Drawing upon social constructionism, this chapter documents the interaction between those who do the defining, and those who are defined. Those weighted negotiations resulted in new identities, as one came to exclude its Others through a particular medium – a scientific discourse. Race was the key 'scientific' concept through which the gradualism of liberalism reconciled itself to the coercion of imperial rule. The language and concepts of Victorian racism served to accommodate the incorrigibles in the metropolitan and colonial social order. The defective constitution of those defined as inferior natives, coupled with a conflated notion of hereditary and of biological determination of conduct, is explored here through early positivistic criminology. It is precisely these forms of representation and the manner in which knowledge production about the Other is constructed, and later appropriated by the agents of the law to police and discipline this Other. Through assessing and contrasting reason with irrationality, the Western through a scientific discourse of dangerousness and savagery, determined appropriate regimes of discipline for the non-Western, in order to secure and maintain its own superior position, in the face of the increasing fear and anxiety it faced when confronted with the natives.

The dominance of these new forms of classification was encapsulated by the philosophical discourses of that time. Metaphysical, classical and utilitarian philosophies and the changing concepts of race all contributed to the development of racial and criminal types in both the metropolis and the colony. As noted in Chapter 3, the penal responses in nineteenth century England in relation to criminality were not rooted in the problem of crime, so much as in the transformation in character through informed rational response (often reflected in legal reform) to the threat of this perceived danger, and the fear of the monster.

Racial Ideologies

Several discursive distinctions need to be made at the outset. Racist ideologies long predated nineteenth-century colonialism. Different scientific racist ideologies contributed to different extents within the colonial project. Racist ideologies are epistemological constructs in seeking to establish difference. As such they can be deconstructed with regard to composition and in relation to debates about racial origins.

Race, from that classic position, can be empirically established. It is a naturally occurring division of humanity. However, the meaning of race itself is problematic. It can be related to particular hereditary features, such as skin colour, or in terms of geographical location. It can have a specific meaning with regard to a collection of given attributes. It can be generalized as, say, 'Indian', to cover both castes and tribes. Culture (especially morality) and intellectual capacities can be imputed from the biological fact of race. In that sense, behaviour of individuals and collectivities is therefore predictable, given appropriate scientific techniques. Further, early research findings claimed a ranking in terms of individual and collective capacities, both physically and mentally. A hierarchy of difference can be established and hence, inequality is a given, based on racial difference. Politically, those races at the apex of the hierarchy believe that they have a given responsibility to deal as appropriately with the lesser races. Racist ideologies are different from the racialist with regard to the existence of such a hierarchy. Racialist arguments are not bound by assumptions of differential racial worth. Racialists, insofar as they recognize hierarchies of difference, appreciate that different capacities of different races may lead to coexisting hierarchies. These two approaches, racialist and racist, however, have a common underpinning. Differentiated races are determined, either by Nature or by God. In particular, destiny determines racial classifications, the process of racial uplift or racial degeneration, characteristics which could one way or another, be passed on to future generations to survive and in others, guiding them to extinction.

Remarkably then, in developing a philosophical basis for the legitimation of power and control in both the metropolis and the colony, a major bifurcation in racist contributions – of the monogenetic and the polygenetic was appropriated to reduce and discipline the Other. Consequently, recognizing that difference over origins leads to different proposals for the legitimation and practice of the colonial endeavour, the monogenetic theories (essentially, biological approaches) held the belief that all peoples have a similar genetic source. For example, difference in physique and especially in behaviour in the age of empire are due to environmental and/or to degenerative factors, whereas polygenetic accounts (mainly anthropological) hold that imputed racial difference is based on different genetic origins. As such, the fundamental binary division between black and whites had different genetic origins.

Predictably, there may be a sliding scale that places some races nearer to animal genetic origins than others – for example the animal-like Asiatics in Victorian England and the native tribes in India. Although there are less polarized versions of such monogenetic and polygenetic approaches, the key point is that at the extremes they lead to quite different forms of social control. Under the monogenetic classification system, the deviant races or individuals have the potential to be reformed, under appropriate tutelage, whereas the polygenetist holds that the inherited characteristics of different races are essentially unreformable and their deviance, which is innate, can only be dealt with by either segregation or by extermination. More pointedly, racists defined deviance as something that deviates from the attributes of the race at the apex of the fixed monolithic hierarchy.

At its core, the concept of racism has a long epistemological pedigree. In particular, there is an extensive monogenetic history of distinct biological groups being classified, based on physical appearances. Enlightenment thinkers, searching for explanations of their own origins, drew on past histories in mapping out physical and cultural transformations from the primitive man in the state of nature, to the modern state of civilization in which they assumed themselves to be the most advanced representatives of the modern world. Both Enlightenment and later imperial scholars claimed an extraordinary pedigree as the foundation for their legitimation of the moral and intellectual superiority of the white races.

Racialist, as opposed to racist, ideologies are commonly traced back to the Greek philosophers, within what in Aristotelian philosophy, became known as the *The Great Chain of Being*. Aristotle argued that there was a natural separation of the characteristics of masters, women, and the slaves, but they all shared a common genetic source. Aristotle proposed that an early functionalist explanation of racial integration offered an alternative explanation of the races, which has often been overlooked by scholars. Given their different capacities ('psyches' – negative, locomotive and rational), all races were functional to the harmony of the social order:

> 'The universe resembles a large and well-regulated family, in which all the officers and servants, and even the domestic animals, are subservient to each other...each enjoys the privileges and perquisites relevant to his place; and at the same they contribute, to the magnificence and happiness of the whole'.[3]

However, racialism as developed by Aristotle is an ideology of difference, not of inequality, when contrasted with racism. Racism promotes the notion that there is a natural preordained hierarchical social order, which naturally separates the races into inferior and superior. The physical characteristics of the different races are linked to other less-observable features – take, for example, the notion that skin colour is a signifier of mental qualities. Hence, moral and intellectual worth could be imputed from physical signs. As part of this logic both the outward signs of difference and inner capacities are innate, and genetic inheritance determines physical and mental attributes.

Later scientific racism drawing, *inter alia*, on Aristotelian insights furnished increasing precision and delineation of given attributes, allowing predictions of future actions and human capacities. Consequently, documented personal and collective histories of different races, which deploy scientific gradations, allowed judgments to be made and policies formulated for the control of the behaviour of inferior groups. The latter signifies the use of scientific or ostensibly scientific findings and methods to support or validate racist attitudes and worldviews. Such scientific racism is also a political ideology utilized to legitimize social inequality.

Racial Types and the Enlightenment

To understand degeneracy and atavism, early Western philosophies refined racialism by introducing the core racist ideas of natural ordering – some were worth morally and intellectually more than others, while some were degenerates, the inferior savage heathen most noticeably, beyond the pale of civilization. Their extinction would encourage the others to be saved. During the Enlightenment period, theological explanations of this natural racial ordering were increasingly replaced by secular/scientific explanations. Coexistence of competing racial ideologies was the norm. In fact, the emerging European colonial powers promoted not just racial difference, but also the concept of a natural hierarchy which affected the practice of domestic social reforms. From metaphysical sources of the seventeenth and early eighteenth centuries, notions of superiority and inferiority became more pronounced and were aimed at the foreigners. Social change was an inevitable process. Evolutionary accounts were coupled with crude typologies – angels and other metaphysical spirits were the primary driving force, while humans were secondary, followed by animals. Typical of such work was that of Richard Eden,[4] in which theological justifications for racial ordering were coupled with empirical observations based on encounters between white and black populations, in the Spanish Empire and in the early African slave trade. Eden argued that while some races survived, the others would perish as climatic determinism thrived. The first English settlers in North America would evolve, because of the climate, to look like Native Americans. The indigenous peoples appeared more susceptible to diseases and to early fatality, as compared with the settlers' natural physical superiority of the white man's body.

Hence, a new secularism diminished the theological source. A schism emerged between monogenetists and the new polygenetists. Despite later contrivances, monogenetic theories of human evolution did not challenge theological accounts while, paradoxically, polygenetic writers did. Typologies of different origin informed polygenetic Enlightenment scholars as the handmaiden of the Western colonialism. The racially distinct colonized were evidently at the end of their life history. As inferior beings, their energy was sapped. European colonization only speeded up an inexorable process. These assumptions reinforced a largely secular view, justifying European pre-eminence and control over other racial groups.

The Colonial Input in Racist Images of Difference

Typical of such early scholars was Francis Bernier (1625–88) in his *New Division of the Earth*. He summarized the key racist themes of Enlightenment philosophy. Human development was primarily secular, and human beings were part of the natural, rather than the sacred world. He developed an arbitrary secular typology, based on physical attributes – the Europeans, North Africans, South Asians, Africans, East and North East Asians, and Lapps.[5] Essentially mental qualities could be read from physical factors. Bernier's confidence that his argument was irrefutable drew on personal experience: he had travelled throughout India and had observed and admired the Indian nobility, while disparaging lower castes and tribes as of different origins. His ideas were popularized, partly because of that unique firsthand experience in India, by the Swedish writer, Carl Linnaeus (1707–78), from within the monogenetic tradition. Linnaeus devised a sophisticated fourfold typology of the continent-based races.[6] Each race had clear mental characteristics – inter alia, Native Americans were stubborn and angered easily, whereas Asians were avaricious, and easily distracted. Whites were seen as clever, inventive and governed by laws and by contrast, the Africans were indolent, negligent and governed by caprice. Linnaeus's obsessive classifications influenced the great philosophers of the time, notably Hegel, Kant, Comte and Spencer, in depicting progress from primitive society to industrialized civilization. Further refinements were later offered by George Comte De Buffon (1707–88). What separated De Buffon from others was his philosophical and empirical pursuit of causes and explanations, in which he argued that human races were located on a continuum of progress. Like other scholars, but more systematically, he used arbitrary observations to determine the new hierarchy and concluded that other races were degenerate relative to Europeans. Probably the most influential polygeneticist of the eighteenth century was Johann F. Blumenbach (1752–1840). Like Buffon, he perceived continuity, rather than distinct types, in delineating five complex hierarchical racial groupings.[7] His interest in craniometry, especially the study and analysis of human skulls to correspond to racial categories, resulted in him declaring that the white race were the common origin.

The ideas that reigned supreme at the time followed that human beings were of different species, and therefore of different origins, which coincided neatly with the Enlightenment ideas of equality, universality and sameness. As a result of these definitions, social progress simply meant that different races proceeded at different speeds on the trajectory of life. Similar arguments were imputed by the Enlightenment philosopher, Immanuel Kant (1724–1804), whose work had major influence. His essay *Of the Different Races of Human Beings,* relies on a monogenetic typology, in which the study of the whites of Northern Europe, the 'copper-coloured' native Americans, the blacks of 'Senegambia' and the 'olive-skinned' Indians, was elucidated. For him, the fundamental differences and inequalities between the races would eventually result in the death of the non-white races. For Kant, the Others were presumed to be incapable of change, given that their physical attributes were linked with behaviour and value systems. Eighty years later that classification was refined by the 'godfather of scientific racism', the French reactionary and aristocrat, Count Arthur Gobineau (1816–82). The imagery that Gobineau consistently used throughout his essay[8] centred around the metaphor of the birth and death of developed civilizations. The principle of life and death comes from continually mixing the blood of races. According to Gobineau's logic, it is only through the adulteration of their blood, mongrelism, that people become progressively more degenerate. Hence, he provides the basic paradigm in which civilizing mental abilities of the racially purer classes are in direct conflict with the degenerate, miscegenated lower-class's tendencies.

Gobineau's deterministic monogenetic views were most evidently challenged by the polygenetist Englishman James Cowles Prichard (1786–1848), who also happened to be a strong opponent of slavery. Using ethnographic material from travellers and missionaries, Prichard confirmed that Europeans were the superior race.[9] His initial work rejected the environmentalist (essentially climatic) explanation in favour of inheritance. Prichard argued that miscegenation would not affect heredity because of the choices different races made to choose cognate mates. This selection would enable the right characteristics to be passed on. The idea that the diversity of human customs and behaviour might be dependent on biology that was opposed to external factors such as the environment encouraged European scientists to consider the polygenetic view of human origins as the answer to their questions. Each race had its own distinct process of creation and homeland. Different races and species were transmuted into different types and difference could be explained materially. Predictably, white races were evidentially superior in all aspects to non-whites. In this way, the mindset of reformers helped them argue that the key question to be resolved was whether the civilizing process would enable dark-skinned races to catch up with light-skinned races.

More pointedly, the obsessive detail with which the allegedly activity of miscegenation and degeneracy was analysed, was subsequently widely reproduced in anthropological accounts of race. Firsthand colonial experiences increasingly intervened in this analysis. Typical of those scholars was the fundamental contribution made by the Anglo-French biologist William F. Edwards (1776–1842). With colleagues, he helped produce a racial map of Europe, in which he outlined the thesis that each race had its own physical and mental attributes. Drawing on the work of philosopher Claude Henri De Saint-Simon, (1760–1825), his views were marginally modified in the political functionalism of Victor Courte de L'Isle.[10] De L'Isle had experienced the high death rates of French colonialists in Algeria and rejected the climatic causal factors of the early monogeneticists. The colonializers had been unable to acclimatize themselves to local vicissitudes. Therefore, racial differences, especially their capacity to survive and perish, depended on genetics rather than the environment. In the case of Algeria, which was France's most significant Other, its very site provided France with a sense of worth and superiority. Each race should be understood as having a place in society and their native capacities recognized. Policy was important. Race scientists had a responsibility to propagate their findings, and their success would ultimately be seen in the stability of the social order, where the threat of a revolution prevailed.

Such views were informed popularly by the ongoing exploitation of England's first colony – Ireland. Observed attributes of the peasant Irish intervened with the process of European imperialism and helped legitimize the colonization processes both at home and abroad.[11] Early colonial administrators contributed to the explanation of the Other, as an adjunct to policy. Amongst others, Edward Long (1734–1813),[12] the Lieutenant-Governor of Jamaica, regarded classification of the races as necessary for governance. He drew up a detailed taxonomy of the English, Spanish, Dutch, Creoles and black races, each with their specific attributes, partly mediated by a degree of interbreeding. Long argued that physical and behavioural characteristics of the different race, were a combination of inheritance and of adaptation to the Jamaican context.

In essence, early studies, such as Long's, demonstrate that the meaning of race and of racial difference, varied according to the form of colonial governance. It is clear that Long echoed Kant in arguing, that those of African origin, had failed to 'improve' despite being subject to Europen colonization for many years.[13] The constant serach for a pure origin continued in the colonies, especially in the way in which one was and can be dehumanized by pratices of imperial othering.

Like imperial administrators, colonial missionaries also contributed to the new racist sciences. Remarkably, there was a relative convergence between evangelists and early positivism. An evangelical view, reconciling Enlightenment secularism with earlier metaphysics, was articulated by energetic missionaries and their institutional backers in contributing to biological ideologies of race.[14] One typical account is from the Baptist, William Carey (1761–1834), who expressed his desire to create India in England's image. Although imperial evangelism had originally targeted European settlers, people like Carey regarded the capture of the heathens in the British empire as the logical next step. Such contributions had a byproduct: missionaries garnished raw data on imperial subjects for the new sciences.[15] Given the intensity of religious observation in the early nineteenth century, such accounts from the missionaries were a primary source of information on the constitution of the Other for a much wider audience. More pointedly, the Evangelicals were recognized as an important source of data and information for state policy. For example, the EIC, despite its protests, was required to allow access to its territories to the evangelists at the end of the eighteenth century.[16] In turn, domestic missionaries, often connected directly with their brethren in the Empire, contributed to popular and scientific discourse in constructing images of the primitive English criminal classes'.

In England, Prichard's Christian monogenetic position was superseded by the polygenetist, Robert Knox (1791–1862). An Edinburgh anatomist and racial theorist, Knox had considerable South African colonial experience in refining Gobineau's typologies. In his most influential work, *The Races of Men,* invoking the work of Buffon, he claims that essentially there is a history of the racial struggle for supremacy, in which different racial types were unaffected by either environmental factors or by interbreeding.[17] In essence, Europeans and Africans were clearly of different species and even different races, set in a state of permanence. Despite some of his own complex views, Knox's work was used by the succeeding Social Darwinists to justify European imperialism. Prichard's work in the *London Ethnological Society* was challenged by other polygeneticists, such as James Hunt (1833–69) who helped set up the *London Anthropological*

Society. What is remarkable and common to both sides in the emerging struggle between monogenetic and polygenetic, and in the emerging academic conflict between ethnologists and anthropologists, was that both argued that their disciplines should be placed at the service of state policies in the governance of both the urban mass of the metropolis and of the colonial Others. Policy pressed for scientific explanation of colonial phenomena. Central to the conditions that incited the modern form of governance are key moments of native resistance and rebellion in both Victorian England and in the colony. There are several instances, such as the rebellious behaviour of the natives at Cawnpur in 1857, and similarly evidence of lascar and ayahs resorting to crimes of survival in the metropolis, which pushed racial thinking to its unrecognizable limits. Rational explanations had to be found. Evident from such works and instances is that racism was not, as in Saidean discourse, simply an imperial creation and projection. Racial discourses were reworked and reformulated in colonial settings, not just by officials, governors, missionaries and transient travelers, but by those who tried to put 'the natives' to work,[18] and also to contain and discipline their wayward behaviour.

The tensions and ambivalence generated by the Other meant that the colonial state itself was in transition. Marked differences existed between the early and late periods of colonial rule in British India, just as between British colonialism in India and Africa. In the colonial context itself, as opposed to the centre of Empire, that imagined native character – not race – was the key issue upon which legislative decisions turned.[19] Together, the new racist sciences intersected with imperialism in several ways, especially as the colonized were evidently at the end of their racial life and such endings should be mentored. Colonization only speeded up an inexorable process, especially as the EIC was dissolved and the British Crown assumed direct control over India in 1858.[20] The problems experienced by both the governing classes and the non-Western needed informed resolution. Given that scientific racism had become regarded as a generality, as a stable and comprehensive paradigm, formulated in Europe, these ideas were extended inexorably into the irredeemable Orient, as well as to subjugate the Asiatics and heathens in the metropolis. Scientific racism was critical to that differentiation process.

Eugenics and the Consolidation of Scientific Racism

The colonial imperium was founded on an explicit racism. Such mid-century views were bolstered with evolutionary inputs from Herbert Spencer (1820–1903) and Thomas Huxley (1825–95), in an interpretation of the (belated) publication of Darwin's (1809–82) *The Descent of Man*.[21] Darwin inferred racial differences and European superiority. Darwin, while denying the polygenetist position, noted that stronger tribes always replaced the weaker. When the savages encountered civilization, they were destroyed.[22] Despite Darwin's reservations on the new emerging racist sciences, enough could be read into his work to lend support and credibility to similar racist ideas. Other sub-disciplines emerged. For example, J. H. Gall's phrenological theories and practices contributed to the stock of imperial knowledge – especially in its commitment to measurement[23] as a basis for policy. The new discipline of social statistics contributed to this form of knowledge production (see Chapter 8). State officials possessed a new instrument of assessment of the inferiority of its local and colonial subjects. In phrenology, colonial ethnographers had an accessible tool, for example, in classifying subject populations as 'barbaric' or 'martial'.[24] More importantly, when one looks at the connection between empire, race and law, it is the adaptation of the new eugenics from Darwin's work by Galton (1822–1911) that provided a missing link. In the name of enlightened civilization, Galton's vivid description of the human faculty serves to provide a hierarchy of both the advanced and the backward races.[25] Galton set out to examine whether human ability was hereditary. From biographical accounts of man, he answered the question in the affirmative.[26] Galton was concerned with collective rather than individual behaviour – tribes and classes rather than individuals, despite his foray into individuation by fingerprints.[27] He was also committed to prediction – how to be forewarned about those who would show traits of hereditary criminality. As a founder of what transiently became known as criminal anthropology, he wished to document the facts of different races in order to predict, and consequently prevent, their future criminality.[28] His rhetoric tended to betray his commitment to scientific objectivity. Later he spoke of a 'recently uplifted savage' as he compiled a ranking of racial abilities, according to each race's distance from its bestial origins from the '...Jabbering, quarrelling, tom-tomming, or dancing negroids to the self-complacency of a steady-going Chinaman'.[29] There was, however, a more encompassing agreement between Galton and Spencer, in which they both claimed that criminals were less evolved than their fellows.[30] However, it was Galton who was the key to the scientific identification of whole genetic groups with an inherited predisposition to criminality – like the criminal classes and criminal tribes. As such, his logic fitted directly for the Victorian commitment to a body of law that pre-assigned certain groups, on the basis of their birth, so as to civilize some from a criminal constituency and segregate those who were deemed to be irredeemable.

Criminal Types and Images of Dangerousness

Without a doubt, the Enlightenment had given birth to the independent scientific domains of anthropology, ethnology and biology, producing (mainly) polygenetic hierarchical classifications, combining both physical and mental characteristics. Increasingly, anthropology dominated discourses on racial difference.[31] By the mid-nineteenth century, such sciences emerged as an important discourse in modernity 'the neutrality and objectifying distantiation of the rational scientist created the theoretical space for a view to develop bodies. Once objectified, these bodies could be analyzed, categorized, classified, and ordered with the cold gaze of scientific distance'.[32] Other academic disciplines contributed. These ideas came to define human history according to the cultural-racial categories of savagery, barbarism and civilization. For example, J. S. Mill's essay, *Civilisation* (1836), had formalized the hierarchy of the historical stages of mankind, bringing geography and history together in a scheme of European superiority, and identifying civilization with race.[33]

Given such forceful observations and accommodations, the new positivist sciences increasingly informed criminological discourse. Criminal behaviour was legible and open to interpretation and comprehension by science. Early criminology absorbed biological and anthropological assumptions over genetic inferiority and superiority, structuring debates not just over racial difference and social hierarchy, but also with regard to criminality and dangerousness. Populations could be split into the binary divisions of the normal and the pathological, reinforcing images of the abnormality of the non-Western, thus mirroring local distinctions between the respectable and the 'criminal' classes. Scientific knowledge formulated an appropriate interpretative framework for continually criminalizing the dangerous types in three ways. Firstly, in categorization of the domestic criminal class,[34] secondly, the identification of its non-Western component within that criminal class; and thirdly of the colonized in colonial India. The concept of dangerousness developed currency in determining identities, especially of the dangerous classes. Scientific racism legitimized the notion of dangerousness.

The new urban bourgeoisie and the urban working class knew their own identity, because they were not the Other – the dangerous class. The term 'dangerous class' had first risen in France in the writings of Fregier, in which he provides a clear distinction between the poor and the dangerous,

> the poor and vicious classes have always been and always will be the most productive breeding grounds of evil-doers of all sorts: it is they whom we shall designate as the dangerous class. For even when vice is not accompanied by perversity, by the very fact that it allies itself with poverty in the same person, he is a proper object of fear to society, he is dangerous.[35]

In the imperial domain, imperial fears were enhanced by the eugenicist ideologies of crime and dangerousness, further enhancing the impetus to control incorrigibles and the racially inferior. Images of racial aberration, combining colonial subjection of lesser peoples and their reduction to the status of savages with evolutionary imagery of the dangerous class required that the subjects, indigenous and non-Western, be removed once and for all, from civilized society and its standards.

More specifically then, dangerousness as a criminal type was not, of course, invented by the new sciences, it was merely refined. Long before the Habitual Criminals Act 1867,[36] informal images of the criminal had been prevalent. For example, the 'sturdy beggar' was an image redolent of Elizabethan history and was sustained well into the nineteenth century. Various descriptions of the dangerous criminal types in the metropolis had been circulated by the *Police Gazette* of the Bow Street Runners in the mid-eighteenth century. A set of basic characteristics were then assigned to each type in the popular common discourse by the Georgians and Victorians. On the one hand, there is the juridical person (the citizen) who can own property and enter into market transactions but with limited right to claim official welfare benefits; and the Other is the irreconcilable deviant criminal who was to be the subject of control.[37] The former might occasionally be aberrational in conduct, but this behaviour could be modified.

The Internal Other

More pertinent to our discussion is the way in which racial stereotyping of the colonials as dangerous develops. My interest here is to demonstrate how the above competing images on law and racial types, outlined above, are marshalled to legitimate different projects of power, with different stakes; and, more importantly for the purposes of this book, different strategies of resistance as will be shown in the following chapters. The image that emerges from the colonial archive on scientific racism proclaims that the non-Western was highly charged and corrupt. It is this image which prompted British legislatures to intervene to stop the threat of this ever-growing dangerous class. Various typologies were constructed internally as well as externally. Imperialism in Ireland (as above) was one source of the new criminal science.[38] Cartoons in Punch portrayed the Irish as having ape-like features, stigmata linked by later phrenologists to a lower evolutionary order and criminality. The Irish in Britain had arrived at a crucial time of the development of the British state, a project directed at developing a homogenized society and culture. Irish Catholic migrants represented by defining the Other, from which the opposite, national unity, could be defined, Britishness and concomitant notions of respectability was defined by what it was not – Irishness. In John Beddoe's[39] *Races of Britain* (1862) that all men of genius were orthognathous (less prominent jaw bones), while the Irish and the Welsh were prognathous and that the Celt was closely related to Cromagnon man who, in turn, was linked, to the 'Africanoid'. Popular culture absorbed and reflected these images. The 'ape-like' Celt became something of a malevolent cliché of Victorian racism, 'I am haunted by the human chimpanzees I saw [in Ireland], I don't believe they are our fault. But to see white chimpanzees is dreadful; if they were black, one would not feel it so much'.[40] The Irish were regarded as 'immature' and in need of proper tutelage. Their emotional selves were contrasted, unfavourably, with English 'reason'. These were all arguments which conveniently supported British rule in Ireland.[41]

At the turn of the twentieth century, Asian and black minorities,[42] the human products of the imperial mission and of mercantile trade, had been a visible, if shifting and unstable segment, within the larger dangerous class within the metropolis. The presence, seen as an intrusion, of the non-Western on England's streets compounded perception of dangerousness. Popular concepts of race embraced varied religious, caste, tribal, national and ethnic identities, all posited as being essentially biological and hereditary. Emblems of blood and of descent thus created a two-tier scheme of racial hierarchy under which non-Western peoples were deemed potentially dangerous to the European race. These racialized differences became a key part of imperial discourse.

More pointedly, criminality as a form of degeneration of the native class (or a lower evolutionary form in the case of the new minority ethnic communities) symbolized the confrontation between modernity and savagery. Criminal policy followed, such as proposing (as in Chapter 3) the segregation, control and incarceration of those whose degeneration or evolutionary stagnation threatened social order. In Fitzpatrick's words

> '...In the colonies the savage was the carrier of the irresolution in occidental identity and the constituting negation of its civilization and, so, had to be maintained as intractably apart from that identity and that civilization'.[43]

Dangerousness itself, and hence the notion of anxiety, constituted the key component of fear of the Other. In the case of race, fear[44] was embedded in the belief that the virgin sanctity of the West would be endangered by the proximity of the non-Western.

It must be stressed that racist science had created a mental chasm between Occidental modernity and indigenous peoples throughout Empire. The concept of dangerousness, when linked with the themes of crime, race and colonialism, opened a vacuum. Criminology, the new science of crime, sought to fill that void, attempting an objective basis for such popular images. Dangerousness was a conflation of the stereotypes of inherited criminality.[45] Further, dangerousness was known by what it was not, rather than by its core features. The West increasingly portrayed danger as stemming from those who had yet to reach the stage of civility and who lacked the contours of modernity. Supposedly primitive and backward races were characterized as dangerous. The West defined that status by reference to its opposite – the civilized standards of modernity, of morality and of progress. The stable facade of Victorian identity concealed, in the process of nation-building, a fluidity of status, of indecision and in turn, an Other against which it defined itself. The social construction of the non-Western as dangerous and primitive was designed to mask and displace Western anxieties.[46] Widespread fear over the apparently rising crime and the unruliness of the colonials was the manifestation of this anxiety. Central to the easing of such concerns was the representation of the dangerous savage. By attributing racial characteristics to biological differences, criminological science turned savagery and civilization into fixed and permanent conditions. These ascriptions of the non-Western as dangerous enhanced hierarchical differences.

Disciplinary Criminology

Criminal sciences were attractive to states that sought to contain the perceived rising tide of crime and social danger riding the heels of modernity. Scientists and governments could cooperate to eliminate, or at least mitigate, the effects of criminality. The new criminological scientists, such as Cesare Lombroso,[47] empirically demonstrated that crime was a non-rational and determinate product of under-socialization and inheritance that could be studied,[48] in much the same way as scientists studied the natural world. Lombroso acknowledged his debt to the Scottish penal physician, J. Bruce Thomson, whose 1870 paper, *The Hereditary Criminal*, refined in criminological form the importance of theories of the inheritance of crime to British imperialism,[49] 'The influence of colonial experience was clear in Thomson's argument, which was peppered with a reference to caste as a way a delineating people... caste... opened up the possibility of the hidden existence of criminal castes at home'.[50] Thomson argues that just as castes were inbred so must the criminal class at home. The criminal, Lombroso argued, was frequently a throwback to a more primitive form of human being, distinguishable through physiological characteristics.[51] Criminality was innate.[52] That scientific discourse furnished a frame of reference within which criminality could both be understood and be constrained. Exalted as the positivist school[53] of criminology, its central theme was that the mind and the body of the criminal should be investigated through the application of the methodology of the natural sciences. Racial classifications were central, especially in Ferri's work, which followed the conventional elaboration of the survival of not just the fittest, but also of the most civilized and superior human types. For example, self-restraint was an evolutionary valuable trait.[54] Crime was always the effect of an anomaly or of a pathological condition, and behaviour that transgressed conventional norms was directly inscribed into the categories of the criminal character, which could be cured and reformed.[55]

In essence, criminal definitions of the pathological deviant came to play a prominent role in imperial criminal justice policies,[56] bolstering the earlier Benthamite commitment to rational crime control. In the colonies, such ideas were bolstered by the development of criminological associates, such as evolutionary anthropometry which classified criminal physiognomy in order to predict different kinds of criminal behaviour.[57] Born criminals, in particular, could no longer be held directly accountable for their actions. They were beyond the pale of modernity and needed to be controlled by appropriate legislative and scientific strategies. Dangerousness was not just a state of mind, of rhetoric, but had a scientific, rational basis. Moreover, scientific arguments moved through generalized categories of difference, to specificities of psychological, intellectual, eugenic,[58] and moral categorization and especially the adaptation of evolutionary theory to the hierarchy of race. This knowledge altered popular perceptions of race and racial differences and ensured widespread acceptance of the new claims of an inevitable and permanent racial superiority and its attendant virtue of civilization.[59] Within a racialized landscape, postcolonial anxieties focused on the savages, both within and the savages without –outside. The discipline of criminology drew on, and evoked, colonial notions of the civilized and the uncivilized, the savage and the modern. Scientific racial differences lent themselves formidably to a Western discourse, which conceived of itself and of its non-Western peoples in terms of enlightened Europeans being charged with the improvement of those dangerous Others. Ideas about racial difference and hierarchy justified the criminalization of the non-Western whilst being instrumental in legitimating social inequality and segregation. Post-Enlightenment society could combine a commitment to legal equality by combining it with a concept of rationality. To be rational meant being civilized, like the West. Ideas of inferiority and superiority were established in which those without rationality, humanity and reason were rendered as qualitatively different from the modern. The dangerous irrational non-Western and the colonial savages and heathens could therefore be excluded. They were primitives, children of a lesser god, requiring management and control, and in some cases, outright extinction.

Criminological and Postcolonial Reflections

This imperial acceptance of scientific explanation and resolution in relation to the Other can readily be explained through more critical approaches. It ignores social constructionist questions of how crime was defined and the presuppositions and power of definers'.[60] It assumed that criminal law constitutes some fixed, discrete and unified category.[61] Social and antisocial behaviour were arbitrarily defined as absolutes. It was a discourse that failed to grapple with problems of partisanship in the construction of deviant individuals, as definitions imposed by different criminal discourses and imperial projects. This shift in defining categories according to class and race was the way in which crime was experienced and understood – made rational. The problem of crime was widely assumed to be an abnormality that could be incorporated into the imperial social order and to criminal justice policies. The West created the dangerous savages against which it set itself. The criminal sciences set the scene in which the non-Western was deliberately constructed as essentially different and inferior, 'the subject projects these outside so as to be able to flee from them, phobic avoidance, and protect himself from them, the subject now finds himself obliged to believe completely in something that is henceforth subject to the laws of external reality'.[62] This projection describes the process whereby the subject attributes to others the intolerable passions[63] and inclinations that she or he is unable to accept in her or himself. A racist self will deny or disavow his or her fears and disposition, repressing them and projecting these intolerable feelings on to the despised racial groups. Mentally splitting the Self and the rest into 'good' and 'bad' represses the anxieties which arise from the proximity of the Other. The 'bad' Self is distanced. The deep structure of the sense of self is built upon the illusory image of the world divided into two camps, *us* and *them*.[64] Within the imperial project, the relationship between the construction of difference and general stereotyping was especially potent when applied to notions of racial difference predicated on physical attributes. Here, differences are constructed through the process of creating distinct categorizations, which assist in the production and maintenance of identities. Scientific racist ideologies, racial myths and stereotypical characterizations in criminal discourse are enactments which echo Western anxieties. Embedded in this psychic process are processes of distortion, contradiction and ambivalence.

Through taking their own identity from the new sciences, Westerners became bound in their own being under the conditions, rules and values with which they oppressed others. In this all-defining project, the non-Western in imperial India and similarly in the metropolis was scientifically constructed as mysterious, belonging to an unknown savage, located at an unknown time and place. The saved were the Westerners in whom truth and light was reflected.

This chapter has provided an archaeology of the key tenets of the positivist school in criminology, especially its scientific basis of racial thinking, which was a key component in the social construction of the Other. Science complemented law, retracing its themes, weight and contexts, in which it reified the criminal. The West has an illusory sense of a superior identity, which needs constant reassurances. This security is, of course, spurious and thus constantly under threat because it is, in reality, highly dependent on the Other. It is the threat of a dissolution in the self-constructed identity which fuels racial supremacy and subsequent criminal statuses. The West was caught on the cusp of modernity which is all encompassing in its inclusiveness of the non-Western in terms of equivalence, and yet at the same time excluding the Other as the primitive savage. The obsession with the latter was part of a racist motif to categorize the non-Western as inherently less able than, and inferior to, a modern West. This helped justify the suppression of the Other, not only in imperial India but also within the metropolitan centre. In both settings, the constant fear of 'dangerous' people established the main institutional frameworks, not only in the police and in the penitentiary, but also in welfare measures established in the name of progress and modernization. Once in place, police controls, prisons and poorhouses,[65] could become more immediate, discipline-specific institutions to manage the 'unruly' savages. Criminal tendencies within an individual required the entire social edifice to contain the frightening, anxiety-producing possibilities. The West's preoccupation with the scientific mode of thought revealed its most oppressive face when the non-Western came to assume the label of a hereditary criminal. It has to be seen in the context of our understanding of the role scientific racism played in the repressive violence that was key element of colonial rule, both at home and abroad. This mode of identity formation was utilized not only in imperial India against the criminal tribes and castes, but similarly employed in identifying the non-Western as part of the Victorian criminal class, which is the subject of the following chapter.

5 THE 'ETHNIC' AS A COMPONENT OF THE 'CRIMINAL' CLASS

> Crowds of Lascars and Malays hang about the grogshops, quarrelling of course, writhing their bodies about like snakes, showing equal venom of tongue and double the wickedness of eye possessed by those interesting reptiles.[1]

Introduction

In 1869, Charles Dickens, like the urban missionaries of the period, voyeuristically foraged with a group of friends into the East End of London. Dickens's observations resulted in his short story, *The Mystery of Edwin Drood*, which portrays a sample of the depravity and primitive ways of imperial subjects lurking in the 'lascars' den'. The work's remarkable impact is obvious. 'The opium den in which Jasper indulges his habit and entertains dreams is a world unto itself, peopled by "Chinamen" and East Indian *Lascars*.'[2] This scene contains all the Victorian nightmares of dangerousness and of the irredeemable imperial Other. As such, opium addiction is the fault of vicious oriental hordes, bound by the exoticism of India and of the Orient. The exotic Occidental account of the dangerous Oriental detracts from more sober description. Fortunately, there is a quite different contemporaneous account of this same lascars' den which treats the occupants simply as working people, conducting crimes of survival. Situated in Victorian Court, in Bluegate Gardens, the 'den' was one of several that the moral guardians of the Strangers Homes for Asiatics regularly attempted to close. Eliza (portrayed vicariously by Dickens) is the common law wife of a lascar, She speaks Hindi, is an expert on her craft, opium-smoking and furnishes what some would regard as a necessary service for stranded lascars.[3]

Dickensian perceptions and scenes provide a link between domestic crime, a kind of psychic division, and the politics of empire, 'psychologically, the indigenous connects with the empire-like repressions that characterizes the "criminal intellect" in all of us'.[4] Similarly, late Victorian detective novelists, such as Edgar Allen Poe and Arthur Conan Doyle,[5] captured the essence of ethnic proclivities and the challenges these heathens, posed to imperial identity. Earlier the poet,

Thomas De Quincey narrates, 'Every third man at the least might be set down as a foreigner. *Lascars*, Chinese, Moores, Negroes, were met at every step, and apart from the manifold ruffianism, shrouded impenetrably under the mixed hats and turbans whose past was untraceable to any European eye'.[6] What is clear, however, from this example of De Quincey's writing in the early nineteenth century, is that this conflation between different races and foreigners was the very processes of Orientialism that Said exposed. The opium scene could have been staged any time in the eighteenth century of alien settlement in the urban metropolis.

The power of representation is all too evident in this configuration, where the debates over ethnic identity acquired saliency during the different phases of migrant settlement in England, especially against the backcloth of the socio-cultural and economic processes of colonialism. This chapter outlines how different ethnic identities were constituted by many of the same legal and criminal justice strategies that constructed the indigenous criminal class in Victorian England. In a notable work of the period, John Salter notes of some lascars,

> in the case of repeated convictions suffer a much longer term of imprisonment and one we know who has no less than seventy-two convictions against him. He has lived more in prison than out of it and has become so vitiated with the vagrant life as to prefer prison to liberty.[7]

His convictions suggest that societal reaction, through various criminal and civil statutes, scientific discourse and literary voyeurism established the identity of the ethnic minorities of nineteenth-century England, not just as subordinate strata, but also by a more complex process, as a variant of the newly emergent criminal class. Further, this labelling and the subsequent criminalization of a diffuse ethnic minority in Victorian England, and its rendering as different under various statutes, from criminal legislation to the Navigation Acts, also lends itself to the creation of the castes and tribes as dangerous in colonial India (see Chapters 6 and 7). The differentiation of the non-Western within the periphery, and in the centre accommodated a particular racial formation, which both encompassed and resisted those constructions. Victorian racial identities were fraught with contradictions and inconsistencies rather than fixed securely to a modernity to which it repeatedly made claims. It was precariously located, therefore, in the dynamics of identity on both sides, and remained unresolved and fractured. More importantly, the governing class's promise of inclusion, made to the non-Western, could not have been wholly ignored, because the law at least had to be seen to be responsive to a variety of situations involving the Asiatics, the lascars and economic migrants in Victorian England. Identities and moralities of visible minorities among the working classes were fragmented. We now turn to specific instances, each involving different people in similar settings. Each setting qualifies simultaneously as a peculiar place connected to empire and law, and each individual so defined was enmeshed in the local and the colonial. A developing literature[8] demonstrates, that caught in England's cities, in the hub of empire, the lascars and the ayahs (domestic servants),[9] found themselves reconstructed as part of the criminal class, and subsequently subjected to disciplinary measures of social control and surveillance. Conceptions of the threat of the non-Western crystallized around the same popular images of savagery and of moral degeneracy, a process reinforced in imperial fiction. Missionary literature such as Salter's iconic work drew on and contributed to the developing sciences of ethnography and anthropology outlined in the preceding chapter.[10] A desire to civilize and improve the peculiar habits of the non-Western followed directly from indigenous precedent.

The Minority Incursion

An appreciation of economic imperatives from the seventeenth century through to the first decades of the nineteenth century, is central to an understanding of how various racist ideologies became fundamental to the self-perception of imperial England. The primary reason for the growth of the black population in England was the development of the transatlantic trade. Ethnic minorities were not a novelty to Victorian England. There were black soldiers and travellers in England long before the eighteenth century.[11] As Fryer shows, there were many blacks (using that terminology to encompass all those with a non-white complexion) in England more than a thousand years before the beginning of the slave trade. Africans arrived as soldiers in the Roman army of occupation and there were black women who had their own maidservants at the early Scottish Court.[12] Between 1200 and 1600 AD, a series of distinct ethnic minority groups made their way to England. Typically in the mediaeval period, 'jews faced particular hostility and "Jew-baiting" became a sport, like cock throwing, or bull-baiting and pelting some poor wretch in the pillory'.[13] Images of the Other had their own history. The status of racial inferiors as slaves was already established in the early fifteenth century, as Davies notes on European relations 'woven in monstrous and phantasmagoric detail, based primarily on fears, fantasies and demons inhabiting the Western mind from St. Augustine to Columbus, this perception became an integral part of Europe's self-identity'. There were early East Indian slaves.[14]

South Asian presence is anecdotally evident early on. The East India Company first employed lascars[15] in the seventeenth century. Initially, that employment arose because of the high sickness and death rates of European sailors on India-bound ships, and their frequent desertions in India, which left ships short of crew for the return voyage.[16] Obtaining a fresh supply of European sailors in India was expensive, costing 50–70 per cent more than sailors recruited in England. In order to bridge the labour gap, the custom of employing some lascars in predominantly British crews began. Later, in the eighteenth and early nineteenth century, imperial navies depleted mercantile ranks. During the Napoleonic Wars, for instance, conscription of British sailors by the Royal Navy was frequent from EIC ships. Lascars were therefore recruited six-fold to supplement European crews.[17] Hence, death rates were extraordinarily high. According to some records, up to 50 per cent of lascars would never return to India, ensuring a recurring demand for new recruits.[18] In India, availability depended upon seasonal opportunities for agricultural work.[19]

When the Company's Charter was renewed in 1813, faced with agitation from other merchants, Parliament stripped the EIC of its monopoly on trade with India. Free trade, coupled with steam power, ultimately proved crucial for the employment of lascars. As trade expanded and India became increasingly central to Britain's global economy, lascars became the mainstay of the labour force in British-registered ships bound for Europe. As naval records demonstrate, they substituted for the 'native' English at the same period.[20] The lascars came to England primarily from India, especially from Gujarat, the Punjab, Serat and Bengal,[21] and also from other parts of South Asia, as well as from Madagascar and North Africa. The attraction for maritime employers was obvious. They were expendable and relatively cheap and abundant.[22] They were more open to coercion, even by the nautical standards of the Georgian era. Like other Europeans at the time, British merchant adventurers found that large profits could be made from importing oriental luxuries via newly discovered sea routes. India provided sugar, spices, dyes and, most importantly, textiles of a quality that could not be produced in Europe. Overseas manpower was an economic imperative. So many were employed that the British government periodically required the company to hire at least one English seaman for every three lascars. Between the years 1794–1814, 2,500 Lascar sailors had visited England, and by the late nineteenth century between 10,000 and 12,000 came to the country annually.[23]

Law's Violence: The Lascars and Collective Identity

Sailors played a critical role in the development of imperial identities. In the seventeenth and most of the eighteenth century, maritime workers were consigned to the periphery as marginal people.[24] But, culminating with Nelson's victories, the sailor became the 'classic example of a patriotic British subject'.[25] Jack Tar came to epitomize imperial spirit and colonial superiority. Alien sailors, such as the lascars, represented a threat to the growing identity of 'Britishness'. They constituted a complex but collective group of maritime workers. Unlike the individuated employment of imperial domestic servants such as the ayahs, they were a workforce that, whatever its many tribulations, enjoyed dynamic group solidarity.[26] Recruited by their fellows, the *ghat serangs*, they worked in the port of origin, lived there and were confined and treated, not as individuals, but as a unit.

In India and in other Asian ports, the *serang* was the gatekeeper to lascar employment, despite several EIC attempts to dismantle his powers over such labour,[27] access to EIC employment (and to other traders, especially with the abolition of the EIC's monopoly) depended upon payment and goodwill to the *serang*, The *ghat serang* occupied a position in the realm of Indian shipping employment akin to that of a labour agent, a lodging-house keeper and a money lender. He made his own bargain with individual seamen for their services (in times of abundance, taking a bribe from the recruit). His junior, the *serang*, was responsible for lascar welfare and discipline, and wielded forcible authority. The *serangs* negotiated wages which were held by him and his ancillary tindals[28] from the outset of the voyage. On board the ship, he was the intermediary between the European officers and the lascar component of the crew, combining the functions of boatswain and crew representative. On shore in Victorian England, for the most part, lascars lived in the same integrated groups under the *serang*.[29] The *serang* was central to the crew and in resisting Occidental definitions. As such he was both hero and villain. As the leader of the lascars, he delivered their requirements to the officers.[30] But he also administered his own chastisements. He was held responsible by the Captain for any perceived dereliction by the crew. In England, after receiving due wages from the Captain, he distributed to the crew (minus his fees). He would also remit to India due payments for lascars who had died. On shore, he acted with informal legal authority over his collectivity and also acted as a spokesman on external legal matters, for example as the key petitioner to the British authorities in cases affecting the lascars.[31] Critically, the *serang* was a countervailing authority to the power of the EIC and its officers, essential to the integrity of identity of the lascars and the focus of authority reaction.

As a collective, the lascars were rarely treated with recognition of their human worth. More pointedly, there are contrary accounts of their actual skills, mainly derogatory.[32] They were not individualized. One of the most extreme recorded cases of the brutal treatment accorded to the lascars is that of Captain Eastwick in 1819. After his ship had sunk on the French coast, Eastwick prevented lascars climbing into the lifeboat and some 310 lascars were drowned.[33] The lascars were treated as subhuman, akin to an animal-like-human, and were not worthy of the place of a European; as a result, killings by officers were not uncommon.[34] Collectivity and subhumanity were maintained in other ways. Lascars were financially determined as inferior. By the eighteenth-century Navigation Acts they were constructed as lesser to those of British or of African descent. 'A Select Committee of the EIC reported that two lascars may be equal to one European, so in a cold climate, the lascars become of no consequence'.[35] As potential for Naval employment, lascars were not considered of similar worth to others. Company officials regarded lascars as less productive than Europeans. Naval authorities valued them as physically weaker and less morally willing to engage in conflicts with enemy ships. Pay levels and food supplies[36] were determined at two-thirds those of other maritime workers. They were legally defined as non-British. Prior to the abolition of slavery in 1805, they could – though the cases might be exceptional – sold as slaves.[37] Identity was reinforced by assumption of financial, physical and moral subordination.

The world of seafaring was harsh and unequal.[38] Ships were oppressive workplaces and officers brutal bosses. Death rates for lascars were extraordinary:[39] 'Thirty Asiatics died on board the Fort William on the voyage to London, bodies of 18 were thrown over board in the English Channel'.[40]

Colonial seamen had not only to endure oppressive conditions at their workplace; they also had to suffer the indignity of being an underclass of 'coolies' denied the sympathy and support, let alone admission to their community, of workers. Imperial treatment in engagements, and discharges, affirmed their image as coolies standing in the penumbra of freedom.[41]

In 1783, regulations for the proper treatment of Indian servants and lascars (seamen) taken abroad came into force. Such regulations proved ineffective. The streets of the metropolis became '...inundated with destitute Asians, and the workhouses, jails and hospitals becoming full of numerous Asian occupants who had been cast adrift and left unprovided for'.[42] Enforced subordination met with resistance.

The Limits of Law: Lascars, Resistance and Agency

Most studies of colonial workers in metropolitan contexts focus on their structural incorporation and subjection. This is a debatable emphasis, a view that carries some dangers, notably the tendency to reproduce shared metropolitan and local elite representations and stereotypes about these workers, their subjectivities, and their capacity for agency. Lascars, throughout the different periods of colonialism, were in an ambivalent status, a confused identity in the eyes of the Occident. But agency was maintained primarily through collective unity. This grouping based on severe working conditions was the primary source of strength of the lascars. Their solidarity onshore, despite the fact that the group could encompass many different regions, cultures and religions, and in the face of the poverty affecting other inhabitants of London docklands, was the key source of resistance.[43] With their complex sources of origin and mixture of cultures, they were clearly alien to the Occident.

Legally (increasingly over the period), they were subject to competing identities and statuses. On board ships, they were subject to maritime legislation, derived harshly, from Britain. On shore, in London and other ports, they were subject to the largely inquisitorial power of English criminal law, like members of the indigenous criminal class

> 'Most Lascars who had voluntarily entered into a maritime labor gang ...Yet once in England, many lascars found themselves or on another kind of servitude. Their term of service was involuntary, indefinite, brutal, and often fatal'.[44]

They enjoyed, formally at least, citizen rights: for example the right to prosecute and appeal in the courts. Formal penalties in those higher courts differed little from the indigenous.[45] However, with the bifurcation of criminal and civil law in the nineteenth century, they had few civil rights. Where they enjoyed legal equality, they were nevertheless frequently treated in derogatory fashion. For example in a Mansion House case, where the *serang* and his colleagues claimed they had been denied wages and provisions (including 'grog') the presiding Lord Mayor made fun of them, including asking why, if they were Muslims, would they require grog. The *serang* replied 'the prophet could never have contemplated that any of the faithful should live in such a wretched country, like this or he would never have prohibited (its) use'. The more theological arguments of his colleagues were openly derided and the EIC had the case dismissed.[46]

At lower legal levels, they had no parish rights for sustenance,[47] but agency and resistance were possible. Law was a contested arena,[48] a location of struggle that could be used calculatively by lascars to maintain their own identity.[49] One of the first recorded cases was in 1750, when up to fifty-six lascars chose Marshalsea prison and all its deprivations rather than being arbitrarily shipped back to India, especially as a series of requests for payment from the attending surgeon attests to their experience.[50] They 'absolutely refuse[d] to go without their prize money',[51] a legal right which was eventually conceded, despite other sanctions.

Criminal law was also a medium of resistance. Despite the responsibility for all aspects of prosecution – costs, finding witnesses and requiring a translator in court – there are a series of Old Bailey cases in which lascars chose to use the Old Bailey to seek redress against both ship-masters and members of the indigenous criminal class.[52] Of course, these were exceptional cases. The vast majority of matters involving criminal and civil law were inquisitorial (see Chapter 3), such as vagrancy and begging, for which few records are available and the law stacked against the accused. Many of the offences for which lascars were charged involved relationships with brothel workers,[53] and other members of the criminal class. Legal petitions were used. In the late eighteenth century, there were many such petitions, normally articulated by the *serang*, to the Directors of the EIC.[54]

Resistance could take other forms. Fisher quotes an incident in 1798, when a British Captain kidnapped lascars for his crew and sailed off. Virtually all other lascars went on strike until punishment for the offender was promised.[55] Equally, such industrial action could result arbitrarily with prison – the powers granted by the Masters and Servants Act could be invoked.[56] There a few reported examples of serious crime by starving lascars.[57] There were several riots[58] – some due to grievances against the authorities,[59] and others inter-ethnic.[60] But there were more positive signs of resistance to the destruction of identity in the frequent ceremonies which embellished religious faiths, such as in funeral procession.[61] Symbols of culture and identity were maintained – as the rejecting of the extraordinary attempts by local missionaries to induce them to conversion.

Domestic Workers: the Ayahs

Servants constituted a second group of Asian migrants. About half of them were women.[62] They were fixed in a halfway house between slavery and indentured labour. They shared with the lascars their eventual fate. Class, sexuality and racial difference can be seen as part of a matrix of ideas in which the colonial female returning from the colonized territory to the metropolis with her status symbol, 'the hard-working ayah', was perceived as the norm. Many Asians were brought by government officials, army and navy officers returning from service abroad and by captains of merchant ships.[63] Indian servants and ayahs (nannies) were brought over by British families returning from India as early as the seventeenth century, for example to attend to the needs of the family on the six-month journey from India. English children were often sent home for their education in the company of trusted Indian servants.[64] By the eighteenth century, the custom of employing Indian servants and ayahs in returnee British households had become firmly established. They were convenient, cheap and totally dependent. The colonial lifestyle could be partly maintained – ayahs were an 'index of rank'. Oriental servants were a symbol of the exalted status of the newly enriched India-returned nabobs. They were exotic[65] a kind of fashion accessory, available only to a few.[66]

The domestic servant, conversely, carried various identities, which were constantly investigated and monitored. Most Indian servants worked in isolation, with a demeaning status, in British households.[67] They were under strong pressure to Anglicize, in a subordinate status of Englishness. Deprived of any rights once the contractual obligation ended, few could afford the fare back to India. 'I was happy in Benares till I hired myself to a sahib, who brought me to England 15 years ago, and he died and left me helpless. I have now an English wife and little girl, and we live by begging'.[68] By the middle of the eighteenth century, an increasing number of families discharged their travelling servants on arrival in Britain, leaving them to fend for themselves.[69] A few received paid returns but most were left wandering in port cities, made destitute by the colonial government in India, who refused the costs of repatriation.[70] With no contracts of employment, abandoned and destitute, they were forced to beg for a passage home.[71] For women, prostitution was the only viable alternative,[72] until they were removed by the police from the streets to be incarcerated under Poor Law powers.[73] Such non-Western normative behavior was repeatedly described as 'immoral' and 'indecent'. Domestic workers from the colonies were unable to verify their 'right of abode'.[74] Those who escaped the harsh realities of the household, encountered major difficulties once out of the private domain.

Crimes of Survival: Ethnic Vagrants and Beggars

By the mid-nineteenth century, there are records of many destitute Asiatics wandering about the streets of London.[75] A House of Commons debate noted 'a large number of lascars wandering about London ... and that some remedy might be found for the sufferings of these poor people'.[76] The 1790s coincided with a rise in xenophobia and the passage of the Aliens Act of 1793, which provided wide powers for the control of foreigners, including deportations of those regarded as undesirable.[77] Later, in the winter of 1850, 'some 40 sons of India' were found dead of cold and hunger on the streets of London.[78] Begging and 'wandering' by the employees of the EIC became a major feature of the English ports.[79]

The social condition of the South Indians and the reactions to such inequality made them more liable to have their activities criminalized. They were an impediment to the process of social change, of capital accumulation, and their conditional and presence undermined the identity of the British. These minorities were socially constructed as a 'criminogenic' population. The moral panics over such social groups were not a new phenomenon. The idle stranger was excluded from membership of the community while a different kind of exclusion applied to strangers by 'race' – both blacks and Indians were deemed inferior and uncivilized, and denied any claim on public funds.[80] This socially unequal status resulted in a self-fulfilling prophecy.

Extensions of inquisitorial statutes had severe and far-reaching consequences for the ethnic minority population. The Vagrancy Act of 1824 in particular furnished ample scope for the criminalization of this class. The police could arrest 'anyone wandering in the public streets or highways, behaving or looking suspicious'.[81] Discharged servants and lascars were therefore contained within reconstructed notions of the dangerous and criminal classes. Lascar vagrancy had been apparent from the mid-eighteenth century.[82] A contract did not guarantee a return passage to India. Discharge slips were often unacceptable. Some were incarcerated for using fraudulent coinage to pay for passages.[83] Economic estrangement ensured that low-caste Indians were unable to find any employment as a means of returning to India. The Reverend Pegg notes that vagrancy and subsequent starvation was a frequent outcome.[84] As Salter noted, 'eight human beings of the same class have perished with cold and hunger in our streets during the present winter'.[85]

As early as 1816, a Parliamentary Committee of Enquiry had attempted to develop specific regulations to control what it regarded as the 'low' criminality of the lascars. The Committee recommended new forms of policing directed specifically at the lascars and proposed moving their accommodation away from St Giles, from where they gained access to the City.[86] These 'strangers' had no financial security and lacked contracts of employment or provision for a return passage. Many were discharged without ceremony after their arrival in England. Under the Merchant Shipping Laws, ship-owners were liable to provide for those who had to wait for the return journey.[87] However, the legislation had little effect. Vagrancy, of course, was highly related to the question of accommodation. The EIC recorded lascars arriving at their Leadenhall Street offices 'reduced to great distress and applying to us for relief'(1782). Improvised accommodation was perceived as morally and physically threatening. 'The shed in which many of the Asiatic are lodged in the East India Dock, is a filthy place, the place is in a worse condition than a pigsty ... more than 100 ... huddled together with no fire and very little clothing'.[88] From 1795, lascar hostels and seamen's homes were established in Shoreditch, Shadwell and Wapping. Inevitably, the poor quality of the accommodation was blamed on the indulgent practices of the lascars themselves.[89] In 1802, the EIC contracted barracks in Shadwell for lascar shelter and food. Around this barracks grew a small commercial community of taverns, brothels and pawnbrokers to serve its needs, and these became targets of the larger criminal class.[90] As the respectable class grew more aware of lascar poverty and the moral threat of the lascars, an appeal was launched by the Society for the Protection of Asian Sailors and the Stranger's Home (founded in Limehouse in 1857). Difference, the non-Western, could be contained in the Strangers Home for Asiatics,[91] where missionaries prowled, as reflected in the work of John Salter[92] and of John Pegg.[93] This home had the specific function of separating, in parallel with the earlier measures against the indigenous class, the deserving from the undeserving, and the indigenous from the non-Western. In the contemporary words of Augustus Sala,

> there are black Ayahs, and Hookabadars, and Lascars, poor, bewildered, shivering, brown-faced Orientals, staring at everything around them, as if they had not quite got over their astonishment yet at the marvels of Frangistan. I wonder whether the comparison is unfavorable to us in their Brahminical minds, between the cold black swampy Isle of Dogs, the inky water, the slimy hulls, the squalid labourers, the rain and sleet: and the hot sun and yellow sands of Calcutta; the blue water, and dark maiden, with her water-pitcher on her head; – the sacred Ganges, the rich dresses, stately elephants, half-naked Sircars of Hindostan; – the rice and arrack, the paddy-fields and bungalows, the punkato, palankeen, and yellow streak of caste of Bengal the beloved'.[94]

In the mid-nineteenth century, Henry Mayhew referred to Hindu beggars as 'deceptive and artificial', claiming that the worse treatment was meted out the sweepers and cleaners (topzees),[95] many of whom were accosted begging in the streets of the large ports.[96] Unlike the criminal laws, the Poor Laws governing social and economic relief did not apply to destitute Indians as a means of relief. They were only applicable to remove paupers between English parishes.[97] Transhipment was therefore possible in England but not Poor Law relocation to India. A later respectable Liverpool observer commented about the resultant nomadism:

> They are deserters from the ships, and these are the men who are scattered over the country begging, thus earning an idle living and selling tracts as an excuse. When they fail in their begging speculations, they are thrown on the parishes and then forwarded to London.[98]

State Reports regularly commented on their destitution and resultant begging and vagrancy.[99] Discarded Indian seamen were assumed to be a threat to civilized standards. Respectable Western identity was threatened by the core elements of this emerging new non-Western criminal class, especially when they ventured out from the Shadwell ghetto[100] where they had established meeting places and centres of worship, coexisting with the larger indigenous criminal class.[101] There were regular complaints that the lascars were not kept under restraint.[102] Images of debauchery and savagery attracted the attention of the wider public and the police. Any tolerance for Asiatcs begging on the streets of London diminished in the early part of the nineteenth century. Judicial attitudes towards the minority people hardened. The immediate result of this panic was the extension of the Vagrancy Act of 1824 to incarcerate destitute Indians as a deterrent to others 'The magistrates at the police courts were continually occupied in punishing those who had been tempted into evil; so the prisons were never free from natives of the East'.[103] Magistrates often resorted to the legally expedient practice of deportation for vagrancy, after indefinite arbitrary confinement.[104]

Popular discourses engaged in the continual suppression of the South Asians by portraying their aberrant native character, especially their supposed cunning, idleness and linguistic peculiarity.[105] The notions of an idiosyncratic language and religion, and indifference to pain, induced beliefs in the Asians of 'unworthiness'. Hardship, such as lack of access to religious practices was regarded as beneficial in a rejection of heathenism. Religious food practices were ignored by shelter overseers. Where they were lodged in a workhouse, the presence of the Indians interfered with the enforcement of discipline because the authorities could not find employment for Asian paupers. As a result, Poor Law authorities shifted the financial and social burden onto the revenues from India. However, the India Office itself refused to use Indian taxpayers' money to relieve the Indians found destitute in England.[106] Illness and poverty were commonly described as pathological problems of the self.[107] Difference could be coupled with pathos as in a letter in *The Times*, 'The Lascars have been landed from the ship ... One of them has since died...the coffin being filled with food and money, under the idea that the food would maintain him till his arrival in the new other world ... Some of the poor fellows have hitherto been shivering about the streets, wet and half naked, exhibiting a picture of misery but little creditable to the English nation'.[108]

Contested Identities

This period of Asian chastisement coincided with a central crisis of imperialism. Intricately interwoven in dominant discourses were definitions of morality and empire. Internal dangers and crises were realized and easily reframed as issues of morality, identity and civility 'The morals of these people were very low, and their temper savage, cruel and disdainful and they have very little regard for one another.[109] Charles Dickens, for example, in *Great Expectations*, in line with the new science of anthropometrics, described how the lawyer, Jaggers kept '...two dreadful casts on a shelf, of faces peculiarly swollen, and twitchy about the nose'. Readers would recognize the alien criminal as something different, to be catalogued and pinned to the wall. Victorian missionaries and reformers articulated a strong sense of the superiority of the white 'race'. The English abroad were still engaged in taming the 'savages' and images of the 'uncivilized' continued to excite and shock. Immoral Orientals, infused with various dichotomies, provided a ready-made danger for the colonial imagination. These haunting images informed the legal regulation of unruly categories and the redefinition of class, race and empire.

As the nineteenth century progressed, problems of class, ethnicity and criminality became more precisely delineated. A clearer distinction was made between masters and servants, the ayahs and the lascars subordinated beneath the trinity of landlords, tenants and waged labourers of empire.[110] Social hierarchies were affirmed and identities clarified. Allusions to theft, and to betrayal by minority groups as part of the service class, vividly captured the imagination of the landed gentry and aristocracy as well as of the new urban bourgeoisie. An attitude of condemnation arose, along with a further articulation of racial discrimination and social diminution with respect to the non-Western. The contractual relationship between the employer and the domestic ayah, the ship-owner and the lascar, was steadily undermined by the notion of difference.[111]

The key fact was the construction of both ethnic domestic and surplus seamen, as a legal adjunct to the indigenous criminal class. Mayhew gives a typical account, locating graphically the criminal position of the stranded Asians. A patronizing racism combines complexly with moral judgment, evolutionary determinism and Oriental romanticism

> Are those spare, snake-eyed Asiatics who walk the streets, coolly dressed in Manchester cottons, or chintz of a pattern commonly used for bed-furniture, to which

> the resemblance is carried out the dark, polished colour of the thin limbs, which it envelops. They very often affect to be converts to the Christian religion, and give away tracts; with intention of entrapping the sympathy of the elderly folk. They assert that they have been high-caste Brahmins, but as untruth, even when not acting professionally, is habitual to them, there is not the slightest dependence to be placed on what they say. Sometimes, in the winter, they 'do shallow', that is stand on the curbstone of the pavement, in their thin, ragged clothes, and shiver as with cold and hunger or crouch against a wall and whine like a whipped animal; at others they turn out with a small barrel-shaped drum, on which they make a monotonous noise with their fingers, to which music, they sing and dance. Or they will 'stand pad with a fakement', i.e. wear a placard upon their breasts that describes them as natives of Madagascar, in distress, converts to Christianity, anxious to get to a seaport where they can work their passage back. This is a favourite artifice with Lascars – or they will sell lucifers or sweep a crossing, or do anything where their picturesque appearance, of which they are proud and conscious, can be effectively displayed. They are as cunning as they look, and can detect a sympathetic face among a crowd. They never beg of soldiers, or sailors, to whom they always give a side berth as they pass them in the streets. From the extraordinary mendacity of this 'race' of beggars – a mendacity that never falters, hesitates, or stumbles, but flows on in an unbroken stream of falsehood. I have, however, many reasons for believing the following statement, which was made to me by a dirty and distressed Indian, is moderately true.[112]

Mayhew's 'Hindoo beggar' provides a unique (and lengthy) oral testimony of transition from service to begging. The degeneracy and the primitive nature of the non-Western were contained through criminal legislation, later informed by scientific discourse, similar to that defining existing criminal class.

What emerges from the above accounts is the extent of the victimization of South Asians in Victorian England as well as the creation of an alien class in which the invocation of legal discourse, especially in the earlier Aliens Act of 1793, facilitated wide powers for the control of 'undesirables'.[113] The social and legal regulation of the non-Western would help tutor them to a British way of life.

The danger and the threat posed by the non-Western to the respectable classes played on fears of the declining morality of the Western nation. The reform movement lobbied for special reformatories to contain and curb those minorities who posed a threat to their way of life. Although the Merchant Shipping Statutes of 1854 and 1855,[114] placed the responsibility for the provision of welfare for those found destitute with the Poor Law institutions, many non-Westerners found themselves confined in the Strangers Home for Asiatics.[115] Ethnic minority groups, socially and geographically, occupied the traditional lower-class territory, the urban ghettos which had always served as a reservoir for policing forays and for Poor Law administration.

The colonial labour migration reinforced a shift in the conditions within which ethnicity and the newly fashionable, legally and scientific, discourse of race became related to varying interpretations. Race was reified. The hidden histories of the 'Other', the perceived subterranean activities of the colonial underclass, contrasted dramatically with the emerging image of the respectable public. A division took place which differentiated the notion of the West as good, decent and respectable, from that of the non-Western as deviant, undesirable, outsider and disreputable uncivilized folk. This dichotomy generated a plethora of discursive constructions based upon racial definitions of blackness, of sexuality, and of related victimization,[116] which later shaped the identities of both the non-Western in Victorian England and of the dangerous castes and tribes in colonial India. This classificatory mechanism opened up a range of approaches to the taxonomy, classification and supervision of visible minorities. Criminal law complemented Poor Law in social control as it had done in a replication of those schemes applied to the indigenous criminal class (as discussed in Chapter 3). Alongside issues raised earlier by Irish and other intra-European migration, and the discourses of the 'Other', was a further reconstruction of the non-Western from slaves and indentured servants to a more institutionalized minority status 'the cultural reservoir of racism was not to be abolished so easily. Indeed, after slavery was abolished racism took on a new and deeper form as it became fused with the image of empire and British domination'.[117]

Power and Discipline in Victorian England

An identical discourse to that fabricated for indigenous criminals can be perceived in the construction of the identity of the non-Western in Victorian England. The enforcement of new policing practices, of legislation and of penal sanctions, not only had far-reaching consequences for the 'dangerous' classes but also had important repercussions for the South Asian and black population of Victorian England.

The ideology of ethnicity, with its various referent points resulted in many non-Western people being labelled as 'surplus'[118] – a type of 'social junk'. Social control, with the cumulative effect of the criminal laws, was to marginalize the non-Western who participated in the production of imperial services – from domestic labour to the manpower of the merchant fleets. Slavery, in particular, had contributed its weight to racist discourse.

The roots of South Asian experience in England itself lay within the larger history of immigrant experience, from the Irish to the increasing numbers of the non-Western. Central to this chapter has been the concern that the non-Western was constructed within an indigenous criminal class by several instruments. The first of these was the racialized discourse, which was interwoven with two forms of legal control (as well as being enforced under the discretionary mandate of the New Police and of Poor Law overseers) in the same way that agencies had been used against the white lower classes. Criminal law, as well as the vagrancy and habitual offenders' legislation, and later the Masters and Servants Act of 1867, was used against the minorities unequally in order to regulate their inferior locations and to further reinforce their identities. Similarly, civil law, as represented by the Poor Law legislation, constructed those minorities as types of beggar towards whom the state and erstwhile employers were frequently exempt from obligations. Navigation Acts were the legal foundation of that differentiation.

The various forms of Panopticon control, criminal and welfare legislation and the institutions of the New Police, prisons, and workhouses were first experienced by the indigenous criminal classes. Increasingly in the early nineteenth century, those controls were then applied to the early migrants – Irish and other non-British Europeans. Later, similar legal controls were applied to the non-Western – the Africans, Afro-Caribbeans and various South Asians. This constitution of difference was not limited to the shores of the English Channel or to the Irish and North Seas, but was an important instrument in the reconstruction of the identities of the servants and subjects of Empire. The internal colonialism, which created the indigenous criminal classes, the vagrant sturdy beggars of the Irish, and the mendicants of the Afro-Caribbeans and Asians, was also an external colonialism. Law, as the epitome of racial ideologies at the centre of English imperial hegemony was a transplant from the local shores to the further reaches of imperial India. The imperial project was decidedly less about bringing the non-Western into the fold of civilization and more about alleviating Western fears and anxieties, which resulted from the proximity of the non-Western both within Victorian England and in imperial India.

Crucially, the depiction of the South Asian migrants not only bestowed demeaning identities on those groups; it also enhanced the status and clarified the identities of the white respectable classes and of their white and ethnic white inferiors. The confusion over local statuses gave way to a hierarchy of difference, both in Victorian England and, at the same time, in imperial India. Difference was sustained through scientific racism and the use of criminal law, which located the 'Other' as dangerous. Central to these debates is the appreciation of the construction of 'criminal' identities in Victorian England, especially its non-Western component. Attention now turns to the conception of the Other in imperial India. It is here that we find similarities, in the differences between the dangerous classes of Victorian England and the criminal castes and tribes in imperial India. What we also find is the simultaneous construction of dangerousness, which lies at the heart of modernity itself.

6 IMPOSING COLONIAL LEGAL IDENTITIES IN INDIA

> Fingerprinting quickly established itself as the universal system of criminal identification. In the technologies of policing, as in many other areas, empire served as an important laboratory for the metropolis. Criminality under colonialism was about both classification and control: the 'criminal' castes occasioned some of the first ethnological monographs, and this anthropology collaborated with policing to provide a science to measure and by measuring to contain the subjectivity of persons whose identities were otherwise fluid within caste boundaries.[1]

Introduction: Modern and Colonial Law as Inchoate

The new criminal sciences, influenced by racist and eugenic theories, shaped much of the criminal justice administration and process in Victorian England. Within the image of the criminal was an identifiable, if diffuse, ethnic class, composed of the ayahs, of the lascars, and of the larger emerging black population of industrial England. Crucial to the articulation of those identities is the history of England as a colonial regime. The discourses of the racial Other and of the criminal type, especially the physiognomic type, once again finds its replica in the Indian subject. The aim of the following Chapters, 6 and 7, is not only to explore the transportation of Victorian legal definitions to imperial India, but also the scientific typologies and categorizations used to subjugate the colonial subject. More pointedly, Victorian definitions of race, related components of eugenic theory and especially anthropometry,[2] eventually came to reinforce a decaying Indian caste system as an instrument of imperial categorization and rule. This way of 'knowing' the Indian society, especially in the census, the imperial gazettes and legislation, fulfilled the needs of the imperial state.[3] With the end of the EIC's sovereignty, the criminal justice process in imperial India accumulated many of the same elements of collective discretionary legislation[4] and of policing controls as were found in Victorian England. The freebooters of the eighteenth century gave way to the bureaucrats of the nineteenth century. In particular, the criminal justice process in pre-colonial India contained many of the same elements of collective discretionary legislation[5] and of policing controls as were found in Victorian England, and these, being conflated, contributed to the construction of identities of both the colonial rulers and of colonial elite under imperial sovereignty in India.

Criminal justice reforms in Victorian England provided a blueprint for colonial India (where caste relations were peculiarly read by the British as social caste), legitimizing the hegemony of a local elite. Pragmatism and agency intervened between theory and practice in legal reform. Legislation relating to the lower social orders was constructed in imperial terms ensuring continuity with the past in maintaining inequality under law. What follows is a brief outline of the Indian legal system, not primitive as it has been often been presented, but rather a modern system, and how it coincided with elements of the English criminal justice process.[6] Central to that outline are several themes. Firstly, the legal system of India in pre-colonial days was a patchwork of jurisdictions, some influenced by Moghal law and some drawing on Hindu law. Secondly, in India historically, the dominant legal process was often counterposed to the 'common law' practices of the majority. Two often conflictual, sometimes symbiotic and complex legal processes conducted an uneasy relationship.[7] Thirdly, and principally, the following analysis demonstrates that India already enjoyed its own version of modernity, with a complex, sophisticated and historically-derived legal process. Imperial rule did not encounter a legal void but sometimes complemented and sometimes attempted to incorporate, the skeleton of Indian legal process.

In that colonial incursion, certain key figures in India were relied upon for their access to *traditional* Indian knowledges. The colonial production of knowledge in India was not a simple process. It included a clash with, and a marginalization of, the knowledge and belief systems of the Indians – but there were complex interpretations of these by the British.[8] A caste system, which was vague rather than absolute, was transformed into a peculiarly rigid social phenomenon through the combined effect of colonial policing and of scientific discourse.[9] Communities and groups, known for their perceived criminal propensities, came to be identified through the discourse of race, caste and tribe. The concept of tribe itself was important. 'Criminal tribe' had particular meanings. The tribe was situated on a lower rung than caste on the evolutionary scale but the term could evoke qualities of savagery, wildness and otherness in a way that caste could not. The term 'criminal tribe' was often used as a sign which could evoke an image in British consciousness.[10]

At the same time, through various aspects of religious authority and of judicial procedure, the EIC came to comprehend Indian communities through an intermediary, the Brahmin caste. At every point, the effort to maintain a dominant position was reinforced by a corresponding effort to reassure the Brahmin community, and to satisfy its legitimacy in terms of social categories, criminality and punishment.

Colonial rule in India involved much coercion and resistance, but at the same time it was dependent on a degree of consent. The solutions developed in response to these assurances reached their apogee in the 1860s, culminating in several criminal justice innovations: T. B. Macaulay's Indian Penal Code; the re-formation of the police and the system of *thanedars;* (the policeman) the Police Act of 1861; and the local Village Chowkidar Act of 1870.[11] The chapter closes with a discussion of how the Indian Penal Code of 1860 and the Criminal Tribes Act of 1871 were appropriated to the systems of prosecution, sentencing and the containment of the Sansi[12] of Punjab.[13]

Indian Criminality: Caste, Crime, and Customary Law

Judicial systems have been described as the cutting edge of colonialism.[14] Law was the cutting edge of the civilizing mission[15] in the nineteenth and early twentieth centuries. The literature on the processes, mechanisms and the factors propelling the change and the reform of the criminal justice system of India remains sparse.[16] The analysis of criminal law under discussion, however, has been partially conducted.[17] Initially, the quest to establish a definable and reliable relationship between the colonial government and the governed entailed the formulation of knowledge about the pre-colonial legal system of India.[18] Central to the control of the people of India was establishing continuity with the ancient regime, which Derret says 'took the orthodox Brahminic learning as the standard of Hindu law'.[19]

Caste lay at the heart of Indian law and Indian unity.[20] It was most evident in the administration of criminal justice. Contrary to the opinion of many colonial judicial functionaries,[21] as well as in the Orientalist constructions of the Other, the authoritative sources of *Manusmriti* contain references which clearly show that a well-defined criminal policy existed in the early days of Hindu society.[22] Central to the Code of *Manusmriti* were not only the ordinances relating to law, but a complete digest of the prevailing religion, philosophy, and customs practized[23] by the *Brahmin,* the *Vaishyas,* and the *Kshatriya.*[24] The Brahmin class became the natural born priestly caste, versed in the scriptures of the prevailing texts. The Brahmin, armed with *shastric* (knowledge) injunctions, assumed for themselves the position of sole interpreters of *Manusmriti* and became the social and political elite, while the *Shudras* (low-caste) were placed at the bottom of the hierarchy. Outside of those gradations were the untouchables and the criminal castes and tribes.

In essence, the administration of justice in pre-colonial India was the duty of the king (or similar personages), and its practice was elucidated and elaborated by the idea of *dharma*:

> Which was a marked feature of the Indian mind and it attaches a spiritual meaning and a religious sanction to all, even the most external social and political circumstances of life, imposing on all castes and functions an ideal, not except incidentally, of rights and powers, but of duty, an ideal way and permanent character – dharma has a spiritual significance.[25]

Dharma, central to the code of *Manusmriti*, represents the religious aspect of Hindu life and the *dharamsastra* is the repository of legal provisions pertaining to this aspect of life. Every aspect of life came to be governed by *dharma* – which expressed the idea of the rule of law, of the rights and duties of the individual and of a social contract.[26] Those defying their duties and rights were construed as suffering from sins committed in their past lives and took on the labels of the *shudras* and the untouchable caste. Their lives came to be associated with backwardness. *Dharma* played a key part in the cohesion of a particular kind of Indian society. It also maintained considerable inequalities in caste identities. The concept of caste and the related notion of *dharma* were the legal key to unlocking pre-colonial judicial India. Central to fulfilling the judicial function was the appointment of the learned Brahmin caste, who expounded the texts of *Manusmriti.* The Brahmin, the sole interpreters of the *Vedas* and the *Shastras* – the Hindi scriptures, became the expositors of the usages and customs which were both secular and religious. However, the duty to uphold law and order, and to maintain the customs and related religious functions, was the sole responsibility of the king. *Manusmriti* enjoined the king to uphold the customs of the country. Thus, the relationship between a hierarchical order of castes, with its focus on the superior position of the Brahmin, on the one hand, and a conception of sovereignty on the other, focused on the Hindu king or the royal functions of the dominant caste, which came to represent an ideological sphere of relations.[27] In the administration of justice,[28] the translations reveal that the king should ensure that there was no danger from thieves, and he should appoint 'policing officers' for the protection of his subjects. High-castes, by virtue of their greater privilege, came to occupy key positions within the criminal justice system. In terms of crime, the 'criminals' portrayed by Brahmin commentators were essentially low-caste and male.

In essence, crimes were seen as a privation, a result of the misuse of man's reason, often resulting from passion. The higher the caste of the victim, the greater the defilement associated with a given sinful act. It was, therefore necessary, according to the penal code of *Manusmriti*, for the punishment to be proportionate to the pollution incurred.[29] The emphasis on the individual's responsibility for his or her actions to the king was complemented by the way in which the scale of punishment was decided. Crimes were classified into three categories: firstly, crimes against the person, which included abuse and assault, secondly, crimes relating to property and, thirdly, sexual offences. Punishment for these three categories of crimes was dependent on the *dharma* of each individual's caste.[30] Caste status contributed to determining the seriousness of the offence. Sentence severity reflected the caste of the offender and victim, hence, the focus was on the character rather than offence. For example, a Brahmin killing a low-caste was awarded light punishment, whereas the killing of a Brahmin by a low-caste was serious.[31] Therefore, the main purpose of punishment was retribution and deterrence. For crimes of theft, the following were observed:

> Penalty for a shudra (low-caste) should be eight times of the value of the stolen goods, the Vaishya sixteen times, Kshatriya thirty-two times, and the Brahmin sixty-four times or one hundred and twenty-eight times on the grounds he was educated to know the consequences of his actions.[32]

Punishments included maiming, disfigurement and a wide variety of physical chastisements. The death penalty and incarceration had limited application. Most offences during the early colonial period, were prosaic and undramatic, often involving cattle-theft, small amounts of food, clothing, money and personal possessions.[33] Various forms of shaming (unlike in Georgian Britain) were the main form of punishment.[34] A typical penalty would be a procession of the offender, tied to a donkey, through the village as symbolic commentary, an allegoric representation of the king's laws. These degradation ceremonies were (and are) followed by gestures of reintegration into the community. Discretion was a critical feature. Feudal patronage, in practice, (as in Georgian England) often protected its subjects from the consequences of their crimes, especially for the higher castes.[35] The dispensation of justice in criminal cases was immediate. Public shaming, which was widely used, served to reaffirm distinctions in identity. Brahmin interpretation of Hindu law and society, however, was frequently unrelated to practice.[36] Local law was often makeshift and pragmatic. Critically, inequality based on character, not offence was a primary and undisguised feature of Hindu law. For the majority, similar legal structures encompassed the lower strata in the Orient and in the Occident.

In sum, the ruler, the policing agencies and the magistrates evaluated and penalized offenders according to caste, to degree of respectability and over conformity to social mores.

Law under the East India Company

The advent of the EIC ensured that concessions were made to the Brahmin caste with their knowledge of *things Indian*. By appropriating the knowledge of the high-castes, the Colonial Office (following the EIC) established key sites of 'law and order'. Caste definitions assumed a more concrete form, not only in a social and political capacity, but also in the construction of caste-related criminality.

Thus, *Halhed's Gentoo* laws were translated in order to unmask the knowledge of Indian laws and religion held by the Brahmins.[37] These translations located the culture of things Indian as things of unchanging order, as well as of disorder, degeneracy and repetition.[38]

In particular, the initial Warren Hastings *Plan for the Administration of Justice*[39] in India assumed that indigenous norms could be incorporated into Western-based legal texts without significantly altering the laws of the Koran with respect to the Mohammedans and the laws of the Brahmin *Shasters* with respect to the Hindus. Hastings[40] provided a hierarchy of courts and listed the civil cases which would fall under Hindu and Muslim law, also indicating the necessity to consult Indian legal experts on those subjects.[41] Thus, Hastings's plan established a hierarchy of civil and criminal courts, whose role was to apply Hindu and Islamic legal norms in all suits regarding inheritance, caste and religion. The impact of these ideas is clearly discernible in the subsequently transformed administration of the judiciary.

In 1790, administration of criminal justice was taken over and centralized by the EIC. The district magistrates appointed by the EIC were given discretionary powers of collecting the revenue and taxes. Consequently, they became the judge, the policing agent and the Collector. The impact of these changes was twofold: on the one hand, it was framed to define the powers of the government and on the other hand, to protect the rights of the individual. The emergence of the judiciary in the role of the protector of the 'rule of law' was to become a fundamental feature of judicial discourse under the EIC. However, the attitude to the practice of Indian criminal law frequently appears to have been determined by agency – the personalities of the Western officials who arrived from the naïve superiority of English public schools.[42] The British colonial servants operated as though they were part of the Indian caste system – thus garnering the mystique of authority without having to rely unduly on force.

Apart from a series of experimental measures, criminal matters were virtually unattended by the governing bodies from 1790 to the 1840s.[43] This was due, in part, to the EIC emphasizing its financial priorities. A total reform[44] had to await the imperial panics resulting from the mid-nineteenth-century revolts in Cawnpur and Lucknow.

The eventual transformation of law, and the development of the duality of the legal system, were a process in which the Company's legal servants and, later, the legal emissaries of the Colonial Office, were successful in maintaining effective control through nominal utilitarian[45] philosophy – the principle of the greatest good for the greatest number. Central to that philosophy was the notion of race', in which biological differences determined the natural capacities and destinies of racial groups (see chapter 4). This scientific, essentialist ideology gained an increasing hold as many Indian judicial institutions were categorized as inferior and to be subjected to imperial reform. An identical scientific policy was used as various castes and tribes were enumerated and brought under imperial gaze. It suffused a developing Western-in-India identity, which assumed Western racial superiority and an imperial mission.[46]

In the period following the rebellion of 1857, the imperial concern with caste and 'race' intensified. The 1857 violence served to prove the essential barbarism of the Indians – their exotic irrational character. Many Europeans, including women and children were killed and tortured by native Indians. For the governing classes in both England and in India, that cataclysm proved that Indians had shown their wayward character, and were not only culturally, intellectually and racially inferior, but needed to be controlled for their own good. This mode of thought imbued outraged Victorian reactions as illustrated in Charles Dickens diatribe:

> I wish I were a commander in chief in India. The first thing ... I would do is to strike that oriental race with amazement... I should do my utmost to exterminate the race upon whom the stain of the late cruelties rested... with ... merciful swiftness of execution, to blot it out of mankind and raze it of the face of the earth.[47]

The low-castes, who were contemptuously referred to as backward, were now located as members of an inferior 'race'. This view would be especially relevant to the formation of criminal identities in India to the emerging view of customary law. Imperial anxieties and fear were managed through legal and scientific sites and through the implementation of various strategies. The substitution of the EIC's mandate by the imperial government, witnessed a legal crusade. This was to reach its apogee in the 1860s and 1870s, culminating in several criminal justice implementations – the Criminal Procedure Act of 1871, the Penal Code of 1860, the Police Act of 1861 and the Criminal Tribes Act of 1871.

Legal Traditions in the Colonial Context

As both Skuy[48] and Baxi[49] note, many commentators dismissed pre-colonial law in India as primitive[50] because it lacked key elements of a modern legal system, which is based on written records and professional pleaders, an appeal system with superior and inferior courts, recognition of precedent and a single set of legal principles.[51] Similarly, Rudolph and Rudolph found no traces in India of the elements, which characterized the universalism, and the impersonality of modern Western legal systems.[52] Colonial India had a notion of authority but not of legality, and it was the supposedly civilizing mission of the white man to inculcate this in India. Typically, EIC Governor Charles Grant[53] wrote that the Indians were depraved victims of a fallen civilization. He proposed that by advancing the policy of assimilation, it was possible to make Indians into 'Black

Englishmen'.[54] Earlier, James Mill had argued that essentially India was a blank sheet for law and believed that the modern, rational body of law could be developed from utilitarian principles to encourage the evolution of lower races towards a European civilized destiny. As Raman comments, Mill was a self-appointed prophet of reform and a critic of the criminal justice institutions of both India and England. He regarded existing English law as not merely dated, but also as anachronistic. India was the opportunity to start again on a clean slate.[55]

In particular, the EIC officials had drawn on an established set of imagined customs, not only as a result of the threat posed by the native Indians but also, and pragmatically, in order to win the support of high-caste Indians.[56] This was in line with the ideas of Warren Hastings about preserving high-caste roles in the bureaucracy, which resulted in confining recruitment to the criminal justice system (as elsewhere) only to such groups.[57] This colonial discourse not only cited Brahminic scriptures as the key to Indian society, but also distinguished sharply between Hindu and Islamic conceptions of law, justice and punishment. More pointedly, the centrality and importance given to Brahmin scriptures by the colonial officers, and the construction of Hindu law from these texts raise the question of the relationship between Brahminic scripture and society in colonial India. The high-caste interests of the new judiciary further suited the political interest of the colonizers, providing the requisite legitimacy to its rule. Others, who were born on a lower evolutionary level, were seen by the colonial officers as tangential. With reference to the Indian legal system, the Western complaints about the nature of Indian justice, and its people, were phrased with the great certainty that 'a gift composed of legal norms' could be imported to India: 'Once the qualities of the real native agency will improve then they can become fit for trust and employment'.[58]

Central to that trust was the perceptions of the Indian inhabitants who had to recognize that their traditional customs and indigenous institutions were on a lower evolutionary level to those of the West. At the same time, they were to be a vehicle for remoulding the Indian system along lines consistent with modern ideas and higher standards. Nandy has explored the perception of 'Englishness' by the Indians from a different point of view:

> In the colonial culture, identification with the aggressor bound the rulers and the ruled in a dyadic relationship. The Raj saw Indians as crypto-barbarians who needed to further civilise themselves. It saw British rule as an agent of progress and as a mission. Many Indians in turn saw their salvation in becoming like the British, in friendship and in enmity.[59]

In keeping with the idea of evolution as continuous, the link between Indian judicial institutions and Western notions of jurisprudence was stressed. The obscurity of customary laws rested not just in the patchwork nature of its sources, but it was maintained and perpetuated by mysterious procedures, which lay at the basis of the monopoly of lawyers against the rest of the people.[60] Thus, a code of law could be arrived at which would define a new clear social and political framework for interaction. It was for this societal interaction that Bentham advocated written codes of law, 'written law is the law for civilized nations and customary law is for brutes'.[61] Indian jurisprudence, wrote James Mill, was a 'disorderly compilation of loose, vague quotations, selected arbitrarily from books of so-called laws'.[62] It was jurisprudence:

> in which the judges have had to take evidence not only to the matters of fact which come in dispute before them, but to ascertain the law, that is, to gather from the testimony of witness what is the custom of the country and of the people.[63]

Given the rhetoric of civilizing the 'backward races', colonial administrative difficulties occasioned by native brutalities against the Europeans, combined to produce an alternative project. Stokes regards Benthamite utilitarianism as the key factor in the replacement of the traditional legal system. The core principles of classical liberalism, as exemplified by utilitarianism reached their prime in India by the mid-nineteenth century. For J. S. Mill, equipped with Bentham's principle of utility, laws in India rested on no authority whatsoever:

> There are certain books called law books, which contain the opinions of certain individuals and are so exceedingly loose, that they afford little or no direction. The customs of India are in fact the laws of India, that by which almost all rights are created and maintained.[64]

Mill further goes on to argue that England was the apex of civilization and India the nadir. Despotism and priesthood had made the Indian people, in mind and in body, the most enslaved members of the human race.[65] This process re-inscribed difference and enjoined a range of influences in the continuing constructions of racialized identities. The production of these views and others that followed them defined an epistemological space, and created a colonizing legal discourse. This, argues Cohn, had the effect of converting Indian forms of knowledge into European objects.[66]

What needs to be emphasized here is that Victorian colonialism was not a uniform process with identical goals in all countries and societies. Nevertheless, certain of its general themes in the legal process are evident in India. The new dominant elite legal culture, reflected in India's social organization, was a mix of both Utilitarian philosophy and of caste tradition, 'The British retained the scaffolding of Islamic law while reforming its inner working'.[67] Colonial civil servants, and their local surrogates crucially moulded the social life and customs of the low-castes. These distinctions were further reinforced by the larger colonial project. This construction was partial, as the high-castes felt threatened by being identified as members of a racial group, that was placed low in the colonial racial hierarchy. However, at the same time as they opposed racial discrimination which affected, or might affect them, they shared the West's prejudice against low-castes. The success of the EIC, like that of the later imperial government, in recruiting many indigenous people by appealing to their religious sensibilities, generated a variety of economic, political and social changes in Indian society, especially in the criminal justice process.

The attempted transplantation of Western legal ideas to Indian courts was part of a much larger administrative strategy. In criminal justice, elites had to be found within Indian society (see above) who could be made to see that they had an interest in the maintenance of imperial rule. Imperial power could only be secured in the administration of justice if it incorporated the power of the Brahmins, and that of the *maulvis,* the Muslim priests.[68]

The Transplantation of Modern Law: Pragmatic Resolutions

James Mill's view of India was partially modified by his son, John Stuart Mill, as the key officer at the East India Office, in respect to those parts of India where stable authority could be recognized by the imperial officers. In those contexts, given J. S. Mill's notion of the law as a means of perfecting human nature (as opposed to the Benthamite emphasis), he recognized the potential input of indigenous legal institutions, where appropriate, parallel to the Western imposition.[69] In Raman's words, Mill's aim was to legitimize imperial rule within an Indian idiom. An indigenous facade was used to mitigate what might otherwise seem to be an alien and threatening institution. However, like his father, J. S. Mill believed that, in newly acquired territories like the Punjab and the Northwest territories (the location of the Sansi) where no existing acceptable sovereignty could be recognized, the transplantation *in toto* of Western law was critical.[70]

However, recent research has challenged the assumptions about the way in which Western laws and concepts were transplanted to India[71] from the 1830s onwards. Raman argues that what was being offered to India was not 'modern' in any conventional sense.[72] It was essentially a patchwork of old (eighteenth-century) legislation[73] and a variety of Benthamite reforms (as symbolized by the commitment to the individuality of law and the codification of separate offences, as opposed to classes of offender). This text criticizes not merely that mode of transplantation but also of the accepted position on the way in which utilitarian ideas were used in an attempt to reform the legislation epitomized by the English Bloody Code.[74] Skuy's view, in brief, is that there were parallels between the speed and ad hoc nature of legal development in both England and India. Taking his cue from critical criminal justice scholarship, especially from Beattie and Langbein,[75] he argues that the state of law in England in the early part of the nineteenth century indicated that reform had been halfhearted and confused, retaining major features of the old legislation. It was not modern[76] in its totality.

Far from England having a coherent criminal code in the period between the introduction of Macaulay's Indian Penal Code of 1860 and the passing of the Criminal Tribes Act of 1871, in practice the legal system was confused, with major inconsistencies between different aspects of criminal law.

In India, Macaulay, when considering the legislation, regarded the existing criminal codes as chaotic and lacking any sense of originality. He argued that it was a patchwork of EIC regulations enacted by each presidency to supplement Muslim and Hindu laws.[77] In each presidency, not only did this amalgam apparently embrace contradictory definitions of criminality, but it also permitted a wide variation in standards. Macaulay also rejected existing English criminal law as being in too great a need of reform itself. Further, Raman argues that Macaulay's Indian Penal Code actually reflected the need for reform of the criminal justice system in England. The Code represented the transplanting of problems of Western law and legal procedures to India, not because Indian law was primitive but because Western law itself needed reform.[78] It was this relative chaos in criminal law that the West attempted to pass to India. One reason why Indian criminal law reflected uneasy tensions between different parts, as transplanted by the West, was not only the resistance of indigenous institutions, but rather because the laws which were being transplanted were also confused. The Indian Penal Code of 1860 was really a code for England, which reflected changes in English criminal law and procedures, and their lack of modernity, and not the needs of the Indian people. Raman claims that in order to understand the Indian Penal Code of 1860 one must therefore begin with the problems of English law.[79]

For our purposes here, and most significantly,[80] there was a clear distinction between the old and the modern in two elements of English law: collectivity versus individuality and the evidence of character versus evidence of an offence.[81] Benthamite reforms individualized key parts of English law.[82] However, they also retained general clauses (although still under the *imprimatur* of adversarial rights) designed to deal with the 'criminal' classes as a collective entity (see Chapters 3 and 4). Specifically, they retained a variety of offences assigned to respond to low-level public orders – the policing of the Victorian street. These ranged from vagrancy powers to those which emphasized the suspicious person, and which also might involve incarceration on the basis of character, rather than through the committal of an offence, as in the Habitual Criminals Act of 1869. As noted in chapter 3 above, local magisterial decision-making commonly and pragmatically ignored legal conventions. The new adversarial notions of the Benthamite era were in accordance with the general commitment to retain those forms of legislation designed to act collectively against the lower classes of Victorian England.[83]

It was this confusion of law, which was exported to India and conflated there with Indian traditions relating to collective criminality, as in the notion of the criminal tribes and castes. Formally, the Government of India Act of

1858 promised Indians the right to enjoy equal and impartial protection under the law with due process safeguards.[84] However, Cohn's[85] account ignores the structural essence of English law, with regard to the criminal class, which was also exported. Like criminal law in England, colonial law was consequently flexible. It combined three elements: firstly, transplanted utilitarianism; secondly, generic powers to deal collectively and inquisitorially with suspected persons and thirdly, indigenous notions of collectivity and hierarchy. Central to the formal apparatus of the colonial legal formation was the pursuit of the individual as a fundamental concept of criminal legal jurisprudence. In this new juridical conception, the subject population consisted of individual citizens with equal rights. However, in the case of the lower castes and other outcast groups, those rights were legally abrogated – collectivity replaced the individual, and rights varied in terms of stratum.[86]

The flexibility in law ensured different modes of treatment for different people – as in Victorian England, modern law for the elite and the underside of adversarial process for the rest. Law followed the English pattern for the social elite in India. However, a quite different standard of law, distinguished again by collectivity rather than by individuality, and by presumption of guilt rather than of innocence, was established for the thugs, the dacoits and later for the criminal tribes and castes. As Mukhopadhyay notes during the period of legal reform in Bengal,

> The judicial system was geared to seize the most likely candidate in a robbery, and members of a criminal tribe, even if their complicity was not proven, generally received a jail sentence on the grounds of suspected livelihood.[87]

As in England, discretion may have been diminished for more specific offences, but it was enhanced for those groups who were to be judged by their character rather than by their actions. Further, Freitag points to the fundamental distinction, both in terms of the allocation of resources and of legal procedures of the Raj (as indeed in Victorian England), made between crime committed by individuals (ordinary crime) and that committed by collectivities (extraordinary crime).[88] Local state functionaries assumed critical positions in discretionary gatekeeping.[89]

Against the background of social criminality[90] the principle of guilt was transferred from an individual criminal act to one of membership of a 'criminal' community. As Skuy euphemistically phrases it in his comparison of nineteenth-century English and colonial Indian law, large parts of nineteenth century English criminal law were primitive in matters defining of offences, especially those parts which related to notions about criminal responsibility that cut across all criminal offences.[91] Most of the shortcomings identified by the first *Royal Commission on Criminal Justice* in 1834 still remained. If the improvements made in the two decades prior to 1862 are ignored, then England's criminal law seems even more primitive. For much of the nineteenth century, English law was not inherently and coherently modern. As in pre-colonial India, the contradictions related to different rules for different strata of society. Consequently, India was not to receive a revelation from a 'modernity',[92] which was located in the West, but a patchwork quilt of the old and the new legislation, which offered formal equality to all subjects but in practice, reaffirmed inequalities through collective discretionary legislation.

In particular, English modern law was not as complete as it appeared. It contained a key contradiction, equality in form and systemically-derived inequality in practice. Transplantation of legislation from England ensured a new form of control and segregation under the guise of legal equality. The idiom of criminality lent itself formidably to a discourse, which conceived of the white race as a discrete, superior, enlightened European people, responsible for the improvement of the 'savages'. At the same time, colonial criminal justice policies were instrumental on a practical level in preserving the principles of social stratification and segregation, in reaffirming collective identities of superiority and of inferiority.[93] The promise of equivalence, universality and modernity in law is a myth, potent but false.

Modernity and its attendant ideals can be seen in the shifting sensibilities, from the idealized criminal justice process to the colonial interpretation, in the legal reaffirmation of a judicial system which was instrumental in the policing and labelling of some thirteen million people as criminal tribes and castes. Behind the conceptualizations were specifically English ideas regarding crime. Two major bodies of knowledge were instrumental in constituting a criminal tribe – ideas about the nature of Indian society derived from colonial anthropology and ideas drawn from contemporary theories of the relationship between caste and crime in Britain.[94] As the image of the criminal had reflected earlier Victorian concerns, colonial anxieties and fears found an expression in the image of a *janam-chor,* the born 'criminal', whose criminal characteristics threatened the colonial collective consciousness. The threat had to be contained. This involved the legal containment of those whose birth and/or degeneration threatened order in imperial India. Constructed in this way, the criminal castes and tribes became observable, quantifiable and accessible to rational control strategies. Mukhophayay notes:

> the investigative modalities of enumeration and surveys deployed by colonial government, relying on the certainty of numbers divided under classificatory subheads, combined the administrative jail reports, covering textual body of knowledge about criminal classes.[95]

Colonial discourse operated as an instrument of oppression which was most evident in policies of law, order and social control, specifically in the ways in which scientific evidence and colonial experience were textualized in the construction of an Indian 'criminal' identity. This shift was crucial to the identity of the criminal tribes and castes and hence to the constitution of the status of the Sansi community (see Chapter 7 below) as 'criminal'. A plethora of political and legal institutions,[96] imported from various colonial territories, was incorporated within the institutional structures of India. For many low-caste Indians, the economic exploitation that characterized colonialism was associated with an equal measure of violence. The new policing system was a primary example through which the violent divide between the colonizers and the colonized was maintained.

Policing Colonial Subjects

The origins of policing throughout much of the colonial world are usually attributed to the London Metropolitan Police Act of 1829 (see Chapter 3 above). Orthodox historiography assumes that that particular policing model was diffused in the replication of Western institutions in the colonies. But while the model actually conflated two different types of policing, the Metropolitan and the Royal Irish Constabulary,[97] indigenous Mughal and other related police institutions had an influence on modern Indian policing which is often ignored. Colonial forces performed several ordinary and routine policing tasks, which were emblematically an important strategy in the legitimation of the colonial state.[98] The resultant policing system quickly became one of the imperial state's largest bureaucracies, with extensive duties and responsibilities.

Policing in India had originally developed from Mughal systems, based upon the theory of communal responsibility. Under this principle, all people living in a community were held responsible for each other's actions through a system of checks, and they were expected to report any crime and likely offenders to their village headman known as the *subeddar*. Collectivity rather than individuality was the key. But India continued to be governed on the ground by a kaleidoscope of systems developed by various rulers and *nawabs*, who controlled the different jurisdictions and principalities. But the common elements of the *thanedar* (policeman) and the *subeddar* (headman) were maintained[99] by the EIC. However, it was the Police Act of 1861, which provided the policing model for the Indian mainland and inter alia significantly affected the policing of other imperial domains.[100] Nevertheless, it was taxation and the maintenance of public order, which remained policing priorities.

Most orthodox explorations of colonial policing in India have ignored the traditional forms of police work. In the early stages of the emergence of the state police function, the differences between English and colonial policing were often minor rather than substantive.[101] Under Lord Cornwallis, the Irish model[102] and the Mughal system of policing were integrated by the civil service, becoming a model for the rest of India. After 1861, in order to legitimize the incorporation of indigenous forms of policing within the colonial police force, it was necessary for the colonizers to portray old policing methods as inefficient. However, like their British contemporaries, the *zillah sipahi* (district constables) were stranded between two forms of social order, that of the locality and that required by higher authorities. In so far as they were perceived to be inefficient, it was because they had to serve two masters, local and colonial.[103]

The development of the new policing, beginning with the urban police forces of Madras, Calcutta and Bombay and consolidated under The Penal Code (XLVIII) of 1860, was therefore the logical solution for the pragmatic, economically-minded colonial officials. If it was confused in its operation, it merely mirrored the social realities with which it was faced. As Gupta argues, this was intended to remould and strengthen the administrative and legal system to ensure, with minimum expense, the effective occupation and administration of the country, and the prompt suppression of all challenges to imperial power and authority.[104] Despite the formal codes – or perhaps because of them – the new structure became racially arrogant at command level, while at the grassroots the police followed the traditional, unequal and discretionary collective practice of the suppression of suspicious caste and tribal members.

Under the Police Act, replicas of the thief-takers[105] of the earlier Victorian cities were initially established to investigate offences relating to the colonial officers. Entrepreneurs combined the roles of thieves and thief-takers.[106] Alongside these developments, a new kind of magistrate, the District Officer, emerged in urban India. While the new police force marked a radical and sharp departure from the practices of the past, many of the essential concepts of the old system were retained under the new legislation.

In rural jurisdictions, policing was organized under the Chawkidar Act of 1870, where a plethora of powers was granted to the village *chawkidar* (watchman) for social order and control of its inhabitants. He was nominated by the local *panchayat* (village court) and appointed by the District Magistrate. Drawing upon English common law practices (as well as local tradition), the *chaukidar* was charged with discretionary powers against those defined as criminal by their character and location, and given ample powers of arresting suspicious characters. Using the police to perform both administrative and regulatory functions[107] was perceived as a useful way of screening local communities. This later led to more effective control measures against criminal tribes and similar groups. The officers of the new Police were informed that their first duty was the prevention of crime, a euphemism for maintaining colonial social order, and for sanitizing the disorderly. Almost all senior appointments in the police force were reserved for colonizers. As stressed by John Strachey in 1868, it would be the beginning of the end for Empire:

> If major executive powers were entrusted to the hands of the 'natives', it was therefore important to keep in the hands of our people those posts such as the army, and magistrates of districts. Their principal executive officers ought to be Englishmen under all circumstances.[108]

Local policing systems and the Western model coexisted. Central to the Indian context, even after the introduction of the major policing legislation, as Sir Thomas Munro stated,[109] a two-tier system of policing continued, with a rural reliance on hereditary local watchmen and similarly in the urban areas where high-caste and Europeans resided. Mountstuart Elphinstone, in his report on the local Indian Police, wrote in 1849 that 'The watchman's duties are to keep watch at night, to find out all arrivals and departures, observe all strangers and report all persons to the Headman.'[110]

These watchmen were under the jurisdiction of the local *panchayats*, and their duty was to report the daily activities of the villagers to the colonial District Magistrate. In turn, this system was subordinate to the central, Western-organized police force. The latter was staffed by the 'best stock', based on the theory of 'martial races'. As in Ireland and Metropolitan London,[111] strangers policed strangers. Brigadier Coke, in evidence to the Peel Commission of 1858 described the central feature of the selection process:

> The selection procedure for the recruitment of police officers ought to uphold in full force the separation which exists between the different religions and 'races' and we should endeavour not to amalgamate them.[112]

A central feature of both the local and metropolitan models of policing was the recruitment of individuals from outside the rank-and-file as officers.[113] This concept of selective recruitment was applied with high-caste constables being deployed in low-caste areas. Sub-inspectors and higher ranks were recruited directly through an elitist system from the sons of country landlords,[114] although some of the senior posts were recruited from England. This system of lateral recruitment was repeated throughout India, perpetuating the domination of the majority by small elite, and simultaneously enshrining the counter-images of the suspect 'criminal' classes.

Similar to England, policing in India was pre-emptive. The network of village *chaukidars* and the police became another instrument of lower-caste oppression, serving as a tool of surveillance and control for the Colonial Office. The *chaukidars* often 'knew' the criminals – the dacoits, the nomads and the thieves. The *chaukidars* worked in collaboration with the 'native' police agency in the suppression and detection of crime, a system which, as in England under the New Police, ensured their pre-emptively determining the criminality of lower castes and tribes.[115] The Police Act of 1861 was primarily a mechanism to impose elite and imperial social order over traditional communal practices in the formal name of the rule of law.[116] The substantive purpose of colonial policing was to maintain practical controls over the local residuum. Order was achieved, as in urban Victorian England,[117] through a police *cordon sanitaire* around the locations and residential areas of the criminal tribes and castes.

New criminal records, especially the registers of gangs and dacoity,[118] were added to the existing registration system to feed government's demand for more information. Arrests were based primarily on the assumption of suspicious characters and of 'known thieves'. Policing was mainly characterized by the arrests of petty thieves and cattle thieves, the dacoits, the beggars and the wandering tribes who were the Indian equivalent of the Victorian vagrant classes, and because of the episodic famines,[119] had become destitute and hence resorted to crimes of survival. But as Arnold argues, petty crime was read as subversion 'For the British, crime and political opposition were always intimately related'.[120] In practice, most rural policing was directed against the nomadic groups. There was a considerable increase in thefts from the mid 1860s due to the food scarcity prevailing in several districts (see Chapter 7). A severe famine in 1866–7 drove the starving population to commit dacoities, robberies and thefts. In the Northwestern Provinces of the Punjab, recorded crime increased in the 1860s to a record level in 1864 and 1865, because of the distress caused by the scarcity and high prices of food consequent on a bad harvest.[121] The price of wheat rose steadily from 1865 onwards. Inevitably criminal offences (social crime), particularly against property also increased by around 30 per cent between 1866 and 1869.[122] There were grain riots in Madras due to high food prices. In the Punjab, scarcity conditions led to a large number of offences against property and riots against grain merchants in 1877. The severity of the colonial economic policies led to a sevenfold increase in reported dacoity and there were many murders reportedly committed by starving mothers killing their hungry children.[123] In the criminal justice system, the colonial administration, though playing only a supervisory role, exercised extraordinary powers and developed elaborate inquisitorial procedures to maintain control over the subordinate people reacting to economic circumstances through social crime.

In essence, the wandering tribes and castes had inherited a perception of inter-generational criminality. Once the groups were labelled, they were targeted, watched, and arrested, on the suspicion of their perceived criminalities. Amongst several tribes targeted by the law, the Sansi were placed at the bottom of the scale. In the Northwestern province of Punjab, in famine conditions, these ascriptions were extended to include the Sansi population within those criminal definitions (see Chapter 7). Scientific notions of racial difference used in Victorian England to control the dangerous classes were systematically applied to various groups in India as imperial anxieties proliferated to newer heights. Scientific debates on race reified the caste system of inheritance. By attributing racial characteristics to caste differences and by insisting on the connection between these factors, once again, science served to turn the dangerous and the 'civilized' into fixed conditions. India furnished a new laboratory for imperial racist science.

Policing through Scientific and Legal Discourse

In the second half of the nineteenth century there was a marked development in India of a racist discourse already identifiable and established in England (see Chapter 4 above). In England, eugenic theories were primarily addressed to questions of class and were viewed as a mechanism to respond to criminality and the moral degeneration of the urban classes. In his early years, for example, Galton had proposed:

> The immediate and resolute segregation of habitual criminals under whatever conditions of surveillance are necessary absolutely to prevent them reproducing.[124]

This language and its implications for social control were readily transferred to India. Eugenicists were prominent in proclaiming the breeding of an 'imperial race'. Eugenicist ideas were powerfully reinforced when the initial setbacks of the rebellious uprising of 1857 in Cawnpur became a cause for imperial concerns. However, the export of racist science was not simply one of imposition by the colonizers. Upper-strata Indians also saw benefits from such attested scientific theories – as they did with wider cultural aspects. Theories of racism and of its attendant biological and moral inferiority, were not exclusive to the English, but also played a profound role in the self-perceptions of Indian subjects of empire such as the Bengal intelligentsia,[125] as were the contiguities of law.[126] 'Such ideas lent themselves to appropriation by particular strata within colonial societies in search of their own political and social empowerment'.[127] In that process of adoption, stark theories of racial science were moderated by local elites (insofar as they applied to themselves) in order to incorporate themselves as part-owners in the imperial project. Similarly, imperial law came to intermesh with indigenous elite perceptions, while coercively challenging local customary law, 'When the early British state attempted to codify and transform extant Indian law, they unwittingly or otherwise struck at the very basis of the communitarian and social aspects of the law'.[128] It was principally the lower strata that suffered from racist science interventions through legal coercion.

As one outgrowth of eugenics, and of Lombrosian positivism, when conflated with a new imperial device for surveillance of the criminal tribes, the science of anthropometry developed a specific Indian offshoot. Anthropometry – a directly 'criminal' science in India[129] – sought to locate the study of man in the biological body. Colonial anthropometry contributed to the construction of social criminality and, in so doing, reinforced the colonial construction of the 'normal' in India. In colonial India, anthropometry had the particular advantage of the caste system in which the character and notions of individuality were considered to be undeveloped.[130] For example, Risley's theories[131] about race and caste were clearly fundamental to the definition of the ethnographic project in colonial India. Risley was confident he could prove, in India, theories about 'race' and the human species which had been merely speculatively proposed in England. In turn, this would feed back into the creation of European identities:

> India is a vast storehouse of social and physical data which only need to be recorded in order to contribute to the solution of the problems which are being approached in Europe with the aid of material much of which is inferior in quality to the facts readily accessible in India, and rests upon less trustworthy evidence.[132]

Thurston in his discourse on thuggee had earlier noted the importance of anthropometry for criminal identification.[133] As in Victorian England, the central intention was to identify habitual criminals who moved from place to place and shifted their identities.[134] In India, the Bertillon[135] system was applied according to conventions established by the colonial sociology of the nomadic 'criminal' castes and tribes. The basic operating principle was that only members of 'criminal' tribes and persons convicted of certain crimes should be so measured. Since most crime was committed by circumscribed groups of people, anthropometry seemed to be the perfect instrument to apprehend the principal suspects. As E. R. Henry, the Inspector-General of Police in Bengal later phrased it, in 1900:

> With anthropometry on a sound basis professional criminals of this type will cease to flourish, as under the rules all persons not identified must be measured, and reference concerning them made to the Central Bureau.[136]

Criminality under colonialism, as in mid to late-Victorian England, was about both classification and control. Criminal tribes and castes were the focus of some of the first ethnological monographs. Anthropology collaborated with policing to provide a scientific means to categorize persons whose identities were otherwise fluid within caste boundaries. Caste was defined, measured and explained in relation to Victorian enthusiasms for the colonized body.[137] In the last years of the nineteenth century, anthropometry began to yield to other means of criminal identification, in particular fingerprinting, which was initially developed in Bengal,[138] as a means of criminal identification and had all the advantages of anthropometry, with none of its difficulties. Fingerprinting was considered error-free, cheap, quick and simple, and the results were more easily classified and quantified. Fingerprinting is normally cited as sourced in experimental work of the judicial officer, William Herschel in India. That functionary's own account symbolizes the miasma of imperial criminal justice developments. He cites one origin of the use of fingerprints in his public school exposure to the classical

English bird engraver, Bewick (Bewick signed his drawings with a thumbmark); Chinese practices with regard to waxed envelope seals; and the local Indian contractor, Konnai. Herschel was concerned with forgery of identity by Konnai's contractors. Herschel then corresponded persuasively with Francis Galton on his Indian conclusion on the effectiveness of fingerprints as a definitive judicial sign of identity. On his return to England, Herschel later demonstrated the efficiency of the fingerprint method of identification to a former Indian civil servant colleague, and then Assistant Commissioner at Scotland Yard, Sir Charles Howard, who consequently adopted fingerprints as a key detective technique in England. Retuning from his role as magistrate in Hooghly in 1877, Herschel claimed:

> In conclusion, it is hard to believe that a system so practically useful as this could have been known in the great lands of the East, for generations past, without arresting the notions of Western statesmen, merchants, travellers and students. Yet the knowledge never reached us.[139]

The adoption of fingerprinting in the early years of the twentieth century, and the creation of a provincial Criminal Investigation Department, further contributed to the expansion and increasing specialization of surveillance and intelligence over the 'criminal' tribes and castes. This accumulation of information and expertise revealed to the police the apparent extent of criminal activity in the Indian countryside, and through it they found self-confirming evidence that certain communities were more responsible for rural crime than others: some were hereditary habitual criminals whilst others were members of criminal castes and tribes.[140]

As Mukherjee explains, British rule in India had constructed a monopoly of violence and the revolt of 1857 shattered that monopoly by matching an official alien violence with the indigenous violence of the colonized.[141] This setback provided fertile ground for the pessimism implicit in eugenics and encouraged the use of social engineering through scientific measurement, categorization and criminal justice controls, to reverse the situation. The colonists assumed the task of methodically taming the savages. The measured attributes of the uncivilized castes provided a fertile ground for the rhetoric (and positivistic precision) of a reform agenda, comprising legal assumptions as well as legal offences, codifications, procedures and new policing technologies. To rationalize the imposition of a new criminal justice system, a reconstruction of the criminal justice processes in India was necessary. This was made possible by a positivistic pragmatism, rather than by operating from the level of general principles. While the underlying premise of the lawmaking process was the subjectivity of the lawmakers, it became scientifically legitimated in format. It resulted in the transformation of imperial mythology into the Criminal Tribes Act of 1871. These new legal constructions and the labelling of acts as deviant, the changing rules of procedure and the shifting arguments and premises to rationalize new rules, would suggest that criminal law was transformed not by the force of legalist ideas and concerns, nor even by expectations of definable goals and impacts. Changes were enforced because of presumptions, which were racial and evolutionary, informed by Victorian experience as well as by local pragmatism. It was the threat and fear of the non-Western that ultimately led to the control and the criminalization of various castes and tribes in colonial India.

Ambivalence and Identities

This chapter has extended the argument from Chapters 4 and 5 on the construction of identities, demonstrating how certain methodologies were critical in both Victorian England and in imperial India. In India, as in England, law was a formal apparatus, which conferred legal equality, the 'master statuses', upon its subjects. In practice, there were two problems with this enunciation. The legal system imposed at various times by the EIC and the new imperial rulers, was inchoate, ill-considered and possibly more relevant to the English experience of recovering from the Bloody Code than it was to India. Pre-colonial law in India was not primitive and yet at the same time neither was English law modern. Secondly, what the legal system in India had in common with adversarial law in England was the way that it provided for formal equality for the upper strata, with appropriate adversarial safeguards for individual citizens, while simultaneously ensuring that the lower subjected groups were legally constrained according to their associations and to their characters, and subject to discretionary legal controls.

Just as there were similarities in the construction of 'criminal' identities in India and in England, entrepreneurs played a lead in the legal process in India, where agents of legal expansion were often police officers, pioneering legislation in their local bailiwicks. Armed with new tools for racial and scientific categorization, the police helped reconstruct the criminal tribes and castes in terms that could be understood through the English 'criminal' class experience. In colonial India, identities were constituted through the use of similar authoritative techniques of legal (criminal and civil law) and scientific methods, as in Victorian England. However, the formation of colonial identities was never fully or perfectly achieved. There were several instances in colonial India where the non-western spearheaded various forms of resistance. The strategies deployed by the indigenous groups were not simply a kind of resistance arising purely apart from the colonial; the resistance itself reflected the constitution of the colonial in its response to the resistance. There are several instances where resistance operated against and within criminal justice structures. Law did not only subjugate, it also responded to alternative voices.

Obviously then, it could be said that the various forms of resistance of the colonized succeeded because they used the juridicial modes and created the conditions under which effective demands were placed on colonial law for it to fulfil its promise of liberal legality. Amin retells the story of the Chauri Chaura, a place where twenty-three policemen were burnt to death by an angry mob.[142] Labelled as criminals by the governing classes, the rioting peasants were removed from the streets only to be relocated within the arena of the law. Here, the peasants admitted to the specific action and acknowledged the legitimacy of the state, but denied that their act constituted a crime. It is clear that the initiatives of the subaltern, both participated and worked to resist colonialism, through various covert, direct and subversive means. The crucial point here is that subaltern agency, at the collective level, engaged in resistance against the order it opposed; in effect, it both worked with that order and displayed its own contradictions. The strategies deployed by the subaltern were not simply a kind of resistance arising purely apart from the colonial; the resistance itself reflected the constitution of the colonial in response to the resistance. The colonial criminal justice machinery can be seen as a space where identities was subverted rather than confirmed or as sites where identities were performed and contested.

7 CONSTRUCTING THE SANSI AS A 'CRIMINAL' CLASS

SANSI, SAONSI, SANSEEAHS, SANSI – (1) A 'criminal' tribe. The Sansi are the vagrants of the centre of the Punjab.[1]

The special feature of India is its caste system. As its traders go by caste; a tribe whose ancestors were criminals from time immemorial, who are themselves destined by the custom of caste to commit crime and whose descendants will be offenders against the law, it was important that the whole tribe is exterminated or accounted for; it is his trade, his caste, his religion to commit crime.[2]

Introduction

This penultimate chapter focuses on the social and the legal construction of the low castes and tribes in colonial Punjab as 'criminal'. That process replicates, in several ways, the experience of the English criminal class of Victorian England. Firstly, this chapter outlines the immediate social history of this process. The earlier experience with the dacoits and the thugs represented a learning process for lawmakers and for enforcement agents in India in the development of the legal construction of the criminal. The major agents were colonial police officers operating with wide, expanding, and discretionary powers, under the pragmatic mandate of inquisitorial law.[3] Other actors played a part. In India, it incorporated the fears and anxieties of upper-caste groups, merging in a generic view of the criminal tribes, while drawing on previous East India Company legislation.

Successively, the Criminal Tribes Act of 1871 legislation is detailed, outlining its discretionary attributes. However, the major aim of the chapter is to furnish a case study of the Sansi as representative of the larger body of criminal tribes and castes. The Sansi were subject to a similar defining process as the English criminal class. They were criminalized as a collectivity in terms of their 'inherited' characters and in their traditional survival practices. The criminalization of the Sansi was the result of two general factors: firstly, there were benefits to Empire in the way that reciprocal identities between 'superiors' and 'inferiors' were constructed, so that the local upper-caste groups were assimilated further into the web of imperial control; and secondly, there were material pressures resulting from the processes of social change in the Punjab. Western strategies for controlling the 'imagined' escalation in caste criminality resulted in the declaration that India's criminal tribes and castes were inherently 'dangerous', and descended from born criminals. Colonial notions of criminality acquired their legitimacy from Occidental evolutionary theories, especially the typologies from what was increasingly becoming known as criminal anthropology. Western notions of criminality and racial theories were extended to incorporate the wandering tribes and low-castes.[4] The construction of the Sansi as a criminal' tribe and the treatment of other low-caste and tribal collectivities was part of the wider programmes of criminal justice reform and colonial intention. The use of scientific notions of 'criminality' and of the *janam-chor* (the born criminal) lurking within low-castes, culminated in the arrest, removal and forcible transportation of several thousand Sansis. The colonial obsession with the maintenance of law and order and the social construction of new identities, within the emergent social hierarchy of Empire, assumed a parallel form to that in Victorian England. Criminal justice, as a means of securing colonial power, became the priority of the colonial judicial system in India.[5] This was supplemented by the various ways in which race and ethnic identities were socially constructed, institutionalized, and maintained. Like the 'criminal' class in Victorian England, the Sansi, as with the earlier thugs and dacoits, were constructed as a collectivity of thieves and criminals by the colonial state and subject to the same medley of legislation as criminal class in England. Images of the 'dangerous' classes of Victorian England imparted an assembly of racialized packages,[6] with copies of contested criminal and legal codes, safely secured in the colonial baggage labelled for India.

From Thugs and Dacoits to the Criminal Castes and Tribes

The key concept of the 'dangerous' and the 'criminal', emanated from early Victorian society (see Chapters 3 and 5). These identities were the product of, and became deeply embedded in colonial perceptions. Imperial reliance on this domestic discourse transformed India's unexplored 'criminal' territories into an imperial site. Legal language and cultural and scientific images framed Indian criminal tribes. The origins of the official labelling of castes as 'criminal' owe much to the early work of Frederick S. Mullaly:[7]

> These notes on the habits and customs of some of the criminal classes of the Madras presidency have been collected at the suggestion of Colonel Porteous, Inspector-General of Police, and put in the present form in the hope that they may prove of some value to Police Officers who are continually brought in contact with the predatory classes, and of some slight interest to much of the public who may wish to know something of their less favored brethren.[8]

Mullaly's book frames the vision of future officials. It categorized the criminal tribes and castes and furnished crude ethnographic detail on the kinds of crimes associated with each collectivity. Mullaly's Victorian typology of the criminal was later reinforced by Colonel Sleeman's several reminiscences,[9] by Thurston's[10] work on different castes and tribes, by Ibbetson,[11] and culminated in Risley's detailed monograph.[12] In effect, the original material was largely regurgitated with little elaboration. Thurston's text was designed as an easy reference work for colonial administrators, revenue agents, district magistrates and army recruiters. Together the several accounts determined official understanding of the problem of the criminal collectivities, while serving as a guide to practice for the various functionaries in recognizing and controlling criminal groups.

Central to the classification of various crimes was an elaborate taxonomic classification of Indian castes and tribes.[13] In Ibbetson's account[14] the reliance on the Anglicized concept of caste for statistical differentiation was mirrored in the establishment of the caste–crime connection. The colonial fear of the heathens became the basis for the management of a more refined criminal policy. The division of groups by caste, and its related notions, became the epistemological basis for the classification of crime. Imperial anxieties and fears demanded that crime be controlled and contained before it polluted neighbouring groups of people. 'Though every Indian could not be known, that was scarcely necessary, as the individual among them did not exist; in the British conception of Indian society, only collectivities existed'.[15] As a result, numerous surveys, censuses and various reports elaborated the caste/crime dichotomy in the *Imperial Gazettes of India*:

> This way of thinking about a particular caste was useful to the administrator, because it gave the illusion of knowing the people; he did not have to differentiate too much between individual Indians – a man was a Brahmin and a Brahmin had certain characteristics.[16]

Further, not only did the colonial imagination focus in reconstructing Indian society through recognizable opposites (as with the dichotomy between criminal and respectable classes of Victorian England); it operated with a further within those collectivities.[17] The 'dangerous' needed to be isolated from the more generic criminal tribe. In turn, the 'criminal' tribes and castes were defined in terms of several features – their nomadism, their outcaste status and the degree of abhorrence shown towards them by other local groups. Several tribes were associated with an inherited propensity to different types of crime,[18] 'It is his trade, his caste; I may say his religion, to commit crime'.[19] For example the Sansi were simply referred to as a vagrant thieving tribe, whereas the Ramosi were armed robbers,[20] both of these 'criminal' tribes and castes representing a lower order of being, possessing both an inferior intelligence and a combination of nature and nurture.[21]

Such views were hardly new. Post-EIC, colonial officials in India regarded criminality as pervasive and irreversible'.[22] Wandering tribes, the vagrants,[23] the homeless and the unregulated people were labelled transgressors and in many cases as 'dangerous'. Subsistence in the form of marginal theft, were transgressions by which various tribes and castes engaged in crimes of survival, the source of criminality.

More pointedly, local and imperial images of dangerousness were amplified – for example that of the '*phansigars*' (the stranglers) and of thuggee reinforced the imperial imagination.[24] Indian society was considered by the colonial state as constituting multiple pathologies in which rehabilitation policies were almost redundant. Thus Warren Hastings's belief in the public execution of offenders (as in the English Tyburn Tree motif) was reconstructed in terms of the necessity of collective symbolic punishment.[25] The principle of deterrence was most evident in the punishment of dacoity. Dacoits who carried out robbery with murder were executed, irrespective of the degree of individual involvement. This spectacle of punishment was intended to create the maximum amount of terror and of respect for the authority of colonial power, in the manner of the English Bloody Code:

> They were directed to be hung by the neck until they were dead and their bodies were exposed upon a gibbet in chains, at such place as the acting agent to the Governor General determined.[26]

However, dramatic penal theatrics were slowly replaced, as in England, with graduated punishments and more precise statutes. Within the new rational calculus, there was affirmed in the language of similar English legislation, a corpus of powers designed to continue the previous century's history of collective legal repression. Similar calls were made to provide for the registration, surveillance and control of certain tribes. Initially these demands came from the North-western provinces, Oudh and Punjab, but they were subsequently extended throughout British-occupied India.

Inquisition and Collectivity: the Thuggee and Dacoity Department

The mode of the social construction of the criminal tribes did not suddenly appear out of a vacuum. For example, the emphasis on gangs as collectivities of 'criminal' groups, long familiar to English legal discourse[27] was simply reproduced by Sleeman's campaign against the thugs and the dacoits.[28] (Invariably, as in the Criminal Tribes Act, colonial officials traced collective criminal origins to the thugs).[29] Sleeman had been given the task of establishing a Thuggee and Dacoity Department. It had been mandated as early as 1829, in which special orders were given to the Thuggee and Dacoity Department to deal especially with the '*phansigars*', drawn from dangerous castes, such as the *Ahariahs*, *Bahalias* and *Bunjaras*. Within its first six years, the Thuggee and Dacoity Department arrested over 2,000 thugs – of whom 1,500 were sentenced to death, while 500 were transported to other British colonies.[30] The Suppression of Thuggee Act of 1836[31] was passed declaring:

> That anyone proved to have belonged at any time to a gang of thugs should be liable to conviction and punished as a general charge including professional dacoits.[32]

An amendment, in the Suppression of Thuggee Act of 1843 by the EIC's judicial body declared:

> Whosoever shall be proved to have belonged, either before or after the passing of the Act, to any gang of dacoits either within or without the territories of the East India Company shall be punishable with transportation for life.[33]

Later amendments increased policing powers. However, Sleeman felt that the sentences passed by judges of the 'native' kind were detrimental to the eradication of thuggee:

> The native judges showed a tendency to deal too lightly with captured 'thugs' and availing themselves of any deficiency in the evidence as to the crime to evade the infliction of capital sentence.[34]

Hence, Colonel Sleeman's staff were granted extra-judicial powers to reward the approvers,[35] and to control crime, by recruiting more civilians as police officers and 'watchmen' in each of the fifty districts designated as 'infected' by 'thuggee'.

Entrepreneurially, the Thuggee and Dacoity Department successfully lobbied to have cases of thuggee and dacoity tried only in front of Special Commissioners and for increasing inquisitorial powers:

> Nowhere in the records of the trials of the thugs is there any mention of anyone acting in defence of the accused. They were brought before the magistrate. The evidence was heard, the accused were asked what they had to say, and sentence was passed. A case could well be built up against the accused, which only the magistrate or the judge, who also filled the role of the jury, could test.[36]

Precedent was established that, although it was still necessary to prove that a particular gang committed a crime, it was sufficient to establish that an accused man belonged to the gang, rather than prove his own culpability. Thugs were to be known by association rather than by direct evidence. In defence of the structural avoidance of adversarial principles, Sleeman argued 'In a country like India, officials who worried about the possibility of the innocent suffering would be unsuccessful in bringing in the guilty.[37] Trusted 'approvers' could be appointed by magistrates to senior positions in the police establishment,[38] to seek out their erstwhile companions,[39] in return for a pardon.[40] The approvers were a unique and valuable source on thuggee and, according to contemporary reports, caused the arrests of thousands of their compatriots.[41] The colonial officials generated information about the thugs and the dacoits through interrogative entrepreneurial activities. Critically, of those arrested, the trials commenced without the due process of law formally required by the EIC and later by the British imperial state.

Although many robber-gangs were accosted and dacoits captured and catalogued by the hundreds, dacoity was not suppressed. Sleeman himself had reservations about the efficiency of the process. There was not a considerable legal step from the suppression of these collectives of thugs through a highly discretionary legal process, to the construction of similar legal processes for the so-called 'criminal' tribes. As Roy notes:

> The construction of 'thuggee' was not simply a novel yet apposite way of reading Indian criminality at a moment when the pressures to reform the East India Company by reforming India were especially marked. For what was at stake in the discovery of 'thuggee' was a philosophical reconstellation of Indian criminality. Thuggee also gave rise to a veritable cottage industry of policing and surveillance techniques as well as ethnographic documentation. Like the system it purported to study, the discourse on 'thuggee' was totalising in its scope.[42]

Permeating the actions against the criminal collectivities of India was a practice of pre-emptive policing, alongside forms of systematic inequality, not simply allowed but also in effect, required by the modernization of law – as it had been in England with regard to the 'criminal' class. Legal process contributed in both contexts to the structuring of both the 'native' and also of the imperial 'self'.

Pressures to Develop the 'Criminal' Tribes Legislation

In essence, the development of the Criminal Tribes Act of 1871 not only drew on the existing legal entrepreneurship of the Thuggee and Dacoity Department, but was also, related to many wider sources. In referring to the castes and tribes whose identity had been encoded in the Criminal Tribes Act, colonial officials almost invariably traced their origins to the thugs.[43] Like much of the criminal legislation, it was inspired by the policing agency itself. There was specific police pressure to develop new legislation to create new criminal constructs. Traditional hierarchical interests reinforced policing powers internally. As Freitag notes, internal legitimacy could be co-opted. There was the Brahmin tradition of control of their own groups, the plainsman's fear of the forest people, and the high-caste's disdain of people without caste, the Hindu's fear of non-Hindus, and their larger governance concern with controlling an ungovernable population which did not appear to abide by the normative rules.[44] Critically, there was the British experience with the criminal classes and habitual offenders. There was the parallel Western tradition of associating migrating itinerant groups with vagabondage and social crime, perceiving them as a 'race' apart.

The development of the Criminal Tribes Act of 1871 was not just a measure intended to deal with crime. As with similar legislation and procedures, from criminal law to Poor Law, it was also a means of rehabilitating the Indian equivalent of sturdy beggars, those who lived off the surplus of others, but did not produce themselves.

In India, legislation was intended to mould unproductive communities into useful and productive contributors to the colonial economy.[45] There was also a concern with colonial authority. The colonial mode of governance tended to assume that collective action by local groups might threaten the legitimacy of their power.[46] As Arnold argues, the police pressed for greater powers to deal with rural crime because they felt that the existing law was inadequate. Few 'criminals' in rural India were arrested, and even fewer were convicted.[47] The attraction of the Criminal Tribes Act of 1871, for the colonists, was that it allowed entire communities to be punished or subjected to exceptional police pressure without individual responsibility being established. Consequently, the innocent would help to coerce the guilty, and indigenous authorities would act as policing surrogates for the sake of the larger collectivity. In terms of limited resources of money and manpower, the police could concentrate on specific communities identified as inherently 'criminal' and 'dangerous'.[48]

Scientific discourse on penality also contributed. Not merely were 'criminals' a 'race' apart, they were irredeemable and had to be isolated for the good of others whom they might pollute. Any redemption could only be achieved when the criminals were tightly controlled and supervised. Finally, borrowing from Freitag,[49] there was also a concern with legitimacy of imperial rule. The colonizers tended to associate collective action by the lower social castes with the normative process of familial and kin networks but also saw it as a threat to their authority. Lower-caste collective action was often perceived to be ultimately a challenge and a threat to the authority of the imperial state. For the colonizers, central authority was the justification and (unlike the previous *Mughals* who had held the local administrators responsible for solving local crimes) they perceived crime-control as essentially a problem for the central organization of the state, to be treated accordingly.

The Criminal Tribes Legislation

The Criminal Tribes Act of 1871 was developed cumulatively,[50] reinforcing de facto, as well as de jure, policing procedures. In December 1855, Colonel Sleeman reported that the magistrate of Janpur had charged the landholder of his district with the task of holding under surveillance the predatory tribe of Baurias who were infesting the lower Doab and Southern India. If similar measures were adopted in every district infested by the wandering tribes, Sleeman suggested, petty crime would soon be considerably diminished.[51] The Judicial Commissioner of the Punjab and the seven Division Commissioners unanimously supported this Report, arguing that a system of surveillance should be extended from the thugs and dacoits to the Baurias and Sansi. In the words of one Commissioner 'The existence of a criminal class, living notoriously on robbery is an outrage on civilized society, and their suppression is urgently called for.[52]

Consequently, under the authority of Circular No. 18 in 1856, all Sansi, Harnis and Baurias were to be registered at the local *thanas* (police stations), the *lambardars* (the headmen) of the villages in which these tribes nominally resided, were to be answerable for their conduct and movements. Registered tribesmen were not to be allowed to sleep away from their villages without a 'ticket of leave'[53] from the *thanadar*, and any tribesman found absent without leave was required to furnish security for good behaviour or, failing that, be sent to jail. This system of control was later extended to cover 'bad characters' and gangs of dacoits by the establishment of punitive police posts near identified villages.[54] Several Punjab district officers proposed reclaiming the criminal tribes by forcibly locating them in settlements on government wasteland under police control, in the expectation of accustomizing them to steady habits of agricultural labour. The Commissioners welcomed this initiative as efficient and productive. Consequently, some years in advance of the CTA, nomadic tribal people were locked overnight in local *thanas* (police posts) and forced to enter settlements until the Chief Commissioner of Punjab declared the measures illegal. This was the result of several years of heated debate between the governments of the Punjab and of the Northwestern Provinces, on the one hand, and the Punjab Chief Court on the other. The main point of contention was that legal rights were threatened by the procedures. The Court feared that the subordinate officials, particularly the 'native' constabulary, would abuse the powers. The Court also feared that forced settlements would be inefficient. The Punjab colonial officers countered that it would be preferable for the police to inconvenience a few doubtful characters than for large numbers of responsible people to be inconvenienced by bad characters.[55] These problems would continue to bedevil the Punjab's system of *kots* (settlements) for the next decade.[56] Meanwhile, however, the Criminal Tribes Act of 1871 had been passed. It provided for virtually the same measures of surveillance, control and reform as had the Circular of 1856.[57] The law was first enacted in North India in 1871, in Bengal in 1876, and then spread to the rest of the county until finally it was made applicable to the Madras Presidency in 1911. This Act was to apply to 150 notified castes of 'hereditary criminals' within the Hindu system. Later, other communities were added to the list. However, in India this was not based on the notion of genetically transmitted crime but rather as a community profession passed on from one generation to the next.

More importantly, the official intention then of the legislation was not so much punitive and retributive as preventative and remedial.[58] Surveillance rather than punishment was the key. Like the discretionary *collective* and *pre-emptive* legislation in England, in its structured departures from the ideals of due process, the CTA gave the police and magistracy extraordinary powers, extending to whole communities. This was the kind of surveillance and control formerly restricted to the confines of the criminal settlements. Thus, much of the popularity of the Act for administrators lay in its expediencies, designed to detect and convict criminals efficiently, not to protect the innocent.[59] The CTA was regarded by some colonial officials as an extraordinary extension of imperial legislation. 'Any other Act on the Statute Book goes so far in giving the police powers to take away a man's freedom. It not only affects the criminal himself, but also those who meet and associate in any way with him'.[60] Section III of the CTA empowered each local jurisdiction to designate 'Any tribe, gang, or class of persons or a part thereof, as a 'criminal tribe' if it had some reason to believe that they were addicted to the commission of non-bailable offences'.[61]

Once notified, members of the tribe (as with the English criminal class) had minimal rights of appeal to the courts. They could only gain exemption by persuading the registering authorities of the Act's non-applicability to them – guilt rather than innocence was presumed. This method of sidestepping legal protections for the accused was so useful that it was greatly expanded in the subsequent amendments of the Criminal Tribes Act of 1911.[62] By adding the word 'gang' to the authorizing legislation, it became possible to proclaim bandit gangs as criminal tribes.[63] On registration, members of the criminal tribe and caste were fingerprinted. Refusal to comply itself constituted a criminal offence, punishable by six months imprisonment or a 201 Rupee fine or both. There were severe restrictions on mobility. Members of the 'criminal' tribes and castes were only permitted to be absent from their home village at specified times and required to reside at approved locations. Section 10(a) of the CTA of 1871 authorized the fixing of hours at which the 'worst' characters and active criminals were to report to the police.[64] Once designated a 'criminal' tribe, the members of a community were placed outside the provisions of the ordinary law and subjected to intensive and indefinite police supervision and direction. Quite apart from the formal restrictions and penalties, like the street legislation targeted at the 'criminal' classes of Victorian England, the Criminal Tribes Act of 1871 exposed those notified to harassment by the police, local landlords and village officers, who were also entrusted with their supervision.[65] However, there is one necessary caveat with regard to this exposition on the CTA. It is clear that the origins of the CTA of 1871, was with regard to maintaining imperial social order. But later legislation was not so clear-cut to its imperatives. Indeed, there is argument regarding the several modifications in later years that a different motivation of the CTA, was solely economic. The later legislative compulsion was dictated less by the need to contain crime than by the demand for labour to reclaim agricultural land and later to supply textile mills and industrial establishments. Private gain rather than social order appears to have become a later priority.[66]

The Constitution of a 'Criminal' Tribe: The Sansi[67] of North Western Punjab

Amongst several tribes targeted by the law, the Sansi and other so-called 'criminal' tribes were placed at the level of the most 'dangerous' category. The colonial image of the Sansi was that of a group of criminals who were beyond redemption '...They are notorious as the worst of criminals'. Thieving Sansi are said to admit any caste to their fraternity on payment.[68] These sentiments echoed the comments made by Sleeman, and the official concern with the Sansi stemmed from the reports in the 1860s, which described them as 'wandering tribes' of the districts of Gurgaon and Gurdaspur. Colonel Sleeman succeeded in portraying the Sansi vagrants of the Punjab as essentially a wandering tribe with no fixed abode and possessing innate 'criminal' characteristics. As early as the 1850s, the Sansi and several other tribes in the Punjab had been subject to official registrations.[69] Even a much more recent text recites objectively 'They commit thefts, burglary, highway robbery and also dacoitism'.[70]

The Sansi were not only the Punjab's largest 'criminal' tribe, with an estimated notified population of 26,000 in the 1860s, but other tribes like the Baurias and Harnis were believed to be offshoots of them. Stereotypical caricatures were essential to reconstruct the Sansi as 'different' and to create a new master status. Official discourse had long portrayed the Sansis as:

> generally dark in complexion with bright sparkling eyes, their faces were recast in the aboriginal mould and were said to be very 'foxy' in expressions; being often eaters of vermin, they could always be detected by their smell which was said to be like a combination of 'musk-rat and rancid grease'; and their religion, mostly a form of Hinduism, was of a very primitive mixed and debased nature.[71]

Social Darwinism and eugenics influenced their social construction:

> The Sansi is still in the suckling stage of human progress, where he expects to receive the means of sustaining life direct from parent nature. To ask a Sansi to work and labour for the daily necessities is as much an anomaly as to ask an infant at the breast to earn the nourishment it receives by personal effort. The stage in the life of the individual corresponds with the evolution of mankind. During his wandering life of

> a few decades, the Sansi was perfectly at liberty to entrap the ownerless creatures of the jungle and to gather any fruits, plants or leaves growing in a wild state. His brief acquaintanceship with a domiciliary civilisation has not been sufficient to impress him with the fact that the same liberty cannot be extended to his neighbour's cattle and crops.[72]

Like the lower classes of Victorian England, the Sansi were at a less advanced stage of human evolution. Only by sustained exposure to a more evolved civilization could the Sansi move towards 'progress'. By importing the early Victorian criminal legislation, the colonial judicial office transformed the Indian lower castes and tribes into lesser individuals, 'born and blood criminals'. According to Ibbetson, in a study of Sansi language reminiscent of Mayhew's account of the 'criminal' class of the Victorian rookeries, the main way to differentiate between the Sansi and urban criminals was that the former had deliberately developed their own dialect, which lent itself '...for the purpose of aiding and abetting crime'.[73]

The main justification for the inclusion of the Sansi in the Punjab jurisdiction was based on the suspicion of their alliance with the local *Mazahbi*[74] thugs, as Major Harvey[75] wrote, in a report in 1860. A later Guide describes them as 'a small caste of wandering criminals of northern India, who live by begging and dealing in cattle. They also steal and commit dacoities and house-breaking'.[76]

Using the power of the colonial officers to guard against collective crimes which they deemed a threat to its authority, the Sansi were continuously arrested for their involvement in crimes of survival,[77] especially so after the annexation of British Punjab.[78]

Further legislation compounded the destitution of the Sansis. The Punjab Laws Act of 1872 restricted the rights of kin to inherit land, in favour of purchase by larger landowners. The stranger who had gained a footing in the village was thus frequently in a position to extend his organizations at the expense of the original landholders of the community. Given population growth (although culled by plague) and coincidental famines, together with the gradual passing away of proprietary rights from agriculturists to non-agriculturists in satisfaction of debts, landless Sansi, was much exacerbated. The level of crimes of survival greatly increased. Settlements were increasingly perceived as the resolution.[79]

However, the Criminal Tribes Act of 1871 was debilitating irrespective of any perceived criminality.[80] A more recent commentator captures the nineteenth century essence of the labelling of the 'criminal' career of the Sansi:

> Crime develops amongst these people through moral weaknesses, induced by circumstances and under corrupt environments. After this they are led on by the impunity of their first offences and then prison association corrupts them further morally and physically. Thus they continue to fall back upon commitment of various crimes and become habitual offenders. The society by abandoning them, after they leave prison, renders them to lead a wretched life.[81]

While the Punjab contained several criminal tribes between 1881 and 1913, the Sansi were the largest. After the designation of the Sansi as criminal, the District Magistrate established a register of them as habitual criminals, under the observation of local policing functionaries. A Pass system was implemented to control their movements,[82] a system which lent itself to local official corruption and false accusations.[83] Sansi movement was essential to their itinerant survival. Later, controls were intensified with the novel development of fingerprinting.[84] Breaches were subject to life imprisonment, as compared to punishment for similar offences by non-criminal tribes members of between three to six months.[85] As in England, legislation differentiated between the roughs and the respectables. In the labelling process, some differentiation was acknowledged in official imprimaturs:

> It would perhaps be more accurate to say that the Sansi should be classified thus: (1) the settled Sansi, who are subject to the Criminal Tribes Act, but who confine themselves to petty crime committed near their own villages and (2) the nomad Sansi who have two main branches (a) the Birtwan and (b) the pure nomads and vagabonds.[86]

Settlement Policy

The creation of a surveillance society in India directly served colonial ends. As Bhukya claims,

> The Criminal Tribes Act (CTA) of 1871 provided for those designated as criminal tribes to be registered with local police stations, to be confined to specific villages, fined, punished, and put in reformatories. Groups that suffered such a fate thereafter found it so difficult to earn an honest livelihood that they became even more likely to commit dacoities.[87]

A contemporary police administrator summed up Sansi experience of criminal justice with a telling anecdote.[88] Gunthorpe claims that they were treated under a similar system to habitual criminals in England. Despite being subject to Pass laws and similar surveillance they have 'in recent years ... passed the limits of forbearance'.[89] Their traditional nomadic character was easily equated with that of the scavengers, who often engaged in 'Cattle poisoning, which was freely resorted to by the population of the district. The serious loss of the agricultural community and the temptation to crime, which are held out to the hide dealing population, require deterrent punishment.'[90]

Under Section 16 of the Criminal Tribes Act of 1871,[91] internal 'colonies' (settlements or *kots*) were set up in which, it was claimed, the de-notified tribes could be trained to earn an honest living.[92] In 1890, by executive order of the Provincial Government, the more stringent provisions of the law were applied to them:

> In a single night, their camps throughout the Western districts were surrounded by a cordon of police, and 1236 men, women and children suddenly found themselves under arrest. The adult males, who were practically all incorrigible criminals, were swept off and interned in the jail at Sultanpur, where indeed they spend the rest of their lives, treated with as much indulgence as was compatible with their safe custody, and allowed to practice any of their petty handicrafts for their own advantage. Similarly, the women and children were removed to a settlement at Farrukabad where they were brought under discipline and educated. Some were apprenticed in the factories at Cawnpur; others were assisted to emigrate to one of the Colonies, with a chance of gaining a respectable livelihood.[93]

Once forcibly settled, the males became involved with labour intensive tasks in agriculture: in weeding, ploughing, watering of fields, stripping sugar cane and other related jobs on the farms.[94] However, Gunthorpe adds two caveats. The young women were a problem for the Magistrates. Suitable marriages (presumably with the intension of breeding criminality out of them) were difficult to arrange. Secondly, to Gunthorpe's evident chagrin, ten years later the Sansi groups was re-classified as 'loafers' rather than criminals, and were released. Gunthorpe laments that the Sansi would undoubtedly then relapse to their old criminal habits.

The settlements would operate much like the factories, the prisons, and the workhouses[95] of England. Confining the tribe would make surveillance more effective on such elusive peoples and prevent the petty crime that was associated with nomadism. 'Work discipline would break their 'thievish' ways and turn them into settled cultivators, basket makers, and weavers.[96] They would redeem nomads, who by hereditary and tradition were 'criminals, robbers, cheats, murderers and highwaymen, each tribe according to its guild and craft'.[97] Several settlements[98] were established in the Punjab, normally consisting of industrial and the agricultural reformatories (for example, the Salvation Army agricultural settlement for the Sansi at Sahibganj). However, the initial settlements, were ad hoc and generally regarded as inefficient in many aspects. As Booth-Tucker claims from a partisan perspective:

> If any of them absconded – as they frequently did – when captured by the police, their captor received a reward of Rs. 5. This led to a system on the part of the subordinate police of leading some of them out into the country and bringing them back as captives in order to claim the reward. It was a common saying among the (tribespeople) that no one need be captured provided he had in his possession Rs. 6 – one rupee more than the reward – to offer to the policeman as a peace-offering.[99]

The Salvation Army settlements were intended to be total institutions, deconstructing individuals in order to reconstruct them, a process that included all the inward as well as outward propensities to criminality, designed to produce self-disciplined workers. Time was to be regulated like thought. Remunerated labour would turn the tribesmen into productive labour.[100] Former prisoners were also sent to the settlement for redemption, especially to the Amritsar Reformatory Settlement. They were divided into two categories – those regarded as settled 'criminals' (given a five-year term) and the nomadic type (ten years). Most members of the criminal tribes were sent to the *Mughalpura* or *Lyallpur* industrial settlements[101] to work in subsistence-paying industrial employment.[102] Increasingly, the settlements had a different, commercial intent in supplying cheap labour, especially under the later Criminal Tribes Act of 1911. The aim being:

> To train them to earn an honest livelihood, first the settler was obliged to work for his living. Reciprocally the Department was obliged to find work for him. For this the settlement officers built good relations with factory managers and other employers up and down the country in whose neighbourhood settlements were established.[103]

Criminal tribe settlements would provide much of the labour required in the industrialization process. Labelling such areas as settlements glosses over their true nature as virtual prisons, as anyone belonging to one of the criminal tribes could be imprisoned for 'escaping' from their reformatory settlement, or for being anywhere 'beyond the limits so prescribed for his residence'. The settlements that were created served as *de facto* labour camps, with contractors requiring cheap manual labour farming out members of the settlement camps. Thus the members of these tribes were caught in the colonial nexus of land reform, the need for cheap labour and the rhetoric of social reform.[104] Hard labour would serve the complementary functions of deterring the lazy and of creating hard-working citizens conditioned to the discipline of industrial life within Panopticon-types structures. 'Criminal castes in India, like vagrants in Britain, represented an obstacle to the institution of the British ethic of work-discipline'.[105]

By the end of nineteenth century, the colonizers had moved from pragmatic, piecemeal solutions to social order to structural modes of control through law, science and the inputs of missionaries.[106] Lower-strata Indians were treated as members of immutable groups with primarily genetically-determined, characteristics.[107] Prominent among those charged with administering the criminal tribe settlements was the missionary Salvation Army.[108] In many ways the Salvation Army collaborated with the imperial government and helped to reinforce colonial power structures. For Salvation Army officials, the settlements were a logical progression from their social service work and followed from the plans of their founder.[109] Commissioner F. Booth-Tucker had suggested:

> The incorrigible 'won't-be-goods' be either transported to some island or settled in remote Himalaya valleys, where they would soon become absorbed by inter-marriage with hill tribes, many of whom really need new blood while the majority of 'would-be-goods' be placed in agricultural reservations like those which had produced the successful and complete pacification of 300,000 Red Indians in the United States of

America. The children of criminal tribes could legally be separated from their parents for the purpose of moral and vocational instruction in special institutions.[110]

Later, Booth-Tucker offered his own discussion of hereditary criminals in his curious 1916 work *Criminocurology: Or The Indian Criminal and what to do with Him*. It included his own classification of Indian criminals – the Incorrigible, the Habitual, the Hereditary, the Ordinary, the Youth and the Child.[111] However, Booth-Tucker maintained that inheritance could be modified by work-habits, discipline, and isolation from eternal influences. This concept of redemption reflected the increasing division in genetic science between the exact contribution of nature and nurture. Even Lombroso, the founder of the inheritance school of criminology had recognized some effect of environment:

> 'There exist whole tribes and races more or less given to crime, such as the tribe of Zakka Kel in India ... In this tribe every male child is consecrated to thievish practices by a peculiar ceremoney, in which the new-born infant is passed through a breach in the father's house whilst the words, 'Become a thief' are chanted three times in chorus'.[112]

The consequences were predictable. The labelling of so many tribal people as 'criminal' and their confinement in settlements led to them being permanently stigmatized. Once released from the settlement, they were denied waged occupation, and their status was irredeemably reinforced.[113] This attitude not only enhanced the dichotomy of 'sin' and 'dharma', but also boosted racial theories and the need to separate the contagious from the healthy members of society.

Identity and Structural Source of Sansi Criminality

The central paradox of Sansi criminality lies in words quoted from Galton's book *Fingerprints*. Galton had encountered a returnee Indian Army officer, Major Ferris, who explained to Galton that the basis for crime in India was the unwillingness of the tribals and the lower castes to surrender their land to the colonial government. If they had done so, much crime would have been eliminated.[114] Tayyah Mahmud responds that paradoxically, the criminalization of these people stemmed from the social changes prompted by colonial economic policies such as state monopolies on commodities and regulation of forest harvesting.[115] State crime was reconstructed as indigenous crime.

At one level, Sansi 'criminality', and the various processes outlined above which produced this designation, must be understood in the context of imperial society's search for new identities for both the colonizers and for the colonized. The phantasmagoric images portrayed by Roy,[116] and in Victorian fiction, suggest an anxiety on both sides. Victorian fears related to the lower stratum of empire and to the insecurity of its own identities. In that fear, the scientification of Indian criminality, located within the positivist modes of social categorization (*curocriminology* in India), ensured the elevation of the colonizers (and their local Brahmin surrogates) in the social hierarchy. It also provided, in a period of rapid social and economic change, the reaffirmation of a demeaning legal status for the Sansi and other criminal tribes. Criminalizing the Sansi through law gave a sense of security to the rulers of the empire and to colonial elite of the caste system. It ensured the latter's own relative status integration,[117] while casting the Sansi and other 'criminal' tribes and castes not just as folk devils, but also as different. Anxieties in the relationship between colonial classes and the Brahmin elite were quelled on their perception of a common enemy, and through a new legal scientific designation for the criminal tribes.[118] Measuring the attributes of the criminal tribes though anthropometry conversely elevated the dominant stratum, in both societies, and assured their identities.

Secondly, there were structural sources in the construction process. In England, the 'criminal' classes had been produced (see Chapter 3 above) through a process of urbanization and industrialization. In India, similar social changes were important. Development in the material bases of existence was critical. Parts of the Punjab were acclaimed by the colonizers as the 'food basket' of India. It was a land rich in grain, and cotton flourished. The Punjab home of the Sansi accommodated agriculture, in which new industries and trade links were being developed. Colonial exploitation necessitated the development of a transportation system, railways, roads and the telegraph, to link the Punjab to the capitalist world market, conversely placing the peasantry at the mercy of world trade. As Hardiman argues, imperial export of food grains and crops, and the consequent high prices of grains, all helped to exacerbate scarcities.[119] The new monetary mode of exchange added to the miseries of the tribal peoples and intensified indebtedness. The market created a demand for credit from the newly emerging commercial groups. Relations between the creditor and the peasant Sansi debtors were of increasing inequality. By subordinating cultivators to *banias* (merchant moneylenders), subsistence loans contributed to the debts and lack of autonomy of the peasant producer. This, in turn, not only provided the merchants with economic control over the peasants but also forced the farmers to dispose of their produce immediately after the harvest, creating later scarcity. The colonial officers assisted by the local *banias* extracted surplus from the cultivator, in the form of land revenue, rent and interest charges.[120]

Shortages exacerbated the dependency of lower-caste and criminal tribes. Between 1860 and 1901, there were frequent famines in the Punjab, partly due to excessive export of grain.[121] Export of grain exhausted local supply. Mortality was greatest within the class of casual and itinerant labour. Similarly the cottage weaving industry collapsed because of imperial free trade. Loss of traditional access to forest lands also subtracted from nomadic livelihood. Consequent deprivation, when combined with stigmatization, drove collectivities such as the Sansi into social crime.

Famine victims were not always passive, for example there are several instances in which several attempts to loot grain stores,[122] involved lower-castes and the Sansi. Offences against property were widespread,[123] reflecting the desperate plight of the poverty stricken people:

> In several places the feelings against the banias and grain dealers, who were accused of raising grain prices for their own selfish ends, was very strong. Grain riots occurred at many places in the district. The famished people in Ferozpur were so hard-pressed that they took to plunder and the owners of the grain-stores asked for a military guard to prevent the disturbances.[124]

In Amritsar, the pauper population was estimated at 20,000 with a further 10,000 internal migrants.[125] Indiscriminate arrests of vagrants were reported of the provincial police.[126] Many surrendered agricultural pursuits and adopted banditry[127] whilst many artisans, weavers and labourers turned to begging. The Sansi, writes Butler 'were driven to dacoity, especially so in hard famine times, they took to it when agriculture was precarious and provisions were few.[128] Colonial anxieties were most evident in reactions to this social crime. In classifying famine-related offences as crimes of dacoity, the authorities predictably blamed the victim. While refusing to intervene in the market economy of revenue and trade, the imperial state confronted the escalating property crime with twin relief and criminalizing measures. Relief measures re-established the Indian equivalent of the English workhouses, as well as the motif of the sturdy beggar. Civil legislation complemented criminal legislation as it had in England, with many public work developments. But the moral tone of empire ensured that only the fit and 'respectable' were employed. Distribution of relief by voluntary agencies[129] followed the inequity of caste divisions, and consolidated social division. There were other effects such as the consequent migration of the Sansi to other provinces in search of food and also to flee state agents.[130]

The victims of agricultural distress who stole grain to survive were now labelled as the most 'dangerous' of criminals, penetrating the collective conscience of the Company officers. Professional interests categorize the low-castes as a kind of social junk, which could be located homogeneously as peripheral and marginal to colonial society, harmful deviants who were criminally threatening, contributing little to the social and economic good of the Punjab. Similar to the criminal class of Victorian England, different factors led to the reconstitution of the Sansi as 'dangerous' under the Criminal Tribes Act of 1871. As summarized above, the first of these was the consequences of imperial polices over trade in which identities of different strata become confused, uncertain and in need of reassertion. Legal process was a key device by which anxieties were quelled and statuses reaffirmed. Scientific discourses, normally adapted in their own language by judicial agents, legitimized paternalistic intervention, a process that was enhanced by the new missionary work in the Settlements. Traditional forms of labour became crimes of survival.

Up to and including the years of Indian independence in 1947, labels attached to the Sansi and to other criminal tribes were affirmed in further legislation. Legal solutions were enlisted to deal with social problems – such as the claim that the Sansi frequently assumed fictional identities to avoid legal controls. The Settlements became controversial over employment policies – or rather the lack of them. However, missionary zeal contained the problem. The Punjab lesson of determining particular groups as criminal tribes spread to cities such as Madras where no criminal groups had previously been recognized.[131] The sledgehammer continued for nearly a century to extend policing powers over the lower social orders. Continuity was maintained as with the Indian Habitual Offenders Act of 1948.[132]

In sum, the transportation of legal definitions from Victorian England was a solution developed in response to colonial anxieties. Crimes of survival by the Sansi were re-defined by imported imperial definitions of criminality. Racial categorizations, which lent themselves easily to scientific racist theories in England, proved beneficial for imperial rule. The idea of the officially-enforced labelling activities, which had first arisen in the 1830s and the 1840s with the discovery, and suppression of 'thuggee' was built and sustained with the colonial administration transforming the Sansi, the wandering tribes, the numerous predatory tribes and castes consisting of the peasants, the poor and the begging population, into 'criminal' communities. The 'natives' had to be collectively controlled for wider benefit. By identifying various groups as abnormal and habitually criminal, and by endowing the police and the magistrates with extraordinary powers to deal with their pathology, the Colonial Office acquired Indian 'sites', in terms not only of geography, economics and education but most of all in law. The Indian tribes and castes were racially constructed within and through criminological discourses. This colonial obsession with the maintenance of law and order and the construction of identities within the social hierarchy of Empire assumed a similar form to that of Victorian England. The 'criminal' tribes and castes of imperial India were legally and socially reified in ways not dissimilar to the 'dangerous' classes in Victorian England.

The construction of the 'dangerous' classes could not have occurred in the way it did without the reference to the simultaneous construction of the dangerous in imperial India. The image of the English 'dangerous' classes drew in part, on 'racial' notions from India and at the same time the legal labelling processes of a similar problem in India relied, in part, on the transplantation of images of dangerousness from the metropolis. While there were clear differences between the two situations, especially in relation to the urban context of one (adjacent to the structures of England's emergent industrial economy) and the other (confined to the periphery of Empire). There were similarities of image, social status and social structure. The similarities between the two cases are more important in explaining their experience of discretionary legislation than any differences. It is in the difference between the two cases that one finds the significance of their similarities. The debates, which gave rise to the Criminal Tribes Act of 1871 in India were similar to the discourse, and reflected the same tensions and anxieties, which gave rise to the Habitual Criminals Act of 1869 in Victorian England.

8 IMPERIAL REFLECTIONS: A COMPELLING INSISTENCE

> 'The hereditary criminal is by no means confined to India, although it is only in that country that they have the engaging simplicity to describe themselves frankly in the census returns.'[1]

Official Statistics and Colonial Census of 1872: Cartography, and the Narration of Caste and Criminal Tribes

The debate about the Census of 1872 in colonial India is exemplary of the argument developed in this text in two ways. First, it is one of the most telling instances of the process of identity construction, especially of the criminal types and the savage tribes. Second, it was hailed by Orientalist scholars as the colonial officials with what they presumed to be a neat distinction between themselves and the people of India. Most notably, and to return to General Booth's comment on the first Indian census, it contains a double irony. At a more general level, it constructs the people of India within an Occidental discourse. Essentially, the census was a British device, framed within British assumptions of the collection of data within modernity. At a more practical level, though, the example of the Census shows how a seemingly hegemonic narrative of the people of India can also function, through its very ideals and values, to open up spaces for alternative voices. What is most revealing about the census is that the people of India so constituted, especially the low-caste as well as the Brahmins, disrupted the chronology and the classification of the census. More pointedly, the subjects challenged, through adopting various techniques of resistance and power, the very forms of identity in which they were supposedly being constructed. Significant is how different technologies of power and modes of resistance were undertaken, by various castes and groups in India to represent themselves in the ever-changing nature of their societies after the arrival of the Europeans. What is often overlooked by historians is how the chronological ordering of the census, an important imperial document, was also disrupted by respondents, who chose to answer questions that reflected their own construction of a response, rather than one that would meet their perception of an identity that could be slotted into the alien instrument. Booth's sardonic comment tells us more about the designers of the census than it does about the respondents. The census of 1872 and its major successor in 1901 together furnish a heuristic structure through which to summarize the key themes of this text.

The Census of 1872 was constructed at the same time, based on similar assumptions and the historical legacy of scientific and legal discourses, as the Criminal Tribes Act of 1871. An analysis of the census illustrates how imperial enquiries can be turned back on themselves, problematizing the identities of those presumed to be conducting the inquisition. Similarly, concepts of criminality, such as the criminal tribes and criminal classes, of dangerousness, of caste and of identity (especially in the case of the census, religious identity), reflect, once again, the tensions and the insecurities of those actively involved in the construction of identities and subjectivities. In this case, they reflect and render uncertain the identities of the officials of the first Indian numerations, which also included dominant indigenous groups operating at regional and local levels, which further point to its limitations. It is in the census that we can trace the history of people who have often been silenced. The census provides an exemplary opening to the wider questions of law's violence and the imperial project, and, between the lines as it were, oppressed voices can be heard.

The first Indian census was actually produced over the years 1868–71, and a successor to considerable early statistical work by EIC officers. Nineteenth-century scholarship in social statistics is a missing ingredient in the earlier account of the scientific discourses within which criminal classes and criminal tribes were constructed. The new statisticians, and political, economic, anthropological and philanthropic investigators such as Henry Mayhew[2] (Mayhew's first employment was with the EIC) made a crucial contribution to the constitution of Empire, both internally and externally. EIC statisticians played significant roles in exchanging data-collection methods between England and India in reinforcing the science of 'difference' (Thomas Malthus was Professor of Political Economy at the East India Company College).[3]

In colonial India, previous statistical work laid the groundwork for the new information order of Empire.[4] In 1807, the Government of Bengal had ordered a survey of the 'Eastern territories', 'We are of the opinion that a statistical survey of the country would be attended with much urgency'.[5] The survey recorded details such as religion, of progress in arts and manufacturing, and the natural history of the region. Marriott notes 'The accumulation of empirical material was the most determined effort heretofore to know the Indian landscape and village life better to exercise economic and political authority'.[6] Missionaries had also contributed.[7] By mid-century, statistics had become an essential tool for the categorization of Empire and especially of the inferior races. Just a few years before the 1872 census in colonial India, compilation of the Imperial Gazetteers had begun by W. W. Hunter. Both the Gazettes and the eventual census reports furnished a variety of statistical data on the people and their circumstances in different parts of India. Although provincial censuses had been conducted in the Northwest Provinces in 1853 and the Punjab in 1855, it was the census material of 1872, which represented a key step in the scattered foci of statistical accumulations within which empire ruled. The central motive for that enumeration was of social order in the colony. Statistically determining the probability of local disorder was an outcome that, it was believed, could be calculated from factors of population and social character. Census compilation and analysis, based on a crude scientific determinism, was a prediction device for social order requirements. Crime levels could be forecast through census data.

However, as Hobson points out, the eventual lack of use of such statistics in relation to disorder, and the depth of apparently extraneous detailed included in the census, seem more to have been propelled by a generic quest for the control of Indian knowledge and of Indian identities.[8] In that enquiry, caste and tribe were regarded as indicators of occupation, of status, of intellectual ability and a critical clue to indigenous identity against which the British themselves could be measured and located on the ladder of progress. For example, questions on religion were enforced in the 1871 Irish and 1872 Indian census but not in the British one. Enquiries on the 'modern' affiliations of the latter being considered an invasion of the rights of civilized people. In colonized nations, no such impediments would be tolerated. Earlier attempts by the British to document the colonial population had been beset by confusion. Inter alia, the physical layout of streets and housing in Indian cities had distorted population numbers, a conundrum that resulted in British administrators resorting to 'known' units of categories and collectivities, as a shorthand technique for assessing individuals. Colonial discourse drew upon indigenous concepts in ways that demonstrated that the British only dimly understood them, but which later had a major impact on the constitution of colonial rule.[9] As Chakrabarty explains, '...the social assumptions on which the classification and organization of census figures rested were fundamentally modern: they showed India to be a collection of "communities" whose "progress" or "backwardness" could be measured by the application of some supposedly "universal" indices'.[10] This was the beginning of the Othering process, which, whilst having far reaching consequences, also posed some serious challenges for the imperial project.

The Objectification of Categories of Caste and Tribe

The caste[11] system furnished a readily accessible typology for the census, one that appeared to draw upon Indian tradition and therefore would presumably be regarded as legitimate on the subcontinent. In the same way that early Victorian writers and ethnographers had referred to the hierarchy of social classes, from the criminal to the respectable, caste and its various levels, including criminal tribe seemed to furnish an Oriental equivalent. Since Victorian society was divided by class, the British in India attempted to equate the Indian caste[12] system to the class system. In contrasting criminal castes with London's criminal class, the British had an extensive body of knowledge to draw upon.[13] They saw caste as an indicator of occupation, social standing and intellectual ability. During the initial days of EIC, caste privileges and customs had been reaffirmed and were encouraged, and the discrimination against lower castes perpetuated. Vague traditions and identities had been given an official *imprimatur*. Thus, it was relatively easy to understand the concept of the criminal tribes through the common concept of dangerousness which was the key device by which the British could make sense of their own criminal class. Caste became a proxy for class. Similarly, as Yang argues, while the term 'criminal' does not appear in the early official accounting in India, criminal tribes by 1871 had become a concrete entity as a specific subcategory of caste, in order to furnish more detailed information.

For British administrators, 'caste was a thing'[14] like tribe, and its reification became one of the dominant modes of representations of Indian society. As Tolen points out, the terms caste, tribe and class were frequently interchangeable. Further, some of the later Gazetteers also used the terms 'criminal caste' criminal tribe, and criminal class as synonyms. However, it was the term tribe which served a distinct representational function. It evoked both an evolutionary stage, with certain attendant values and images. Hence, tribe was situated on a lower evolutionary rung than caste in which the same logic of evolution and images was used to explain crime with tribe. Significantly, tribes committed crime, because it was in their nature and, moreover, it was dictated by their caste to do so. Caste rather than tribalism was the distinctive causal feature of this breed of criminality. But the discourse 'of tribe could evoke qualities of savagery, wildness, and otherness in a way that caste could not. The term "criminal tribe" was often used because of the signs it was able to produce in British consciousness'.[15] Further, given the crime scientists' view of inheritance, caste membership would give guidance on future group behaviour. 'From the outset, the Census had a strong interest in ethnology as a means of organizing a massive amount of seemingly disparate data ... in addition to age, marital status, and sex, the 1872 Census included details of caste [and tribe], and religion in spite of the very real uncertainties that existed'.[16] The British saw caste and tribal affiliations as a technique for breaking down a large population into meaningful aggregates, which had specific characteristics,[17] comprehensible within the Occidental paradigm. By the time of the 1872 census, caste (and to some extent, tribe) had become the primary subject of imperial classification and social knowledge. It had become a hybrid concept. Although caste existed before colonialism, Dirks argues that it was thoroughly reconfigured by British rule, and caste was 'a conscious design of British colonial policy' which was invented to facilitate colonial rule.[18] The caste system, however, embodied highly artificial assumptions in the eyes of its administrators. It was a social construct that simply did not fit the disparate Indian populations. It was a European convenience based on a belief in the ultimate symmetry of Occidental and Oriental social structures.

Firstly, the assumption about inherited features within the caste system was based upon the repetitive hearsay dressed as the empirical science of the born criminal. In fact, indigenous practice largely forbade intra-marriage within castes. Direct inheritance of characteristics was therefore unlikely – even if the science held true. However, if Europeans were aware of the genealogical problems, they did not perceive them as an obstacle to census use for predictions based on inheritance. Secondly, it correctly focused on the rural village as the dominant site of Indian social life. But the Census constituted it an arena driven by caste and religious division, a setting for caste relations rather than the primary building block of Indian society. The village became portrayed as an interstice of conflict between castes, tribes and religions rather than of coexistence between different peoples.[19] As Washbrook states, the British perspectives 'missed the finely honed status differentials within caste, which gave the system flexibility, and above all, missed the webs of interdependency which linked numbers of castes together in an economic and social structure'.[20] British social evolutionary theorists insisted upon inter-caste conflict as a key dynamic of Indian society. The colonial authorities were so committed to that view that where evidence of such rivalry was not immediately obvious, they felt constrained to assume or even invent it. Thus the declaration by senior members of the Secretariat of the Madras Presidency that they would look favourably on appeals directed against caste 'aggression' produced a new dimension in local politics. Washbrook comments 'Once the language of large scale communal hostility, of broadly defined castes competing against each other had been introduced, there was no end to the number of situations it could be used to describe'.[21] Without suggesting a golden age thesis, there is little historical evidence of sustained communal hatred operating at the popular level prior to colonial rule.[22] The Census of 1872 created a difference between the majority and the minority in village communities as in the total jurisdiction, 'in pre-British India, communities had 'fuzzy' boundaries and in British India, they became 'enumerated'.[23] The term 'fuzzy' is taken to mean boundaries that do not admit of clear identities. The census or enumeration gave birth to discrete identities and subjectivities.

However, collecting data for the census was far from straightforward. There was confusion over caste, which was multiplied by the initial assumption that Muslims were merely low-caste Hindus, the product of conversion, and to be accounted for accordingly.[24] This view had extraordinary later repercussions.[25] In any case, the religious categories represented an English construction. Hindus were not a homogeneous collectivity. The boundaries between different religions, especially between Hindus and Sikhs, but also between Muslims, were at best blurred. Other problems arose in interpretation. Several commemorators after the 1901 census suggested that Hinduism was a dying race, not only in fertility and mortality rates, but also in terms of conversion.[26] The British census produced a complex construction of Muslim religious and ethnic identity playing on both the assertion and the denial of difference. The very function of the census was to show, through enumeration, that the assertion of 'difference' – the idea of Muslims as outsiders, was propagated by Indian Muslims themselves. Once this was established as a specifically Muslim claim, that declaration of difference was promptly denied by the categories adopted in British census-taking, which sought to demonstrate that the bulk of the Muslim population came from local converts.

There were other imposed Occidental categories within the census that created a different alterity. Age questions were a key feature. O'Donnell, the Bengal census superintendent in 1871 remarked that 'the ignorance or carelessness of even native gentlemen of position and education in regard to their ages is a notorious fact, and even when they know them accurately, so strong is the force of habitual forms of expression, that it is doubtful if they would state them accurately'.[27] Chronological age affected longevity of populations, of famine relief requirements, pensions of local civil servants, and especially the experiences of women with regard to health and related issues. After the 1872 census in Bengal, Beverley, the provincial registrar, observed that '[t]he population of Bengal rose in one day from 42 to 67 millions, and quipped that the Lieutenant-Governor … suddenly found that he had unconsciously been the ruler of an additional population more than equal to that of the whole of England and Wales'.[28] Concepts of annual aging were, like other Census components, a form of categorization constructed within the Enlightenment. Finally, the Census employed assumptions about occupation. 'Man' has a single occupation from which indices could therefore be understood. But the Indian population, and especially rural people, could have several different occupations. However, in European eyes, the occupation was the primary signifier of identity. Thus an individual who pursued a nomadic existence, a complex of occupations, could be reduced to the simple label of criminal. Here again, the perception of the Brahmin census-taker would affect occupational definitions. 'Criminal castes were said to engage in legitimate occupations, but only to divert attention from their 'real' occupation of crime'.[29] Predictably, an intelligent Brahmin census-taker knew how to sniff out the 'real' occupation of those they regarded as being of criminal inheritance.

Violence and Resistance

By the time of the 1901 census, it was clear that caste had attained its colonial apotheosis. Not only was race the basic category of caste difference, religion was the primary source of values that was seen to support the ascribed caste system. The census was part of a larger scholarly enterprise in which the Victorians, as children of the Enlightenment, sought rational principles that would provide a comprehensive and comprehensible way of fitting everything they saw in the world around them into ordered hierarchies. The existence of empire by imparting a sense of urgency to the process spurred on this creation of knowledge and at the same time the unequal power relationships of imperialism helped shape the categories within which that knowledge was constructed.[30] The census was a device that relied on authoritarian implant. But agency could affect its structural mandate. It could be, and was, manipulated locally. On one hand, the actual census-takers were the local literati, mainly Brahmins,[31] who could shape the questioning and the results to their own advantage.[32] By establishing themselves as authorities on the caste system they could then tell the British what they believed the British wanted to hear, and conversely what would most enhance their own position. The British would then take this information, received through the filter of the Brahmins, and interpret it based on their own experience and their own cultural concepts.[33] Indeed, as Tolen notes, nearly all the earlier ethnographic studies of nineteenth-century India depended upon Brahmin assistants to conduct the fieldwork. Such consequent material therefore was often little more than the product of prejudice, hearsay, anecdotes and innuendo.[34] The police were also a major source of ethnographic information and in turn could have been expected to ensure that the selected information benefited their own careers. At best, such police information would have been constructed within the prevailing British colonial policing paradigm. (Indeed the very concept of criminality both in India and in London was a construct shaped by official presumptions. As noted in Chapter 3, the London Metropolitan Police was very similar in its imagery of the 'criminal' to the colonial police of India).

In effect, the census could also be resisted by evasion or avoidance techniques, as in the succeeding 1901 census, by a multitude of petitions complaining about caste assignation. The 1871 census received a kaleidoscope of answers, frequently not phrased in caste terms, as a means of – in Indian terms – asserting their own actual identity. Definitions of 'self' were grounds for contest, not simply the assertion of 'fact'. To the colonial officers, this merely demonstrated the lesser intelligence of their Indian subjects, rather than the lack of relevance of the question. The view of the latter was that identity was based on caste tradition, not on current occupation or other factors – as with the born criminal of imperial scientific racism. The Occidental paradigm was intended to capture the key concepts of Indian society, and to be able to translate and interpret it within the hierarchy of imperial identities, a project which was informed by existing British identities located within modernity.

However, the various forms of resistance undertaken by the subalterns within the census-gathering exercise has the potential to open up a newly established set of relations, not only between the colonized and the colonizers, but also between and within the agency of the non-Western subjects. In all this, it must be remembered that the census provided the imperial project, with a highly potent framework, to control, to contain and in some cases the outright extinction of the most irredeemable, during one of its key turbulent moment, the Cawnpur uprisings of 1857. The census enumerated communities and Indian subjects into collectivities which was most evident in the reality of colonial violence and oppression. Like the pretensions of law, the real impact of the period was to integrate pre-existing concerns and techniques into larger discourses, transforming them into the process of empire building.

Law and Empire: the Persistence of the Postcolonial

To return to our original interdependent questions outlined in Chapter 1. Firstly, why do we find similar legal constructions of 'dangerousness', in the Habitual Criminals Act of 1869 and in the Criminal Tribes Act of 1871, in Victorian England and in imperial India respectively? Secondly, was this construction simply a matter of accident, the duplication of contiguous legal codes, or was there a near-identical problem perceived by the dominant social formation in each context to which a similar legal arrangement was the solution? Thirdly, why was this legislation characterized by inquisitorial assumptions of guilt prior to any perceived infringement? The primary concern of the text has been to focus on one aspect of the construction of identities – how similar processes appear in both imperial India and in Victorian England. In India, the constructions concerned the Sansi and their rulers, and in Victorian England, they are seen in the construction of the 'criminal' class, along with its ethnic component. In both cases the effect of the construction on the identity of the Other was explored. English criminal law (given its particular structural concealment of inequalities), and racist science, were fundamental to the construction in 'criminal' identities.

Focusing on the construction of identities of the non-Western in the London 'criminal' class and the Sansi as a criminal tribe in imperial Punjab, furnishes the case study material. This following, final, discussion covers the complex role of law in the construction of the 'master statuses' of the Occident and of the Orient and in its ability to conceal inequality within a formal structure of equality. The dimension inherent in the colonial encounter, both within and outside, was enhanced by a growing sense of European exceptionalism. This had the effect of further increasing the distance between the ruled and the rulers. Given this focus, the text has explored socio-legal issues to determine how particular legal devices were used to construct and constrain the identity of both rulers and the ruled in imperial India, and of the respectable and the 'dangerous' in Victorian England.

Alterity, Hybridity and Ambivalence in the Constitution of Identities

Through an analysis of 'dangerousness' in both settings, legal and scientific images on identity and the 'criminal', led to the labelling of 'others' through which the Western identity was sustained. In relation to those who are seen as on the border of modernity, the preceding chapters demonstrated the inside/outside dichotomy of Western discourse which led to a construction in which the identification of the 'criminal' classes in Victorian England and the 'criminal' tribes and castes in imperial India as 'dangerous', stabilized Western identity. What is more, the inequality of the relationship was reinforced through its definition as an absolute opposition. The non-Western, the savage heathen, was viewed as opposite to the Western subject.

Having drawn upon the recent debates in postcolonial theory and the work of the Subaltern School to develop a critique of the framework, which underlies the comparative analysis between the 'criminal' condition of the Indian tribes and the 'dangerous' classes, what has been learnt so far? This text evidences that there were parallel developments in legislation in both Victorian England and in imperial India. The traditional and orthodox belief that the Orient was shaped by a determining West is gradually being replaced by a critique which recognizes that contribution but challenges the certainty of Western identity itself. There was no fixed Western identity against which India was being measured. Not merely was the identity of the non-West and its component formations being reshaped, but so also was the character of Western society. Identities were not constructed in a void. Defining the non-western as 'inferior', imposing demeaning characteristics and focusing on their undesirable traits, was not merely an exercise in the display of power – for whatever reason, it also constructed and elevated the identities of those engaged in defining the 'Other'. Entailed in this self-construction was not only a violence of the subordination of the non-western but an anxiety for all which could possibly have resurfaced to disrupt the identity of the West and expose it as a self-construction. The over-determination of difference, in both case studies, concealed the fear and the tensions inherent in the identity of the West. The discourses of empire are constructed in response to a set of anxieties and fears about the possibilities of failure which threaten the very existence of imperial identities.

In Victorian England, industrialization (and the concomitant processes of urbanization and social disorganization), the birth of industrial capitalism and the transformation of empire from an agglomerate of private trading companies to direct imperial control in India, characterized a major period of social change. This was marked in particular by dramatic changes in the class structure, with consequences for the problems of social order. Social hierarchies were in flux. Patterns of social stratification were changing. The new urban middle class was accompanied by the tentative incorporation of a new industrial proletariat – waged labour, the foundation of industrial capitalism. A new moral order, characterized elsewhere by the Protestant ethic, provided the moral underpinnings of the economic structure. The upper and middle classes were deemed to be threatened by the Other, those outside the wage economy, not just by the lack of commitment displayed by these 'outsiders' to the new industrial ethic, but also because their normative behaviour might infect the emerging patterns of waged discipline. Where morality was defined using the language of 'health', a determinate medical metaphor became popularly associated with the characteristics of the 'Other', especially involving the terminology of diseases, which were also deemed to be threatening.

As Durkheim has argued, in times of social change when morality is in flux, only by defining a group outside the pale in terms of its morality and perceived threat, does new morality appear.[35] Similarly, only when the characteristics of the new out-groups are identified and established, within recognizable parameters of imagery, do other dominant parties of the social order (along with the incorporated lower strata such as the respectable working class) contrive their own identity. Identity is defined through what the out-group is not, that is, it is defined by its new constructed opposite. Anxiety over status and social hierarchy, in the process of social change, is only relieved when the dominant group knows what it is not – it's opposite. This tension neither originates nor ends there. Despite the fact that the 'criminal' classes were a construction of 'dangerousness' by which new social formations could be made sense of and given recognizable characteristics within the demonology of the new moral order, at the same time, those labelled as 'dangerous' were conscious agents in creative tension with the powerful. In both case studies, there were instances of resistance, which created conditions in which the powerless placed great demands on law to dispense justice. In these respects, the non-West appears to have contributed to, modified and challenged the West rather than confirm the 'criminal' labels. For Bhabha, the formation of colonial subjectivities as a process is never fully achieved, all of which, for our purposes here, is a way of restoring the agency of the excluded. There is scope for making visible the position of the marginalized, those labelled as 'criminal' and as 'dangerous', not only in colonial India and in

Victorian England, but also in the continuity of those demeaning labels used by various elite groups, both between and within our fast-changing present.

Non-Western in the 'Criminal' Class in Victorian England

In England, the twin processes of urbanization and of industrialization had displaced earlier social formations and had constructed a so-called 'criminal' class. This class survived outside the waged market economy through crimes of survival, such as prostitution and begging, rather than by crimes of appropriation. The 'criminal classes' did not represent a specific threat to the social order but were marginal to the process. Sanitized by the new police, they represented only a threat to the identity of the respectable class; they did not represent a real physical threat.

Law forms a key social censure in the process of defining people. Law locates in concrete form what other social pressures can only create as epiphenomena. Focusing primarily on two statutes and the more general legal processes of the Habitual Criminals Act of 1869 in Victorian England and the Criminal Tribes Act of 1871 in imperial India, this text has demonstrated that not only were identities formed through legislation but also that legal enshrinement was the major way in which differences were affirmed and imperial anxieties over different statuses of the non-Western alleviated. Within the social constructionist perspective, legislation had little to do with concrete experiences of crime. Like the wider criminal class, the lascars and the ayahs were largely confined to crimes of survival, as amplified by legal and moral entrepreneurs. As this text has demonstrated, within the Victorian 'criminal' class, there was a group of South Asians, playing roles constructed as much through racial myths of India as through concepts of 'dangerousness', who had similarly been affected by social change. Displaced from waged labour, *lascars* were cast out from employment by the vicissitudes of mercantile trade, and *ayahs* were left out on the London streets having been made unemployable in mercantile households. Like their white peers, they were forced to practise forms of 'criminality', from begging to vagrancy, for survival and posed no tangible threat to the physical order, but rather like the larger 'criminal' class, they epitomized a different morality. Racism was a key feature in this process. Myths, metaphors and allegories of Victorian notions of the Orient (East) were used to construct the identities of the non-Western in both England and in India. The image of the opium den involved a very specific transposition; the lascars are the corruptors of the native Victorian folk. Such views became the commonsense of the society. The non-Western, as part of the larger 'criminal' class, played an incremental part in the formation of judgements about inferior identities as well as in elevating the local and in eliminating Western uncertainties and anxieties.

This process was reflected by the way in which law constructed the non-Western as different, as seen in criminal and civil law, proactive policing by the new forms of Benthamite agencies, and in the incorporation of 'scientific' rationalization into legal discourse. In classifying the non-Western as outcasts, law created those outside the 'criminal' class as inside 'respectable' Victorian society. Reifying the 'dangerous' through law as habituals consigned offenders to being 'criminals' by their nature and by their birth. The West in a major period of social change only knew who they were because they were not like the 'criminal' class. Defining the non-Western as primitive and lacking the contours of civilization allowed the West to project itself as civilized and modern to the rest of the world. The West in its claims to civility and modernity, in the celebration of its past and the claim to a future, engaged in the oppression of the non-Western in both Victorian England and in imperial India.

The Sansi as a Criminal Class in Colonial India

In imperial India, the Sansi (used here as representative of the larger agglomeration of 'criminal' tribes) only received legal affirmation as 'criminal', the ultimate censure, after a long process of construction by both local and colonial authorities. As with the identification of the Victorian 'criminal' classes, the new forms of economic and political order in imperial India had also displaced the Sansi group. Under the impact of colonial policies and exigencies, traditional occupations were lost under new environmental legislation and changing economic imperatives with regard to trade and communications. 'Casual' labour as a means of sustenance had been transformed into crimes of survival. Again, despite the earlier moral panics inherited from the colonial imaginative construction of 'thuggee', offences were largely limited to crimes of survival, not of depredation.

The Criminal Tribes Act of 1871, entrepreneurial colonial policing, the new scientific disciplines of anthropometry and new policing techniques in fingerprinting, ensured that the Sansi, like the 'criminal' class in Victorian England, were reified as different. Both 'criminal' tribes and 'criminal' classes were legally and scientifically constructed as occupying a clearly demarcated inferior status. In India, this designation did not only affect the colonial masters, it also allowed the higher castes to identify themselves with their colonial masters, thus placing the 'criminal' tribes and castes outside the notion of modernity and progress. The legal constitution of the Indian 'criminal' tribes reflected Western confusion not only about making sense of Indian society but also about their own social division and imagery – especially with regard to changing notions of the 'criminal' classes and of the 'dangerous' poor. India could be understood through imagery drawn from the West in the same way that the West could be understood through categories of measurement from imperial India. The constitution of criminal identities was a two-way process.

Reifying Inequality in the Construction of Identities

In the constructivist process, modern law also acted in less obvious ways to help achieve a particular kind of result. In conferring on the non-Western 'equality as citizens of empire', it affirmed them collectively as social unequals. In offering the safeguard of adversarial process, the law ensured the marginalization of its subjects to a process bereft of due process rights. Legal process for both the 'criminal' classes and the 'criminal' tribes treated them as collectivities rather than as individuals, conferring social inequality under the guise of legal equality. However, as we have seen, the reality ensured that the non-Western, in practice, became unequals, as legal process sought to demean them rather than to elevate them as equals. The adversarial safeguard, ironically, simply reaffirmed that they were to be regarded as guilty until proven innocent.

More importantly, it appears from the two case studies offered in this text that in the reformed edifice of Western law, the criminal types in both Victorian England and in imperial India, were denied trial as social equals. The non-Western on the street of the urban metropolis, and tribes in distant areas of the Empire, found that law reform merely confirmed on them the array of public order legislation with its discretionary characteristics. Criminal charges could be vague. Definitions of the offence were as constructed in the eyes of the enforcer. Action against the non-Western and the tribes was conducted on the basis of 'suspicion' rather than on evidence. The burden of proof was reversed. Trial was based on aspects of character, spatial location and affinities rather than of evidential action. The conflated powers of criminal and civil law encompassed the non-Western within a legal state of guilt rather than a presumption of innocence. Discretion in law, as argued in Chapter 2, was both an accident of statutory downgrading, a flawed outcome and a necessary feature of the way in which legislation aimed to reinforce rather than deny inequalities. The inquisitorial legal process was effectively disguised as adversarial, not so much a remnant of a previous form of law but rather representing continuity from pre-industrial legislation to the present day.[36] Freitag has suggested that in imperial India this was because a covert legal structure had somehow managed to coexist with due process.[37] However, Singha[38] has recognized the strength of the structural argument – suggesting that the discretionary demeaning forms of legality in India are integral to the wider structure of adversarial legislation. It was this force of law, which was instrumental in the 'criminalization' of both the non-Western in Victorian England and in imperial India.

Finally, the text borrowed from the legal approach to demonstrate a link between the construction of identities both in Victorian England and in imperial India. This reasserts the view of Skuy who argues that, far from England possessing a solid and established legal system in the Victorian period, it was undergoing major convolutions and experiencing uncertainties about its own legal structures.[39] Law, in the social constructivist tradition, had the ability to construct and to reify universal identities. Law was a master status, one that was accepted both by the definers and the defined. The definers believed that the legal label represented a status which was elected above social problems and social disputes. The defined internalized the notion of legal inequality as being right and just, as determined by an impartial measure. Postcolonial theory, demonstrates the way in which the creation of law operates as the defining moment in which identities, superior and inferior, are internalized as objective statements of the truth – a truth that seems to come from and reside in the West. In its claims to be modern and civil, law, which emanates from the West, engages the non-Western to become the same as itself. However, that engagement is based on a relationship of inclusion and subordination in which the West has the upper hand. In imperial India, it was through law that the colonial officers managed to overcome their own uncertainties and anxieties. Conversely, it was through law (while also now knowing its own worth) that the non-western was expected to recognize its inferiority on a 'rational calculus'; the non-western had been tried and found wanting by the impartial standard of due process. It was also in and through law that the non-western articulated various forms of resistance and challenged subjectivities.

Law, Modernity and the Postcolonial: The Larger Jigsaw

No research is conclusive. One study leads to another. This text is no different. It leads to a number of questions for future research. The law is not merely a law that must, to claim originality, disguise its own origins, but needs to continually reinvent itself. Secondly, with regard to the postcolonial debate, more evidence is needed about how such a process affected the Occident, and more generally on the processes of power-driven negotiation between unequals. This is especially so with relation to the criminalization of various castes and tribes in imperial India. Thirdly, there is also the question of how history informs the present day functioning of the legal system. The evidence presented here needs to be developed further, in order to show the similarities of those earlier constructions of identity, which affect the present day experiences of minorities in both England and in India. To what extent can one explain the present day position in the social structure of England and Asian minorities through the use of the 'criminal' label to relieve Western anxieties?

Fourthly, postcolonial theory is based on the assertion that the project of Western colonization to the rest of the world was based upon the social and cultural construction of a fundamental distinction between the West and the non-West, with the latter occupying the position of the West's Other, and serving as the social point for distilling the opposites of all those moral, superior qualities that gradually accreted to constitute the very core of the West's own self-image. Structurally, contributions from critical legal studies combined with postcolonial studies provide the theoretical and conceptual resources necessary to study crime, the 'criminal' and criminal law. By making explicit, for example, the forms of rationality and the assumptions which underpin identity and which also permeate criminal judicial practices, postcolonial studies not only help to expose the contingency of the current social and legal order, they also provide crucial insights into the historical dimensions of social relations and legal structures in both imperial India and in Victorian England. Finally, a sustained empirical focus on the historical 'criminalization' of the non-Western, can assist in giving postcolonial studies more contemporary relevance through investigations of the relationships between power, discourse, and the institutions of criminal justice. An engagement with the continuity from colonial to postcolonial legal conditions could be a step forward for postcolonial theory, critical legal studies and criminology. As Spivak has so rightly said, how to place the label 'post' for a state which is not yet fully present and linking it to something which has not fully disappeared,[40] but in many ways, this paradoxical in-between-ness is precisely what characterizes the postcolonial world. Taken together these studies have the vital role of challenging and disrupting the Western sense of where the 'centre' of things lies. The next significant steps could involve centring what has previously been denied, ignored and marginalized as well as the rethinking and rewriting of law's past with the overall intention of decolonizing the disciplinary space. Borrowing from Fanon and his question of the condition of colonial subjectivity, *Nervous Conditions* explicitly invokes the conditions in which to understand the traumas of colonial encounter. To understand legal practice, as reflected in the content and enforcement of criminal justice structures, and crimes of imperialism, we must start with 'dangerousness', identities and subjectivities. Only then will we have a better understanding of the debates on modernity, law and colonialism.

More importantly, and to return to our original position, the criminal justice systems can be seen as a space where identities were subverted rather than confirmed, or as sites where identities were performed and contested. Here and elsewhere, the West's constant search for a pure undifferentiated identity is destined to fail, for it depends on its recalcitrant Others. Last but not least, the historical parallels between the 'dangerous' types, in both Victorian England and imperial India, are illuminating and insightful. Reacting against and through this postcolonial legacy, the persistent failure of the academy to adequately address the crimes of imperialism, may finally find a voice. There are other sites and other imperialisms than the ones offered here. While the two entities cannot be equated, the predicament of the non-Western in both settings evokes the memory of something that should not be forgotten, or be laid to rest and consigned to the past, at least not until we have given it its rightful place in the postcolonial. The postcolonial predicament is forever present in the periphery and the centre – just as much as it is evident in the contemporary ghetto and in the increasingly globalized territories.

NOTES

1 Imperial Miasma

1. F. Fanon, *Black Skin, White Masks* (London: Pluto, 1986).
2. See D. Chakrabarty, *Rethinking Working Class History: Bengal 1890–1940* (Delhi: Oxford University Press, 1989).
3. See D. Kirkby, and C. Colebarn, *Law, History and Colonialism* (Manchester: Manchester University Press, 2001).
4. P. Fitzpatrick and E. Darian-Smith, 'The Laws of the Postcolonial: An Insistent Introduction', in E. Darian-Smith and P. Fitzpatrick, *Laws of the Postcolonial* (Ann Arbor, MI: University of Michighan Press, 1999).
5. See Chapters 6 and 7, below. For a detailed account of the practices and the religious beliefs of the 'criminal tribes', see M. Kennedy, *The Criminal Classes in India* (Delhi: Mittal Press, 1908); S. Nigam, 'Disciplining and Policing the 'Criminals by Birth', Part 1: The Making of a Colonial Stereotype', *The Indian Economic and Social History Review*, 27 (1990), pp. 131–164; S. Nigam, 'Disciplining and Policing the 'Criminals' by Birth', Part 2: the Development of a Disciplinary System, 1871–1900', *The Indian Economic and Social History Review*, 27 (1990), pp. 257–87; and M. Radhakrishna, 'Surveillance and Settlements under the Criminal Tribes Act in Madras', *The Indian Economic and Social History Review*, 29 (1992), pp. 171–98.
6. On the 'dangerous' classes of England, see Chapters 4 and 6, below and C. Booth, *Life and Labour of the People in London*, vol. 1 (London: Macmillan Press, 1889); J. Pratt, *Governing the Dangerous: Dangerousness, Law and Social Change* (Sydney: The Federation Press, 1997), suggests that by the mid-nineteenth century, the concept of the 'dangerous' class was giving way to a notion of 'dangerous' criminals. However, the literary evidence cited by him suggests otherwise.
7. The metaphors 'sanitize' and 'legal prophylactic' were first used by R. Storch, 'The Plague of the Blue Locusts: Police, Reform and Popular Resistance', *International Review of Social History*, 20 (1975), pp. 61–90.
8. For example, agency plays a varying part – especially in the chance presence of both James and John Stuart Mill in the India Office. See J. S. Mill, *The History of British India*, 6 vols (London: Madden Press, 1840), vol. 2.
9. See T. R. Metcalf, *Imperial Connections: India in the Indian Ocean Arena, 1860–1920* (London: University of California Press, 2007), p. 7. See also A. Burton (ed.), *After the Imperial Turn* (Durham, NC: Duke University Press, 2003).

10. For a classic summary of Marxist views on imperialism, see N. Etherington, *Theories of Imperialism: War, Conquest and Capital* (London: Croom Helm, Routledge, 1984).
11. See R. Hyam, *Empire and Sexuality: The British Experience* (Manchester: Manchester University Press, 1990).
12. See A. L. Stoler, 'Between Metropole and Colony: Rethinking a Research Agenda', F. Cooper and A. L. Stoler (eds), *Tensions of Empire: Colonial Cultures in a Bourgeois World* (Berkeley, CA: University of California Press, 1997), p. 8.
13. Cooper and Stoler (eds), *Tensions of Empire.*
14. See Select Committee on the Police, 'Report From the Select Committee on the Police of the Metropolis', *British Parliamentary Papers* (600) vol. XXII, 1834. p. See also Frederick Engels's comment on the slum of St Giles and especially his chapter on Irish immigration in F. Engels, *Conditions of the Working Class in England* (Oxford University Press: Oxford, 1999). Inhabitants of the St Giles rookery in London and similar districts became known as what Lea later summed up as 'police property': see J. A. Lea, 'Some Structural Aspects of Police Deviance' in C. Shearing (ed.) *Organizational Aspects of Police Deviance* (Toronto, ON: Butterworths, 1981), p. 11.
15. Foucault uses this phrase in relation to the increase in government power. Foucault defines governmentality as the way in which the conduct of individuals is ever more marked in the exercise of sovereign power. This form of governing is at once totalizing and individualizing, involving technologies of domination of others as well as the governing of the self. Governmentality also includes a growing body of knowledge that presents itself as 'scientific', and which contributes to the power of government. This new kind of governmentality is made possible by the creation of specific 'knowledges' as well as the construction of experts, institutions and discipline – in medicine, psychology and psychiatry – so that individuals whom we think of as experts can claim the knowledge necessary to command the power in government. See M. Foucault, 'Governmentality', *Ideology and Consciousness*, 6 (1986), pp. 5–21; also see M. Foucault, *Discipline and Punish: the Birth of the Prison* (London: Penguin, 1978).
16. See R. Yin, *Case Study Research: Design and Methods* (London: Sage, 1994).
17. R. J. Young, *Colonial Desire: Hybridity in Theory, Culture and Race* (London: Routledge, 1995).
18. This Act designated the criminality of the state of vagrancy and divided the offenders into categories: the idle from the disorderly, the rogues from the vagabonds and the incorrigible rogues. See Chapter 5.
19. The 'residuum', was applied to those among the poor who were seen to have remained in poverty because of their indolence, incorrigibility and moral corruption. As the term implies, however, this 'residuum' was widely assumed to be an ever-diminishing proportion of the working class: the recalcitrant fraction of the criminal incorrigibles.
20. See, for example, Foucault, *Discipline and Punish*; and *Governmentality.*
21. See R. Storch, 'The Plague of the Blue Locusts'.
22. The Habitual Offenders Act of 1869 in *Session Papers* (10th December 1868–9), vols 1 and 11.
23. In 1600, a group of merchants incorporated themselves into the East India Company and were given monopoly privileges on all trade with the East Indies. The *Regulating Act* of 1773, provided for greater parliamentary control over the affairs of the Company.
24. See V. A. C. Gatrell, B. Lenman, and G. Parker (eds) *Crime and the Law: The Social History of Crime in Western Europe Since 1500* (London: Europa, 1980) and V. A. C.

Gatrell, L. Radzinowicz, and R. Hood, *The Emergence of Penal Policy in Victorian and Edwardian England* (Oxford: Clarendon Press, 1990).

25. The East India Company first employed lascars in the seventeenth century. The term is believed to derive from the Persian lashkar, meaning an army, a camp or a band of followers. In Urdu, the word lascar is a derivatve of *lashkar* or *lashkari,* which usually refers to soldiers but was used for sailors as well: *Oxford English Dictionary*, 2nd edn (Clarendon Press, Oxford, 1991), p. 666. The first European use of the term dates back to the Portuguese employment of Asian seamen in the early 1500s. They came to England primarily from India, especially from Bengal, Gujarat and Punjab, but also from Malaya and related countries. Victorian usage of the term sometimes misleadingly includes Chinese and North Africans under that heading.
26. See, R. Visram, *The Ayahs, Lascars and the Princes* (London: Pluto, 1986).
27. See P. Fryer, *Black People in the British Empire* (London: Pluto, 1989), and I. Law, and J. Henfry, *A History of Race and Racism: 1650–1950* (Liverpool: Multi Cultural Research Council, 1981).
28. See Visram, *The Ayahs, Lascars and the Princes,* as well as J. Pegg, *The Asiatics Cry to England* (London: Ward and Company, 1844); R. M. Hughes, *The Law Relating to Lascars and Asiatic Seamen Employed in the British Merchant Services or Brought to the UK in Foreign Vessels Smith* (London: Smith, Elder and Company, 1855).
29. See, L. Charlesworth, 'Why is it a Crime to be Poor?' *Liverpool Law Review*, 21 (1999), pp. 149–67.
30. The Atlantic residuum is defined in the work of P. Linebaugh and M. Rediker, *The Many-Headed Hydra: The Hidden History of the Revolutionary Atlantic* (London: Verso, 2000).
31. See P. Linebaugh, *The London Hanged: Crime and Civil Society in the Eighteenth* Century (London: Allen Unwin, 1991).
32. See, J. Davis, 'Race and Poverty: The Underclass and the Making of Victorian England' Paper given at the conference on *Underworld, Overworld or One World* (Cambridge: University of Cambridge, 1996).
33. In the same way that the Habitual Offenders Act of 1869 had been part of a medley of constructionist legislation, so too was The Criminal Tribes Act of 1871 in India. On the detail of the Criminal Tribes Act of 1871, see S. T. Jassal, 'Caste and the Colonial State: Mallahs in the Census', *Contributions to Indian Sociology*, 35 (2001), pp. 319–54. Similar legislation aimed inquisitorially at particular groups included The Contagious Diseases Act of 1875, The Cantonment Act of 1869 and The Female Infanticide Act of 1870.
34. For the 'martial races' see S. Alavi, *The Sepoy and the Raj: Tradition and Transition in Northern India 1770–1830* (Oxford: Oxford University Press, 1997), p. 35.
35. See D. Chakrabarty, *Rethinking Working Class History* (1989).
36. See, for example, Arnold, *Police, Power and Colonial Rule: Madras, 1859–1947* (Delhi: Oxford University Press, 1986).
37. See M. Brogden and P. Nijhar, *Community Policing: International Approaches and Models* (Cullompton: Willan Publishing, 2005).
38. R. J. Tolen, 'Colonizing and Civilizing the Criminal Tribesman: The Salvation Army in British India', *American Ethnologist,* 18: 1 (1991), pp. 106–25.
39. See N. B. Dirks, *Castes of Mind: Colonialism and the Making of Modern India* (Princeton, NJ: Princeton University Press, 2001). William Booth was the founder of the Salvation Army. Schemes for the criminal tribes in India followed the pattern laid down by William Booth for the English poor. This similarity will be taken up in Chapters 4–7

of this book. However, it is worth noting in advance that the scheme for settlements outlined in Booth's text (and eventually adapted for the Sansi) coincides remarkably with Francis Galton's plans for labour colonies as a means of redemption. See Galton's late and uncompleted 'science fiction' prophecy 'A Thousand Years Hence, Being Personal Experiences Narrated by Nunsowe Green', noted in K. Pearson, *Life, Letters, and Labour of Francis Galton*, 3 vols (Cambridge: Cambridge University Press, 1914), vol. 3, pp. 420–613, and T. R. Booth, *The Mukti Fauj: The Salvation Army* (London: Salvation Army, 1922).

40. See J. Leopold, 'The Aryan Race Theory in India', *The Indian Economic and Social History*, 7 (1970), pp. 271–86; K. Malik, *The Meaning of Race: Race, History and Culture in Western Society* (Basingstoke: Palgrave Press, 1996).
41. A discourse of stereotypes regarding the Sansi is available in secondary academic literature. See S. Singh, *The Sansis of Punjab* (Delhi: Munshiram Manoharlal, 1965), Kennedy, *The Criminal Classes in India*; D. C. Ibbetson, *Report of the Criminal Tribes of the Punjab* (Delhi: Mittal, 1881).
42. See A. Yang (ed.), *Crime and Criminality in British India* (Tucson, AZ: University of Arizona Press, 1985); S. Freitag, 'Collective Crime and Authority in North India' in Yang (ed.), *Crime and Criminality*, pp. 227–61.
43. See Chapter 7 of this book.
44. See R. Singha, 'Providential Circumstances: The Thuggee Campaign of the 1830s and Legal Innovation', in *Modern Asian Studies*, 27 (1993), pp. 24–49; R. Singha, *A Despotism of Law: Crime and Justice in Early Colonial India* (Delhi: Oxford University Press, 1998); and see Chapter 5 of this book.
45. See A. Yang (ed.), *Crime and Criminality*.
46. Curiously, in an instance which betrays something of the sexuality of imperial administrators, eunuchs were also designated under The Criminal Tribes Act of 1871.
47. See *Punjab Famine Report* (PFR), 1878–9 and M. Davis, *Late Victorian Holocausts: El Nino Famines and the Making of the Third World* (London: Verso, 2001). This theme is taken up in chapters 6–7.
48. See, for example, M. Radhakrishna, 'Dishonoured by History', *Hindu* (16 July 2000); and similarly with K. Marx, *Critique of the Gotha Programme* (Peking: Foreign Languages Press, 1972); also see P. Linebaugh, 'Karl Marx, the Theft of Wood and Working Class Composition', *Crime and Social Justice*, 7 (Autumn–Winter 1976), pp. 56–71.
49. See, for example, *The Amritsar Massacre: 1919* (London: Stationery Office, 1920).
50. See S. Sen, *Colonialism and Convict Society in the Andaman Islands* (Delhi: Oxford University Press, 2000).

2 Theory and the Constitution of Difference

1. R. Kipling, *Under the Deodars* (New York: United States Book Company 1891), p. 210.
2. For an important discussion on the relationship between the methodologies of the Warwick social historians and the school of Subaltern Studies, see R. Chandavarkar 'The Making of the Working Class: E. P. Thompson and Indian History and Related Essays', in V. Chaturvedi (ed.) *Mapping Subaltern Studies and the Postcolonial* (London: Verso, 1999).
3. See for example, D. Hay, 'Property, Authority and the Criminal Law' in D. Hay, Linebaugh, J. Rule, E. P. Thompson and C. Winslow (eds), *Albion's Fatal Tree: Crime*

and Society in Eighteenth Century England (London: Allen Lane, 1975). For a critique see J. Langbein, 'Albion's Fatal Flaws', *Past and Present*, 98 (1983), pp. 96–120 and J. Innes and J. Styles, 'The Crime Wave: Recent Writing on Crime and Criminal Justice in Eighteenth Century England', *Journal of British Studies*, 25 (1986), pp. 115–34.

4. Hay, 'Property, Authority and Criminal Law', p. 67.
5. On the number of black deaths, see E. P. Thompson, *Whigs and Hunters: the Origins of the Black Act* (London: Allen Lane, 1975).
6. See M. Brogden, *The Police, Autonomy and Consent* (London: Academic Press, 1982).
7. See J. M. Beattie, *Crime and the Courts in England 1660–1800* (Oxford: Oxford University Press, 1986).
8. See D. Skuy, 'Macaulay and the Indian Penal Code of 1862: The Myth of the Inherent Superiority and Modernity of the English Legal System Compared to India's Legal System in the Nineteenth Century', *Modern Asian Studies*, 32 (1988), pp. 513–57.
9. J. Sharpe, *Judicial Punishment in England* (London: Faber and Faber, 1990).
10. E. J. Hobsbawm and G. Rude, *Captain Swing* (London: Penguin, 1973).
11. H. Bhabha, *The Location of Culture* (London: Routledge, 1994).
12. E. Said, *Orientalism* (New York: Vintage, 1979). Said designated the entirety of this process of understanding the Orient as 'Orientalism', which he defined as the complex of knowledge and institutions by which European culture was able to manage, and even produce, the Orient in terms that could be understood within the frames of the post-Enlightenment period. He also argued that these representations have continued to play a part in the global hegemony of Western Europe in postcolonial times. A. R. Jan Mohamed, argues in *Manichean Aesthetics: the Politics of Literature in Colonial Africa* (Amherst, MA: Massachusetts University Press, 1983) that 'Manichean Allegory' sees the world as divided into mutually excluding opposites – if the Western is ordered, rational, masculine and good then the Orient is chaotic, irrational and evil. All is reduced to a division of black or white and good or bad, which is observed from the vantage point of Europe. It would certainly be an exaggeration to claim that Said began postcolonial discourse, which includes, among others, Franz Fanon, especially his engagement with Martinque and then Algeria, C. L. R. James, Chinua Achebe, W. E. B Dubois, Talat Asad, Romila Thapar, K. M. Panikkar, Aime Cesaire, as well as a range of commonwealth scholars.
13. Said, *Orientalism*, p. 1.
14. Ibid., p. 3.
15. See E. Barkan, *The Retreat of Scientific Racism: Changing Concepts of Race in England and the United States between the World Wars* (Cambridge: Cambridge University Press, 1991), p. 93. Barkan notes that the limitations of universal modernization had been recognized in the 1890s by the British, who sought to accommodate to the pressures of allowing oriental diversity; their perspectives, however, were limited by the reigning theories of social Darwinism.
16. See Bhabha, *The Location of Culture.*
17. Ibid., p. 24.
18. See, E. Said, *Orientalism.*
19. See Bhabha, *The Location of Culture,* p. 171.
20. This is what Bhabha refers to as 'not self and other but the 'otherness' of the self'. See Ibid., p. 44.
21. Ibid., p. 12.
22. See P. Fitzpatrick, *The Mythology of Modern Law* (London: Routledge, 1992).
23. See P. Fitzpatrick and E. Darian-Smith, 'Laws of the Postcolonial', p. 1.

24. See E. Said, *Orientalism*.
25. See, W. H. Sleeman, *The Thugs and the Phansigars of India* (Delhi: Deep and Deep, 1839).
26. See, for example, L. Mani, 'Contentious Traditions: The Debate on Sati in Colonial India', *Cultural Critique*, 23 (Fall 1987), pp. 25–45. Also, see R. S. Rajan, 'Representing Sati: Continuities and Discontinuities', S. Goodwin, and E. Bronfen (eds) *Death and Representation* (Baltimore, MD: Johns Hopkins, 1993).
27. See, for example, L. S. Viswanath, 'Efforts of Colonists to Suppress Female Infanticide: Use of Sacred Texts, Generation of Knowledge', *Economic and Political Weekly*, 33 (1998), pp. 12–24.
28. See, for example, J. Davis, 'The London Garrotting Panic of 1862: A Moral Panic and the Creation of a Criminal Class in Mid-Victorian England', in V. A. C. Gatrell, B. Lenman and G. Parker (eds) *Crime and the Law: The Social History of Crime in Western Europe Since 1500* (London: Europe, 1980), pp. 190–213.
29. See P. Fitzpatrick, *Modernism and the Grounds of Law* (Cambridge: Cambridge University Press, 2001).
30. See R. Dayton, 'Science and the European Empires', *Journal of Imperial and Commonwealth History*, 13 (1995), pp. 134–45. Dayton argues that as a symbol of primitiveness, danger and madness, the criminal classes and criminal tribes operated within a racialized landscape in which they embodied colonial anxieties about 'natives', 'savagery' and the 'dangerous'. In turn, 'scientific racism' was used to demonstrate England's superiority to others.
31. See T. Macaulay, in his 'Minute on Indian Education' February, 2, quoted in *British Parliamentary Papers*, 1837–38, vol. 40 (1835), p. 305.
32. E. Pashukanis, *Law and Marxism: A General Theory* (London: Villiers Publishing, 1978).
33. See P. Fitzpatrick, 'Racism and the Innocence of Law', *Journal of Law and Society*, 14 (1987), pp. 119–32.
34. See D. McBarnet, *Conviction* (London: Routledge, 1981).
35. T. B. Macaulay's draft of the Indian Penal Code is called Macaulay's Code or the 1837 Indian Code. The final Indian Penal Code was enacted in 1860 and came into effect 1 May 1861. James Mill (1773–1836), together with Jeremy Bentham, argued that one could deduce rational principles for restructuring societies, which could then be implemented without regard for local variations. For Mill, the value of a 'civilization' could be measured by the degree to which it exhibited rationalism and individualism. Finding neither of these two values in India, he condemned it severely, arguing that contemporary as well as ancient India, whether in science, religion, government, law or political economy, was thoroughly unenlightened and barbarous. His text, which was the first comprehensive history of India, became the hegemonic narrative of 'Indology' for nearly eighty years. It was required reading at Haileybury College, where until 1855 officials of the East India Company were trained. See, for example, J. M. MacLeod. , G. W. Anderson and F. Millet, 'Notes on the Indian Penal Code by the Indian Law Commissioners' *Miscellaneous Works of Lord Macaulay*, ed. Lady Trevelyan (New York: Harper, 1880). See also A. C. Patra, 'An Historical Introduction to the Indian Penal Code', *Journal of the Indian Law Institute*, 3 (1961), pp. 351–67; G. G. Rankin, 'The Indian Penal Code', *Law Quarterly Review*, 60 (1944), pp. 37–50, and R. Singha, *A Despotism of Law*.
36. See Skuy, 'Macaulay and the Indian Penal Code'.

37. See Singha, *A Despotism of Law*, p. 299. It is important to note here that Singha argues that Macaulay set out to codify the criminal law in India hoping it might induce the English to reform their own law as well.
38. See Fitzpatrick and Darien-Smith, 'Laws of the Postcolonial', p. 39.
39. Discussions of British interpretations of India include three widely known interpretations: the Orientalist, the Utilitarian and the Evangelical. See R. Inden, 'Orientalist Constructions of India' *Modern Asian Studies*, 20 (1986), pp. 436–65, and see also A. Callender, *How Shall We Govern India: A Controversy Among British Administrators, 1800–1882* (London: Gowland Publishing, 1987).
40. See P. Fitzpatrick, *Modernism and the Grounds of Law*, p. 12.
41. See M. Morris, 'Metamorphoses', *New Formations*, 10 (1990), pp. 110–23. Morris argues that 'modern' is always portrayed as something that has already happened somewhere else. Also see the work of Malik, *The Meaning of Race*.
42. See M. N. Srinivas, *Caste in Modern India and Other Essays* (Bombay: Media Publishing House, 1962). and C. J. Fuller (ed.) *Caste Today* (Delhi: Oxford University Press, 1996).
43. See O. Mendelsohn, 'The Pathology of the Indian Legal System', *Modern Asian Studies*, 15 (1981), pp. 822–63.
44. See Said, *Orientalism*.
45. Ibid., p. 65.
46. For details on the caste system, see Fuller (ed.), *Caste Today*.
47. See Fitzpatrick, *The Mythology of Modern Law*, p. 160.
48. See I. Balbus, *The Dialectics of Legal Repression* (New York: Transaction Books, 1977).
49. See EIC records and *British Parliamentary Papers* and legal debates from the mid-nineteenth century, which are drawn upon in Chapters 4, 5, 6, 7 and 8 of this book.
50. See R. Guha, quoted in U. Baxi, 'The Law's Emissary: the Place of Law in Subaltern Studies', *Journal of Subaltern Studies*, 7 (1993), pp. 247–64. , p. 249.
51. Beccaria, as discussed in M. Weisser, *Crime and Punishment in Early Modern Europe* (London: Harvester Press, 1979), p. 21.
52. See McBarnet, *Conviction*, p. 12.
53. Here the term Benthamite subsumes many other key figures from Sir Henry Blackstone to Sir Henry Maine.
54. See Fitzpatrick, 'Racism and the Innocence of the Law'.
55. See M. Brogden, T. Jefferson, and S. Wallkate *Introducing Policework* (London: Unwin Hyman, 1988) In their account of nineteenth century policing, they refer to this as an 'accidental' history as opposed to Whig (institutional) and revisionist.
56. See M. McConville, A. Sanders and R. Leng, *The Case for the Prosecution* (London: Routledge, 1991); and A. Ashworth, *The Criminal Process: An Evaluative Process* (Oxford: Oxford University Press, 1994).
57. Aberrations result from a few individual mistakes but structural problems are inherent within the criminal justice system itself.
58. See J. Baldwin and M. McConville, *Negotiated Justice* (Oxford: Martin Robertson, 1977) and McConville, et al. *The Case for the Prosecution* (1991).
59. For example, the conviction of Judith Ward in Liverpool, in November 1974, for a terrorist bombing in which the evidence seemed almost entirely related to her Irish associations.
60. See Pegg, *The Asiatics Cry to England*.
61. See Fitzpatrick, 'Racism and the Innocence of Law', p. 129.

62. See R. Reiner, *The Politics of the Police* (Brighton: Wheatsheaf, 1985), and T. Jefferson, *Interpreting Policework* (London: Unwin Hyman, 1987).
63. See McConville et al., *The Case for the Prosecution* (1991).
64. See McBarnet, *Conviction*.
65. See Ibid., p. 6.
66. See McConville et al., *The Case for the Prosecution*, p. 36.
67. How colonial police officers as state agents pioneered the use of discriminatory legislation against indigenous peoples is discussed in Chapter 6 and 7 of this book.
68. See McConville et al., *The Case for the Prosecution* and Chapter 5 of this book.
69. See Brogden, *The Police, Autonomy and Consent*, 1982.
70. See McConville et al., *The Case for the Prosecution*, p. 155.
71. See D. McBarnet, 'Arrest: The Legal Context of Policing', in S. Holdaway (ed.), *The British Police* (London: Routledge, 1979), pp. 24–40.
72. See I. Smith, 'Race, Crime and Statistics', in R. Morgan et al. (eds), *The Oxford Handbook of Criminology* (Oxford: Oxford University Press, 1997), p. 749.
73. See, for example, Sections 1 and 8 of the Crime and Disorder Act of 1998 which adopt a similar legal approach; also see R. Leng, R. Taylor and M. Wasik, *Crime and Disorder Act 1998* (London: Blackstone Press, 1998).
74. See McBarnet, *Conviction*, p. 45.
75. See McBarnet, 'Arrest', p. 39.
76. This is especially true given that the period under consideration, the early nineteenth century, represents a legal space long before checks, balances and safeguards were implemented resulting in The Police and Criminal Evidence Act of 1984.
77. See, for example, Hay, 'Property, Authority and the Criminal Law' (1975).
78. C. B. Beccaria (1738–94) an Italian jurist, as a key exponent of the Enlightenment wrote *Dei Deliti E Delle Pene* (Essay on Crimes and Punishments). His main idea was that punishment for crime should not exceed what was necessary to maintain public order. People are rational, capable of calculating what is *really* in their self-interest, and therefore can be considered to be *free*. The social contract is fundamental. Thinking of government as a social contract allows Beccaria to shift the power of the state away from the traditional authorities of the sovereign and the church, to the *legislator* – the people's representative and the maker of rational laws. Laws bind all members of society equally. Law is blind to rank or class. See C. Beccaria, *Of Crimes and Punishments* (New York: John Wiley, 1963), available from http://www. constitution. org/cb/crim_pun. htm
79. See G. Jones-Steadman, *Outcast London: A Study in the Relationship between Classes in Victorian Society* (Harmondsworth: Penguin 1984).
80. See Beattie, *Crime and Courts in England*, and see Chapter 6 below.
81. There is a wealth of literature on the subject of social constructionism. The most prominent labelling statements are: H. Becker, *Outsiders: Studies in the Sociology of Deviance* (New York: Free Press, 1964); H. Becker, *The Other Side: Perspectives on Deviance* (New York: Free Press, 1964b); H. Becker, 'Labelling Theory Reconsidered' in P. Rock and M. Macintosh (eds) *Deviance and Social Control* London: Routledge, 1974); J. Kitsuse, 'Societal Reaction to Deviant Behaviour: Problems in Theory and Method' *Social Problems*, 7 (1962), pp. 112–25; D. Matza, *Becoming Deviant* (London: Prentice Hall, 1969); K. Erikson, 'Notes on the Sociology of Deviance', *Social Problems*, 9 (1962), pp. 307–14.
82. See Quinney, *The Social Reality of Crime*, p. 12.
83. See Becker, *The Other Side*.

84. Ibid., p. 10.
85. See E. Durkheim, *The Rules of Sociological Method* (New York: Free Press, 1966).
86. See K. Erickson, *The Wayward Puritans* (New York: Wiley Sons, 1966), p. 34 and H. Garfinkel, 'Conditions of Successful Degradation Ceremonies', *American Journal of Sociology*, 61 (1956), pp. 420–44. Degradation ceremonies can be of two types. Firstly, they refer to entry as an inmate into, for example, a penal institution. But secondly they can also refer to any process in which an individual is made by an official process into accepting an inferior social status.
87. See Chapters 6 and 7 below.
88. See the summary on why expulsion and defining is necessary for social stability in L. Coser, *The Function of Social Conflict* (Glencoe: Free Press, 1956).
89. See D. Cannadine, *Orientalism: How the British Saw Their Empire* (Harmondsworth: Penguin, 2001), p. 67.
90. See *Punjab Famine Report*, 1878–9.
91. See S. Spitzer, 'Towards a Marxian Theory of Crime', *Social Problems*, 22 (1975), pp. 369–401. Spitzer refers to the youth and the elderly as the 'social junk', as unproductive members of society.
92. See Cannadine, *Orientalism*, p. 32.
93. Quoted in P. Ackroyd, *London: The Biography* (London: Chatto and Windus, 2000), p. 708.
94. See P. Roy, *Indian Traffic: Identities in Question in Colonial and Postcolonial India* (California: California University Press, 1996).
95. See Davis, 'The London Garroting Panic of 1862'.
96. See K. Rushby, *Children of Kali: Through India in Search of Bandits, the Thug Cult and the British Raj* (India: Penguin, 2003).
97. See Bhabha, *The Location of Culture*, p. 18.
98. Ibid., p. 21.
99. Ibid., p. 8.
100. See E. Lemert *Human Deviance: Social Problems, and Social Control* (Englewood Cliffs, NJ: Prentice Hall, 1972, p. 89.
101. Under the Vagrancy Acts, once one had been defined a suspected person, one would always remain a suspect. Under the 1824 Act it was simple reputation of the offence, which led to the classification of the convicted vagrant. Previous offences of vagrancy meant a harsher classification ('incorrigible') and a harsher sentence. See Charlesworth, 'Why Is It a Crime to be Poor?'.
102. R J. Tolen 'Colonizing and Transforming the Criminal Tribesman: The Salvation Army in British India', J. Terry and J. Urla (eds) *Deviant Bodies: Critical Perspectives on Difference in Science and popular Culture* (Bloomington, IN: Indian University Press, 1995).
103. See R. Quinney, *The Social Reality of Crime* (Boston, MA: Little Brown and Company, 1970), p. 34.
104. See R. Quinney, *Critique of Legal Order: Crime Control in Capitalist Society* (Boston, MA: Little Brown and Company, 1973), p. 21.
105. See M. Cain, 'Trends in the Sociology of Police Work', *International Journal of the Sociology of Law*, 7 (1979), pp. 143–67 and M. Brogden, 'An Act to Colonise the Internal Lands of the Island: Empire and the Origins of Professional Police', *International Journal of Sociology and Law*, 15 (1987), pp. 179–208.
106. See R. Erickson, and P. Baranek, *The Ordering of Justice: A Study of Accused Persons as Dependents in the Criminal Process* (Toronto, ON: University of Toronto Press, 1982).

3 Imagery and Law in the Creation of Identities

1. H. Mayhew, *London Labour and the London Poor: A Cyclopedia of the Conditions and Earnings of Those That Will Work and Those That Cannot* (London: Griffen, Bohn and Wiley, 1861), p. 68. Comparison between the metropolitan 'criminal' class and the 'criminal' tribes is a key feature of the discourse of the explorers of outcast London; again see, for example, Booth, *Life and Labour of the People in London*, p. 41. 'The hereditary criminal is by no means confined to India, although it is only in that country that they have the engaging simplicity to describe themselves frankly in the census'.
2. Summary justice in the sense of the downgrading of many offences to be dealt within the Magistrates Courts occurred by the Criminal Justice Act of 1856. It was merely a part of a larger process of depriving a lower-class suspect of adversarial rights, in placing him or her at the disposal of a local notable on the Bench.
3. See M. Weiner, *Reconstructing the Criminal: Culture, Law and Policy* (Cambridge: Cambridge University Press, 1991), p. 46.
4. See P. Linebaugh, and M. Redikar, *The Many Headed* Hydra, and M. H. Fisher, *Counterflows to Colonialism: Indian Travelers and Settlers in Britain 1600–1857* (Delhi: Permanent Black, 2004).
5. See Weiner, *Reconstructing the Criminal*, p. 56.
6. Quoted in S. Thome, 'The Conversion of the Englishman and the Conversion of the World Inseparable: Missionary Imperialism and the Language of Class in Early Industrial Britain', in Cooper and Stoler (eds) *Tensions of Empire*.
7. See R. Storch, 'The Policeman as Domestic Missionary: Urban Discipline and Popular Culture in North England 1850–80', *Journal of Sociological History*, 9 (1976), pp. 481–509.
8. Mayhew claimed that the dangerous class consisted of some 30,000 denizens of the rookeries, apart from a wandering population of vagrants. However, the numbers are as elusive as the concept. One authority provides the figure for the mid-1850s of the total criminal class as 'Known thieves and depredators, 22, 959, receivers of stolen goods 3, 095, prostitutes 27, 186, suspected persons 29, 468, vagrants and tramps 32, 938, making a total of 122, 646'. J. Greenwood, *The Seven Curses of London* (London: Adamant Media Publishing, 1869), ch. 11.
9. See C. Booth, *Life and Labour of the People in London*, p. 39 as cited in J. Marriot, and M. Matsmurra, *The Outcast and The Poor* vol. 5 (London: Pickering and Chatto, 1999), p. 49. Typical of the classification system was Booth's notion of a 'criminal' class. However, unlike in India, the classification system remained largely in the realms of popular discourse rather than in official legislation.
10. Quoted in C. Emsley, *Hard Men: The English and Violence since 1750* (London: Hambledon, 2005).
11. See Mayhew, *London Labour and the London Poor*, p. 320.
12. Ibid., p. 87.
13. W. Miller, *Cops and Bobbies: Police Authority in New York and London, 1830–1870* (Ohio: State University Press, 1999).
14. See Davis, 'From Rookeries to Communities: Race, Poverty and Policing in London 1850–1985', *History Workshop Journal*, 27 (1991), pp. 62–79.
15. See J. Turton's account of the Irish as part of the criminal class drawing on Mayhew in R. Swift, and S. Gilley (eds) *The Irish in England: The Local Dimension* (Dublin: Four Courts Press, 1999).

16. See Davis, 'From Rookeries to Communities', p. 69.
17. Engels, *Condition of the Working Class in England*. For a partisan missionary view of the Irish lower class in London, J. Garwood, *The Million-Peopled City* (London: Wertheim and Macintosh, 1835), especially chapter 5.
18. See J. Salter, *The East is West: Work Among the Asiatics and Africans in London* (London: Partridge, 1886).
19. See W. T. Stead, Victorian publisher, journalist and exposer of the underlife of the rookeries, especially young female prostitution as discussed in J. R. Walkowitz, *Prostitution and Victorian London* (London: Cambridge University Press, 1980).
20. See Salter, *The East is West*, p. 39.
21. See C. Emsley, *Crime and Society in England: 1750–1900* (London: Longman, 1987), p. 60.
22. See J. London, *The People of the Abyss* (1903; Chicago, IL: Chicago Review Press, 1995), p. 234.
23. See Weiner, *Reconstructing the Criminal.*
24. Ibid., p. 87.
25. See M. Leps, *Apprehending the Criminal* (London: Routledge, 1994).
26. See Weiner, *Reconstructing the Criminal*, p. 5.
27. See E. Hobsbawm, 'Social Criminality', *Bulletin of the Society for the Study of Labour History*, 25 (1972), pp. 5–6.
28. See S. Tobias, *Crime and Industrial Society in the Nineteenth Century* (Oxford: Oxford University Press, 1967).
29. See B. Harrison, *Drink and the Victorians* (Oxford: Oxford University Press, 1971), especially ch. 14.
30. The Suppression of Vagrancy, *The Times*, 20 October 1870.
31. See Davis, 'From Rookeries to Communities', p. 76.
32. E. Hobsbawm, *The Age of Empire: 1875–1914* (London: Vintage, 1989), p. 35.
33. For example the Town Police Clauses Act of 1848, a system of preventative professional policing. See V. A. C. Gatrell, 'Crime, Authority and the Policeman State', F. M. L. Thompson (ed.), *The_Cambridge Social History of England 1750–1950* (Cambridge: Cambridge University Press, 1990).
34. See E. P. Hennock, 'The Measurement of Urban Poverty', *Economic History Review*, 40 (1987), pp. 208–27.
35. Transportation was abolished in 1853.
36. See L. Mathur, *Kala-Pani: History of the Andaman and Nicobar Islands with a Study of India's Freedom Struggle* (Delhi: Eastern Books, 1987).
37. See D. Gilling, *Crime Prevention: Theory, Policy and Politics* (London: Routledge, 1997), p. 109.
38. See L. Radzinowicz, 'A History of Criminal Law and Administration from 1750', in J. S. Cockburn (ed.) *Crime in England 1550–1800* (Manchester: Manchester University Press, 1977).
39. See Beccaria, *On Crimes and Punishments*.
40. Utilitarianism refers to the social philosophy of Jeremy Bentham and John Stuart Mill with the key principle that the overall utility or benefit produced by an action ought to be the standard by which we judge the worth or goodness of moral and legal action. The happiness of the community as a whole is nothing other than the sum of individual human interests. The principle of utility, then, defines the meaning of moral obligation

by reference to the greatest good of people who are affected by performance of an action. Similarly, Bentham supposed that social policies are properly evaluated in the light of their effect on the general well being of the populations they involve. Punishing criminals is an effective way of deterring crime precisely because it alters the likely outcome of their actions, attaching the likelihood of future pain in order to outweigh the apparent gain of committing the crime. Thus, punishment must 'fit' the crime by changing the likely perception of the results of committing it.

41. See J. Bentham, *Of Laws in General* (London: Athlone Press, 1970).
42. The humanitarian period was characterized by beliefs such as the presumption of innocence, punishments based on restorative reasoning and punishment intended to fit the crime. The structuralists argued that the penal changes were part of the process of discipline and punishment.
43. See D. Garland, *Punishment and Welfare: A History of Penal Strategies* (Aldershot: Gower, 1985), p. 238.
44. This was most obvious in Booth's plans for convict settlements in the Salvation Army's industrial farms.
45. Brogden, *The Police, Autonomy and Consent.*
46. The treatment model consisted of preventative as well as therapeutic and surgical operations based on the notion that society would consistently need those remedies.
47. See, for example, the discussions on the penal system in Garland, *Punishment and Welfare,* and D. Garland, *Punishment and Modern Society* (Milton Keynes: Open University Press, 1991).
48. See Weiner, *Reconstructing the Criminal,* p. 378.
49. See the Gladstone Report of 1895 in Weiner, *Reconstructing the Criminal.*
50. as in the work of Mayhew, *London Labour and the London Poor* and Booth, *Life and Labour of the People in London.*
51. See J. Bentham 'The Panopticon: Or the Inspection House 1787', M. Bozovic (ed.) *The Panopticon Writings* (London: Verso, 1995).
52. See Weiner, *Reconstructing the Criminal,* p. 231.
53. See M. Ignatieff, *A Just Measure of Pain: The Penitentiary in the Industrial Revolution 1750–1850* (New York: New York Press, 1978), p. 212.
54. See Weiner, *Reconstructing the Criminal.*
55. See Ignatieff, *A Just Measure of Pain,* p. 31.
56. See Wiener, *Reconstructing the Criminal,* p. 11.
57. See J. Bentham as quoted in Weiner, *Reconstructing the Criminal,* p. 53.
58. See V. A. C. Gatrell, Crime, 'Authority and Policeman's State' (1990).
59. See Tobias, *Crime and Industrial Society in the Nineteenth Century,* p. 67.
60. See Ignatieff, *A Just Measure of Pain,* p. 45.
61. Ibid., p. 46.
62. See Beccaria, *On Crimes and Punishment,* p. 13.
63. See M. Timmons, *Conduct and Character* (Oxford: Oxford University Press, 1987), p. 102.
64. See Durkheim, *The Rules of Sociological Method,* p. 12.
65. See Beccaria, *On Crimes and Punishment,* p. 10.
66. See J. Bentham, as quoted in E. McLaughlin, and E. Muncie, *Controlling Crime* (Milton Keynes: Open University Press, 1996a), p. 45.
67. Ibid., p. 106.
68. Ibid., p. 104.

69. See Beccaria, *On Crimes and Punishment*, p. 41.
70. See Mayhew, *London Labour and the Landon Poor.*
71. See R. Cloward and F. Piven, *Regulating the Poor: the Functions of Public Welfare* (London: Tavistock, 1971), p. 34.
72. See Garland, *Punishment and Welfare,* p. 12.
73. Social discipline would be produced not just through direct control or punishment but also through social intervention, which will be discussed below.
74. See Garland, *Punishment and Welfare*, p. 56.
75. Lascar Papers, British Library, Home Miscellaneous series, 501, vol. 1, ff. 69–75, p. 38.
76. See Hay, 'Property, Authority and the Criminal Law', and D. Phillips and D. Storch, 'Whigs and Coopers: the Grey Ministry's National Police Scheme, 1832', *Historical Research*, 67 (1994), pp. 75–99, for details of the previous policing system.
77. As supported later through the new stop-and-search powers in the Town Police Clauses Act of 1848.
78. See Weiner, *Reconstructing the Criminal*, p. 215.
79. See Patrick Colquhoun as quoted in D. Phillips, 'A New Engine of Power and Authority: The Institutions of Law Enforcement in England, 1780–1830', in V. A. C, Gatrell (ed.), *The Decline of Theft and Violence* (London: Routledge, 1980), p. 1.
80. See Weiner, *Reconstructing the Criminal*, p. 87.
81. See Gatrell, 'Crime, Authority and the Policeman's State', p. 19.
82. See Phillips and Storch, 'Whigs and Coopers', p. 38.
83. See D. Davies, *Classes and Police in Manchester 1829–1880* (London: Routledge, 1990).
84. See V. Bailey, 'The Fabrication of Deviance: 'Dangerous Classes and 'Criminal Classes' in Victorian England', J. Rule, and R. Malcomson (ed.) *Protest and Survival: The Historical Experience Essays for E. P. Thompson* (London: Merlin Press, 1993).
85. See Weiner, *Reconstructing the Criminal*, p. 32.
86. See W. Greg (1869) as quoted in S. Petrow, *Policing Morals: The Metropolitan Police and the Home Office, 1870–1914* (London: Clarendon Press, 1994), p. 101.
87. See J. Bentham, *An Introduction to the Principles of Morals and Legislation* (1789; Oxford: Blackwell Press, 1948), p. 32.
88. See Hay, 'Property, Authority and the Criminal Law', p. 87.
89. See Said, *Orientalism*, p. 332.
90. See Emsley, *Crime and Society in England*.
91. See Davis, 'The London Garroting Panic of 1862', p. 191.
92. See L. Radzinowicz, and R. Hood, *The Emergence of Penal Policy in Victorian and Edwardian England* (Oxford: Clarendon Press, 1990).
93. Under the Vagrancy Act of 1824, the police could proceed against 'anyone wandering in the public streets or public highways or in any place of public resort and behaving in a riotous and indecent manner'. See J. D. Roberts, 'Public and Private in Early Nineteenth Century London', *Journal of Social History*, 13 (1988), pp. 273–94.
94. See E. J. Hobsbawm, *Primitive Rebels* (Manchester: Manchester University Press, 1974), especially ch. 3; J. Innes, and J. Styles, 'The Crime Wave: Recent Writings on Crime and Criminal Justice in Eighteenth Century England', A. Wilson (ed.), *Rethinking Social History: English Society 1570–1920* (Manchester: Manchester University Press, 1993), on social crime, see D. Hay, 'War, Dearth and Theft in the Eighteenth Century', *Past and Present*, 95 (1982), pp. 117–60.

95. As in the previous century, the falls in grain prices lead to control over customary rights of gleaning. See Wilson, *Rethinking Social History in English Society.*
96. Ibid., p. 57.
97. See Mayhew, *London Labour and the London Poor*, p. 67 as well as H. Mayhew and J. Binny, *The Criminal Prisons of London and Scenes of Prison Life* (London: Smith, Elder and Company, 1862).
98. See Weiner, *Reconstructing the Criminal*, p. 149.
99. The Habitual Criminals Act of 1869 and the succeeding Prevention of Crimes Act of 1871 provided for a register of those who had been designated habitual criminals, people who had been convicted on indictment of a crime, and against whom a previous conviction could be proved. It would enable police to identify and take action against repeat offenders. It contained details of crime and sentence, of age, of occupation, of height, of colour of hair, of eyes, of complexion and distinguishing features such as scars and tattoos (used as the main means of criminal identification until the general development of the fingerprint system in the early 1900s). As an instrument of criminal identification, it proved inadequate and haphazard and was replaced with Bertillon's system of measurement and Galton's 'finger mark' system. The Habitual Criminals Act introduced a system of police supervision for repeat offenders after their release from prison, allowing them to be summarily imprisoned if they were found acting suspiciously. In practice, as recent research now shows, the majority of repeat offenders under the Act were not actually 'hardened criminals' but typical members of the casual poor and criminal classes whose involvement in crime was minor and intermittent. See S. Stevenson, 'The "Habitual Criminal" in Nineteenth Century England: Some Observations on the Figures', *Urban History Yearbook*, 12 (1986), pp. 37–66.
100. See P. Devlin, *The Criminal Prosecution in England* (London: Routledge, 1960).
101. Greenwood, *The Seven Curses of London*, ch. 11.
102. See Petrow, *Policing Morals*, p. 81.
103. See Lea, 'Some Structural Aspects of Police, in C. Shearing (ed.) *Organisational Aspects of Police Deviance* (Toronto, ON: Butterworths, 1981), p. 67.
104. See S. McConville, *A History of Prison Administration: 1750–1877* (London: Routledge, 1981), p. 25.
105. See W. D. Morrison (1891) as quoted in Tobias, *Crime and Industrial Society,* p. 57.
106. Quoted in Weiner, *Reconstructing the Criminal,* pp. 232–3.
107. See P. Bartrip, 'Public Opinion and the "Ticket-of-Leave" Scare', in V. Bailey (ed.), *Police and Punishment in Nineteenth Century England* (London: Routledge, 1991).
108. See Garland, *Punishment and Welfare,* p. 60.
109. See Chapter 1 above on the notion of policing used in this book.
110. See Bentham, *An Introduction to the Principles of Morals and Legislation*, p. 25.
111. In part, the Poor Law concern with the assumed relation between crime and unemployment owed its origins to the other and less developed features of Bentham's argument, the proposal for a National Charity Commission in which labour from indigent inhabitants would be provided in return for provisions of relief by private contractors.
112. For a detailed study of social control through the imposition of relief given to the poor, see Cloward and Piven, *Regulating the Poor.*
113. See G. Himmelfarb, *The Idea of Poverty* (London: Faber and Faber, 1984), p. 163.
114. See L. Morris, *The Dangerous Classes* (London: Routledge, 1994), p. 37.
115. See Booth, *Life and Labour of the People in London,* and Chapter 2, above.
116. Ibid., p. 57.

117. See L. Howe, 'The Deserving and the Undeserving', *Journal of Social Policy,* 14 (1985), pp. 49–72.
118. See Jones-Steadman, *Outcast London*, p. 11.
119. The Gladstone Report in 1895 marked a key transformation in British penal policy. The Report argued that the reformation should coexist with deterrence and rehabilitation should be made a priority. It proposed more scientific methods of treatment. For details, see Weiner, *Reconstructing the Criminal.*
120. See M. C. Finn, 'The Authority of the Laws', in P. Mandler (ed.) *Liberty and Authority in Victorian Britain* (Oxford: Oxford University Press, 2006), p. 163.
121. See V. A. C. Gatrell, 'Crime, Authority and Policeman's State', and V. A. C. Gatrell, *The Hanging Tree: Execution and the English People 1770–1868* (Oxford: Oxford University Press, 1994).
122. For an examination of the records from Sussex and London, see G. Rude, *The Crowd in History* (New York: John Wiley, 1964), p. 12.
123. See Freitag, 'Crime in the Social Order', p. 256.

4 Scientific Racism and the Constitution of Difference

1. J. Hoffemister and F. Hamburg, 'G. W. F. Hegel', Hegel's Einleitung in die Geschichte der Philosophie (1962), p. 189.
2. Quoted in J. Oppenheim, *Shattered Nerves: Doctors, Patients, and Depression in Victorian England* (Oxford: Oxford University Press, 1991), p. 56.
3. See R. McKeon, *Aristotle: The Basic Works of Aristotle* (London: Random House, 1941).
4. R. Eden quoted in G. Mariscal, 'The Role of Spain in Contemporary Race Theory', *Arizona Journal of Hispanic Cultural Studies*, 2 (1998), pp. 7–22.
5. See F. Berner, 'A New Division of the Earth', *Journal Des Scavans*, 29 (1684), translated by T. Bendyphe, *Memoirs Read Before the Anthropological Society of London*, Vol. 1 (1863–4), pp. 360–364.
6. See J. L. Graves, *The Emperor's New Clothes: Biological Theories of Race at the Millennium* (New Brunswick, NJ: Rutgers University Press: 2001).
7. See J. F. Blumenbach, *The Anthropological Treatises of Johann Friedrich Blumenbach* (London: Anthropological Society, 1865).
8. See J. A. Gobineau, *The Inequality of the Human Races, 1853–1855* (London: Heinemann, 1915).
9. See J. C. Prichard, *The Natural History of Man* (London: Bailliere, 1843).
10. Cited in H. F. Augstein, 'Clio Medica: The Wellcome Series in the History of Medicine: James Cowles Prichard and Apos' *Anthropology*, 48, pp. 57–104.
11. See for example, P. Bennett, 'The Negro Never Knew': Emily Dickinson and Racial Typology in the Nineteenth Century', *Legacy*, 19:1 (2002), pp. 53–61 and A. H. Sayce, *The Races of the Old Testament* (London: Adamant Press, 2005), p. 12.
12. See E. Long, *The History of Jamaica: Reflections on its Situations, Settlements, Inhabitants, Laws and Government* (Montreal, QC: Queens University Press, 2003).
13. See Le Mercier Du Quesnay, Frederick. The Longs of 'Longville'. 1964. http://jamaicanfamilysearch.com/Samples/fred02.htm
14. See in particular the House of Commons *Report from the Select Committee on Aborigines*, 1837.
15. S. Thorne, *Congregational Missions and the Making of an Imperial Culture in Nineteenth-Century England* (Stanford, CA: Stanford University Press, 1999).

16. See P. Carson, 'An Imperial Dilemma: The Propogation of Christianity in Early Colonial India', *Journal of Imperial and Commonwealth History*, 18, 2 (1990), pp. 169–90.
17. See R. Knox, *The Races of Men* (London: Renshaw, 1850), p. 53.
18. J. Crush, 'The Global Raiders: Nationalism, Globalisation and the South African Brian Drain', *Journal of International Affairs*, 56 (2002).
19. M. Brown, 'Crime, Governance and the Company Raj; The Discovery of Thuggee', *The British Jorunal of Criminology*, 42 (2002), pp. 77–95.
20. See Government of India Act of 1858.
21. A. Desmond, *Huxley: From Devil's Disciple To Evolution's High Priest* (Reading: Addison-Wesley, 1997).
22. Darwin was himself a monogeneist, believing that all humans were of the same species and finding 'race' to be a somewhat arbitrary distinction among some group. See C. Darwin, *The Descent of Man and Selection in Relation to Sex* (New York: Appleton, 1883).
23. Gall used the term, 'cranioscopy' but his younger colleague, Spurzheim, coined the word 'phrenology' as he went abroad to evangelize and elaborate upon Gall's concepts. He attributed specific localizations of cerebral functions which he thought were indicative of the underlying attributes of the human personality. See C. Combe, *Essays on Phrenology* (Philadephia: np, 1822). This book popularized by the growth of phrenology in Britain from 1815. Phrenology also postulated that the structure of the skull, especially the jaw formation and facial angles, revealed the position of various races on the evolutionary scale.
24. See E. Long, *The History of Jamaica*, p. 23.
25. See C. Darwin, *On the Origins of Species* (London: n. p. , 1859).
26. Galton coined the term eugenics in1883 and set down many of his observations and conclusions in a book, F. Galton, *Inquiries Into Human Faculty and Its Development* (London: Macmillan, 1883).
27. F. Galton, 'Fingerprints and their Registration as a Means of Personal Identification', *Transaction of the Seventh International Congress of Hygiene and Demography,* 10 (1892), pp. 30–43.
28. A final important development was that of the anthropometrics. This is developed in relation to India in Chapter 5. According to the anthropometrics, a 'criminal' could be recognized, and hence deterred.
29. See F. Galton, 'Hereditary Talent and Character', *Macmillan's Magazine*, 12 (1865), pp. 327–412.
30. However, Galton also believed that human beings could regress. See Weiner, *Reconstructing the Criminal*, p. 43.
31. See D. Goldberg, *Racist Culture: Philosophy and the Politics of Meaning* (London: Blackwell, 1993), p. 29.
32. Ibid., p. 50.
33. J. S. Mill, as quoted in Young, *Colonial Desire*, p. 35.
34. See Booth, *Life and Labour of the People in London*, which offers an estimate of the size of the criminal class – complete with metaphors of empire – as in 'darkest England, then, may be said to have a population about equal to that of Scotland. Three million men, women, and children, a despairing multitude in a condition nominally free, but really enslaved', pp. 18–19.
35. quoted in M. A. Fregier *Des Classes Dangerous de la population de la Grande Vills 1840* cited in J. Rowbotham and K. Stevenson (eds) *Criminal Conversations: Victorian Crimes, Social Panic and Moral Outrage* (Ohio: Ohio University Press, 2005), p. 5. For a detailed

account see C. Emsley, *Crime, Police, and Penal Policy: European Experiences 1750–1940* (Oxford and New York: Oxford University Press, 2007), especially ch. 8.

36. See G. Pavlich, *The Accusations of Criminal Identity* (2006), http://www.mcgill.ca/files/legal-theory-workshop/Pavlich-Accusations-Criminal-Identity.pdf (accessed 21 October 2008). Pavlich sees the Act as the legal affirmation of the term.
37. Edward Higgs, for example (2008), in his continuing work on the history of identification quoted in Pavlich, *The Accusations of Criminal Identity*.
38. See A. S. Wohl, *Racism and Anti-Irish Prejudice in Victorian England* (1990) available at: http://www. victorianweb. org/history/race/Racism.html (accessed 24 October 2008).
39. The President of the Anthropological Institute (1889–91),
40. See Charles Kingsley in a letter to his wife, quoted in L. P. Curtis, *Anglo-Saxons and Celts: A Study of the Anti-Irish Prejudice in Victorian England* (Bridgeport, NY: New York Press, 1968), p. 84.
41. See Wohl, *Racism and Anti-Irish Prejudice in Victorian England* (1990)
42. See Chapter 5 of this book.
43. See Fitzpatrick, *Modernism and the Grounds of Law*, p. 179.
44. See U. Beck, *Risk Society* (London: Sage, 1992), p. 21. Fear, argues Beck, becomes a systematic way of dealing with hazards and insecurities that are introduced by modernity itself.
45. See Pratt, *Governing the Dangerous*, p. 32.
46. See Chapter 2 of this book.
47. See C. Lombroso, *The Criminal Man* (New York: Putnam, 1911). Lombroso is regarded with pragmatic disdain by many of his contemporaries in Britain.
48. See E. Ferri, *The Positive School of Criminology* (Chicago, IL: Charles Kerr Press, 1917).
49. L. A. Jackson, 'The Medical Origins of Criminology', *MetaScience*, 16:2 (2007), pp. 281–4.
50. S. A. Cole, *Suspect Identities: A History of Fingerprinting and Criminal Identification* (Harvard, MA: Harvard University Press, 2001), p. 94.
51. See Lombroso, *The Criminal Man*, p. 12.
52. See H. Mannheim, *Comparative Criminology* (Boston, MA: Houghton Press, 1965), p. 213.
53. Positivism as a distinct 'school' is principally associated with the work of Italian scholars Ferri and Garafalo, who had a major influence on the institutionalization of criminology in the early years of the twentieth century.
54. See Leslie Stephen in M. Weiner, *Reconstructing the Criminal*, p. 161.
55. See Ferri, *The Positive School*, p. 34.
56. See the summary of Beccaria's work on 'Crime and Punishment', L. Radzinowicz, 'A History of Criminal'.
57. See Pratt, *Governing the Dangerous*, on how eugenics meshed with the new criminal statistics in the development of biometrics.
58. According to Galton, eugenics was the study of agencies under social control, which may improve or impair the racial qualities of future generations either physically or mentally. See Galton, *Inquiries into Human Faculty*. For a recent study of the criminological implications of Galton's work, see Pratt, *Governing the Dangerous*, pp. 39–42.
59. See A. P. Thornton, *Doctrines of Imperialism* (New York: Wiley and Sons, 1965).
60. As developed in Chapter 3 above.
61. See E. Sutherland, and D. Cressey, *Criminology*, 8th edn (Philadelphia, PA: Lippincott, 1970), for a definition that influenced labelling, societal reaction and the criminal law.

Its use is qualified here because of the critical differences in criminal law, between the 'majority' and those who are subject to legal discretion, as discussed in Chapters 2 and 7 of this book.

62. See J. Laplanche, and J. Pontalis, *The Language of Psychoanalysis* (London: Karnac Books, 1988), p. 352.
63. Intolerable because passions are considered as manifestations of the bad Self.
64. See S. Gilman, *Difference and Pathology: Stereotypes of Sexuality, Race and Madness* (Ithaca, NY: Cornell University Press, 1985), p. 17.
65. For example the settlements for the Indian Criminal Tribes and castes, see Chapter 7 of this book.

5 The 'Ethnic' as a Component of the 'Criminal' Class

1. See W. Phillips, 'The Wild Tribes of London', in M. Marriot and M. Matsumura, *The Metropolitan Poor: Semifactual Accounts 1795–1910* (London: Pickering and Chatto, 1999), p. 11.
2. See R. R. Thomas (ed.), *Dreams of Authority: Freud and the Fictions of the Unconscious* (Ithaca, NY: Cornell University Press, 1990), p. 226.
3. R. Rowe, *Life in the London Streets* (1881) especially ch. 1, 'Saturday Night at the East End' available at http://www. victorianlondon. org/publications/lifein.htm (accessed 21 November 2008).
4. Dickens's unfinished 1870 story of the *Mystery of Edwin Drood*, ed. A. J. Cox (Harmondsworth: Penguin Press, 1974). Two years later the Governor of the Stranger's Home claimed the dens had now all disappeared thanks to the work of his staff, see letter to *The Times*, 28 October 1872.
5. See A. C. Doyle, *The Adventures of Sherlock Holmes* (London: Wordsworth Editions, 2001), p. 63. Also see Ballew, William. 'The Not So Rascally Lascar', *P&D*, No. 143 (August 1990), 7. 'The rascally Lascar was a man, vital to the beggar's plan'.
6. T. De Quincey and R. Morrison, *On Murder* (Oxford: Oxford University Press, 2006), p. 100.
7. See Salter, *The East is West*, p. 45.
8. Inevitably, the vast majority of evidence on the Lascars' experience is from Imperial records, and subject to appropriate reconstruction.
9. See Visram, *The Ayahs, Lascars and the Princes.*
10. R. H. Lindeborg, 'The 'Asiatic' and the Boundaries of Victorian Englishness', *Journal of Victorian Studies*, 3 (1994), pp. 381–404.
11. See R. Seagel, *The Black Diaspora* (London: Faber and Faber Press, 1996). Also see R. Visram, *Asians in England: 400 Years of History* (London: Pluto Press, 2002), which documents the presence of Asians in London as early as the sixteenth century.
12. See Fryer, *Black People in the British Empire*, p. 45.
13. See D. George, *London Life in the Eighteenth Century* (Harmondsworth: Penguin Press, 1996), p. 45.
14. 'In 1701, he went away from his Master Yesterday Morning at 4 a Clock, an East-Indian Boy nam'd Cæsar, about the Age of 16, wearing his own short Hair, a sad-colour'd Fustian Frock over a black Wastecoat, a Fustian pair of Breeches, and grey Stockings. He has a handsome Face, and is tall for his Age. Whoever takes him up, and brings him to Mr. John Waterhouse's, in Aylif-street Goodman's-Fields, shall have 10 s. Reward', available at http://www.mernick.org.uk//thhol/miscellany01.html.

15. The term is believed to derive from the Persian 'lashkar', meaning an army, a camp or a band of followers. The first European use of the word dates back to the Portuguese employment of Asian seamen in the early 1500s. 'Lascar' means an Indian sailor (from India) serving in the British merchant marine. For a detailed definition of the etymological origins of the word 'Lascar' see, H. Yule and A. C. Burnell, *Hobson-Jobson; A Glossary of Colloquial Anglo-Indian Words and Phrases, and of Kindred Terms, Etymological, Historical, Geographical and Discursive* (New Delhi: Munshiram Manoharlal, 2000), pp. 507–9. The word derives from the Persian *'lashkar',* meaning an army or a camp. The meaning came to be expanded to any foreign sailor from east of the Cape of Good Hope, whether East African, Indian, Malaysian or from anywhere in the East Indies.
16. Attempts to curtail Lascars recruitment, such as by the Navigation Act of 1660, were notable only by their failure.
17. See N. Myers, *Reconstructing the Black past: Blacks in Britain 1780–1830* (Abingdon: Routledge, 2004), p. 115.
18. M. H. Fisher 'Working Across the Seas: Indian Maritime Labourers in India, Britain, and in Between, 1600–1857', *International Review of Social History*, 51 (2006), pp. 21–46.
19. See Visram, *The Ayahs, Lascars and the Princes*, p. 53.
20. P. J. Marshall, *The Making and Unmaking of Empires: Britain, India and America, 1750–1783* (Oxford: Oxford University Press, 2005), p. 66.
21. There was an early Bengali presence in 1616, for example the Mayor of London attended St Dionis Church in the City for the baptism of 'Peter', an East Indian from the Bay of Bengal.
22. See Fisher, *Counterflows to Colonialism.*
23. See, Myers, *Reconstructing the Black Past,* p. 106.
24. Unemployed seamen, like former soldiers, were perceived as some of the lowest in the Georgian social hierarchy, being regarded as a threat to stable English society. See D. Marshall, *English People in the Eighteenth Century* (London: Longmans, 1956).
25. See I. Land, 'Customs of the Sea: Flogging, Empire, and the "True British Seamen" 1770 – 1870', *Interventions: International Journal of Postcolonial Studies*, 3:2 (2001), pp. 169–85, p. 170.
26. Indeed, Lascars were different from other sailors, as the latter were individually recruited.
27. In 1783, under the Ordinances issued for recruiting and fixing the wages of 'native' seamen employed on 'Country' ships, Warren Hastings attempted to reform the system of Lascar recruitment. A Western-style registration office was set up where lascars could sign on. Wages were fixed and paid directly to individual lascars through the registration office agent, cutting out the middleman. But the reform ran into the vested interest of the *ghat serangs*, while in London the EICs considered the regulation inconvenient and expensive for Europe-bound chartered ships, risking delay and the possibility of not obtaining good seamen. On the attempts to short-cut the *serangs*, see Fisher, 'Working Across the Seas' p. 35 and p. 39.
28. In modern terms, 'gangmasters'. H. Melville, *Redburn: His First Voyage* (London: Penguin, 1976), gives a detailed account of a *lascar* crew on arrival in Liverpool. He notes inter alia that the *serang* appeared to be of a higher caste than the others. He also details the number of dead Lascars on the voyage from India and that they were of varied backgrounds although they conversed in Hindi, see especially ch. 34. On mixed composition of work groups, see also Fisher, *Counterflows to Colonialism*, p. 161.

29. See Fisher, *Counterflows to Colonialism,* p. 141, estimates that Lascar gangs of workers numbered between sixteen and fifty-six members and rose proportionately as ship sizes increased over the years.
30. For an illustration of the serang's function at sea and sources of conflict with the Captain, see Old Bailey Reference Number: t18530404–509 1853. The issues involved in the case were brutal and led to many of the Lascars seeking to desert.
31. See Fisher, *Counterflows to Colonialism,* p. 36.
32. See the opposing letters – 21 February 1881 that derides as 'skulking' in bad weather as opposed to 30 May 1893, which praises their seafaring skills and claims that British sailors were invariably drunk. Nearly all such information draws on partisan British sources.
33. See Fisher, *Counterflows to Colonialism,* p. 138. Eastwick's own chronicle – *A Master Mariner: The Life of Capt R. W. Eastwick contains* unique accounts of barbaric European treatment of *lascars* on board ship (London: Unwin and Crompton, 1891).
34. See *The Times* letters 27 August 1813; 28 September 1853; 24 October 1874 (a most curious affair when, contrary to medical evidence, the Captain claimed that the nine Lascars had died of an imaginary 'Indian Plague'); and 28 November 1874.
35. B. P. P. *East India Company Affairs, Minutes of the Evidence of a Select Committee on the East India Company Affairs,* 11 vols (IUP: East India, 1832), vol. 6.
36. See letter in *The Times,* 9 December 1814 for a detailed account of the living standards of Lascars on both ship (forced to live on rice and ghee) and land and lack of medical assistance on board.
37. The earliest recorded case of the sale of Lascars as slaves is by Captain Lord of the *St George* after they had been forcibly enlisted in Surat. In that case, the EIC interceded and freed the lascars. An advertisement in Steele's and Addison's Tatler in 1709 read: 'A black Indian Boy 12 Years of Age, fit to wait on a Gentleman, to be disposed of at Denis's Coffee-house in Finch Lane near the Royal Exchange'. Some rare advertisements even show Indian domestics with slave collars. At baptism (which also implies prejudice against the 'heathens') Indians were sometimes given their masters' names with the words 'belonging to . . . ', I. Chatterjee and R. M. Eaton, *Slavery and South Asian History* (Bloomington, IN: Indiana University Press, 2006). For examples of Lascar slavery and the EIC's formal opposition to it (on Christian grounds) see Fisher, *Counterflows to Colonialism*, pp. 47–8. and in detail see also Ackroyd, *London.*
38. See Land, 'Customs of the Sea', p. 184.
39. Lascars. IOR/H/501, *Proceedings of the Committee of Shipping 26th May and 2nd June 1802 relative to alleged ill-treatment of lascars on board the country ships Union and Perseverance, including letters from John Luke (Master of the Union) 6th April 1802, Nathaniel.* Date range: 1800–02, pp. 1–93.
40. Ibid., p. 45.
41. G. Balachandran, 'South Asian Seafarers and their Worlds: 1870–1930s', in J. Bentley et al. *Seascapes: Maritime Histories, Local Cultures, and Trans-Oceanic Exchanges* (Hawaii, University of Hawaii Press, 2007).
42. See Fisher, *Counterflows to Colonialism* , p. 65.
43. Ibid., pp. 142, 161.
44. See Chatterjee and Eaton, *Slavery and South Asian History*, p. 189.
45. There is an extraordinary of *lascars* under the Sernag protecting outside the London Mansion House and later in courts of lacks of payment of dood and brutality on boards ship 'beaten with thick ropes and whips'. Their interpreter, a Naval Captain convincingly

undermines their evidence by saying in English that he had much experience of such 'natives' and only beating would make them work, They were in cases 'dissolute' Their wages had been withheld to stop them 'wasting' it. Letter, *The Times*, July 26 1824. See also *The Times* November 22 1822.

46. *The Times*, 25 July 1823.
47. This ambiguous legal status was made the responsibility of the EIC in 1834.
48. See F. O. Shyllon, *Black People in Britain* (Oxford: Oxford University Press, 1977).
49. See Fisher, *Counterflows to Colonialism*, p. 38. Quotes – a presumably unique – case from 1679 in which an armed Lascar desecrated the symbols of British rule in St Paul's cathedral.
50. Navy Board: Bound Out-letters ADM 354/143/294 amongst others.
51. Navy Board: Bound Out-letters ADM 354/143/227 As the Out-letters demonstrate, there were a series of similar cases both before and after this date of lascars resisting their deportation before receiving their prize money.
52. Old Bailey – Reference Number: t18270913–241 and Reference Number: t18360509–1233. For particular cases, see Fisher, *Counterflows to Colonialism*, p. 66.
53. See letter to *The Times* 3 June 1854 on a fight between Lascars and prostitutes in Shadwell.
54. See Fisher, *Counterflows to Colonialism*, p. 40. On one occasion, the Royal Family was petitioned by a *serang*. In this case, as presumably in several others, when the Lascars won formal justice, in practice, they suffered other consequences from the ship-owners.
55. Ibid., p. 71.
56. Letters to *The Times*, 22 March 1834 and 16 September 1896.
57. For example, *The Times*, 13 December 1815 and letter to *The Times*, 15 December 1815.
58. For a detailed account of one such riot, see http://www.mernick.org.uk//thhol/miscellany01.html (accessed 13 October 2008).
59. Fisher, *Counterflows to Colonialism*, p. 160.
60. For example, *The Times* 7 October 1808, involving a major conflict between 'hundreds' of Lascars and Chinese.
61. Fisher, *Counterflows to Colonialism*, p. 161.
62. Ibid., p. 65.
63. See Fryer, *Black People in the British Empire*, p. 19.
64. William Thackeray, the writer, came home from India as a child in 1817, accompanied by his 'Calcutta serving-man'.
65. Fisher, *Counterflows to Colonialism*, p. 43, notes the many hand paintings featuring such women (and men).
66. In a single year, 1771, for the two months of April and May, the EIC received eighteen applications from its employees to return their servants to India, fifteen male and three female.
67. Fisher, *Counterflows to Colonialism*, p. 54.
68. See J. Salter, *The Asiatics in England* (London: Seeley, Jackson and Halliday, 1872), p. 116.
69. See letter to *The Times*, 5 September 1855 regarding an Ayah being promised work by such a lady and immediately being abandoned on the London docks.
70. See Salter, *The Asiatics in England*, p. 112.

71. After several petitions for a passage home, EIC Directors were forced to provide passage at their expense to 'prevent reflection on us in this respect from the people of India'. They also introduced a bond of £50 as a surety, with little effect.
72. On the isolation and individuation of Indian servants, see Fisher, 'Working Across the Seas', p. 55.
73. Colonel Hughes as quoted in Visram, *The Ayahs, Lascars and the Princes*, p. 22. See also Public and Judicial Department Records: *Lascars* destitute on London streets IOR: L/P&J/2/49, f. 7/281 letter, dated January 1869, in connection with 'native servants' abandoned and left destitute, begging in the streets of London. He suggested a reintroduction of the system of deposit to provide their return passage.
74. Visram, *Asians in England* , p. 34. Also see Sections 3 and 6 of the 1824 Act.
75. Visram, *The Ayahs, Lascars and the Princes*, p. 24.
76. House of Commons Debate, 03 March 1842, vol 60, c1377 available at http://www.archive.org/stream/introductiontoth010910mbp/introductiontoth010910mbp_djvu.txt.
77. Pegg, *The Asiatics Cry to England*, p. 89.
78. www.towerhamlets.gov.uk/data/discover/downloads/bengali-eastend-walk.doc (2006).
79. letter to *The Times*, November 1847, complaining of Lascar beggars. A year earlier, the EIC, had stated that the problem had been resolved. Such letters (for example, 28 August 1858) typically claimed that they deliberately dressed for role of beggars, earning more money at that occupation than they could do proper work back in India.
80. Morris, *The Dangerous Classes*, p. 57.
81. Visram, *Asians in England*, who, after a trawl through the Old Bailey Session papers for the early 1800s, notes the regular appearance of the names of *Mahomet* and *Sheikh*, amongst the list of those convicted.
82. Visram, *Asians in England* p. 45.
83. Salter, *The Asiatics in England,* p. 121.
84. Pegg, *The Asiatics Cry to England*, p. 7.
85. Coroner for East Middlesex as quoted in Salter, *The Asiatics in England*, p. 20.
86. Hughes, *The Laws Relating to Lascars and Asiatic Seamen*, p. 5.
87. Ibid., p. 18.
88. Magistrate Ballantine of the Thames Police as quoted in Pegg, *The Asiatics Cry to England*, p. 9.
89. Parliamentary Committee on Lascars and other Asiatic Seamen, 1814–15.
90. Old Bailey case 13 September 1827. Reference Number: t18270913–241.
91. R. Visram notes, unlike other writers, several Stranger Homes, including one for ayahs in the latter part of the century. Their existence caused much distress – for the respectable classes – because of their location near to the city's commerce and they were later closed and re-established adjacent to the docks. See Visram, *Asians in England*, p. 51.
92. Salter, *The Asiatics in England,* p. 67. Lindebopr notes that Salter appeared to measure achievement more in terms of the amount of oluitarure given away rather than in terms of the numbers converted.
93. Pegg, *The Asiatics Cry to England.*
94. G. A. Sala, *Gaslight and Daylight: With Some London Scenes They Shine Upon* (London: Chatto and Windus, 1872).
95. Mayhew, *London Labour and the London Poor*, p. 440.
96. Ibid., p. 18.
97. Ibid., p. 79.
98. J. Cooper, as quoted in Pegg, *The Asiatics Cry to England*, p. 27.

99. For example, in 1886, report from a Committee comprising of representatives from the India Office, the Colonial Office, and the Local Government Board.
100. See Salter, *The Asiatics in England*, p. 183.
101. A book published in 1761 entitled, The Servants Pocket-Book, alludes to, the wonted haunts of Moormen (Muslims) and Gentoos (Hindus).
102. See Visram, *Asians in England*, p. 13.
103. Quoted in Salter, *The Asiatics in England*, p. 61.
104. Ibid., p. 56.
105. See Visram, *Asians in England*, p. 13.
106. See Salter, *The Asiatics in England*, p. 110 as well as Arnold, *Police Power and Colonial Rule*. The Government of India at the expense of the Indian taxpayer was already sending English vagrants found destitute in India back to England.
107. Letter dated 28 November 1809 from Hilton Docker, medical doctor to the lascars describing lascar conditions on board and in England, linking lascars poverty to '... every excess in drinking and debauchery, and contact to a violent degree those diseases (particularly venereal) which such habits are calculated to produce' (L/MAR/C/902, vol. 1, ff. 25–6).
108. Letter to *The Times* (15 March 1836).
109. See Salter, *The Asiatics in England*, p. 55.
110. See Arnold, *Police Power and Colonial Rule*, in his account of the use of the Vagrancy Act of 1869. Curiously, Arnold notes the experiences of European sailors who experienced a similar fate when discharged in Indian ports. Arnold argues that 'vagrancy' was synonymous with European destitution.
111. Ibid., 12.
112. Mayhew, *London Labour and the London Poor*, pp. 494–5, says those engaged in crossing sweeping were always afraid of the police for they 'could not ask for money' if 'there's a policeman about'.
113. See Hughes, *The Laws Relating to Lascars and Asiatic Seamen*, p. 15.
114. See P. Panayi, *Immigration, Ethnicity and Racism in England, 1815–1945* (Manchester: Manchester University Press, 1994), p. 21.
115. See Salter, *The Asiatics in England*, p. 14.
116. See K. Ballhatchet, *Race, Sex and Class Under the Raj* (London: Weidenfeld and Nicholson, 1980).
117. See Law and Henfry, *A History of Race and Racism in Liverpool 1650–1950* (Liverpool: MCRC, 1981), p. 10.
118. See Spitzer, 'Towards a Marxian Theory of Crime'.

6 Imposing Colonial Legal Identities in India

1. See Dirks, *Caste of Mind*, pp. 187–8.
2. See Pinney 1991 on the confluence of anthropometric techniques and official theories of caste as a means of making comprehensive to imperial officials the indigenous peoples of British India. C. Pinney 'Colonial Anthropology in the 'Laboratory of Mankind', in C. A. Bayley (ed.), *The Raj: India and the British, 1600–1947* (London: National Portrait Gallery, 1991)
3. See Freitag, 'Crime in the Social Order of Colonial North India', pp. 227–61.
4. See Singha, *A Despotism of Law*.

5. Ibid., p. 34.
6. On the origins of legal authority in India, see, S. K. Purohit, *Ancient Indian Legal Philosophy: Its Relevance to Contemporary Jurisprudential Thought* (New Delhi: Deep and Deep Publications, 1994), pp. xii–xiii.
7. A. Mukhopadhyay, *Behind the Mask: The Cultural Definition of the Legal Subject in Colonial Bengal, 1715–1911* (Oxford: Oxford University Press, 2004), p. 223.
8. Warren Hastings had arranged for his own translation of Indian law but the accuracy of that interrelation has been debated in S. Sen, 'Retribution in the Subaltern Mirror: Popular Reckonings of Justice and the Figure of Qazi in Mediaeval and Precolonial Bengal', *Journal of Postcolonial Studies*, 8 (2005), pp. 439–58.
9. N. B. Dirks, 'Castes of Mind', *Representations*, 37 (1992), pp. 56–78.
10. Tolen, 'Colonizing and Transforming the Criminal Tribesman', pp. 82–3.
11. *Public and Judicial Department Records*, hereafter known as L/P and J/6–171, 393.
12. Chapter 7 of this book, and A. Ali, *The Mews of Mewat* (Delhi: Oxford University Press, 1978), p. 28. The Sansi, however, became of prime concern to the colonial officers following their militant activity in Cawnpur in 1857.
13. Chapter 7 of this book.
14. Fitzpatrick, *The Mythology of Modern Law*.
15. P. Darby, *The Three Faces of Imperialism* (New Haven, CT: Yale University Press, 1987). See also the work of P. Fitzpatrick, 'Custom as Imperialism' in J. M. Abu-Nasr, U. Spellenburg, and U. Wanitzek (eds) *Law Society and National Identity in Africa* (Hamburg: Helmet Buske Verlag, 1990).
16. S. Rajula, *Essays on the Indian Penal Code* (New Delhi: Vikas, 1962), and T. Banerjee, *Background to Indian Criminal Law* (Calcutta: Calcutta University Press, 1963).
17. for example, Yang (ed.), *Crime and Criminality in British India*, as well as J. Fisch, *Cheap Lives and Dear Limbs: The British Transformation of the Bengal Criminal Law 1769–1817* (Steiner: Wiesbaden, 1983).
18. Until the last quarter of the eighteenth century the criminal justice system in India was primarily based on the normative rules of the Mohammedan criminal code. It was administered, financed and enforced by the Nawabs (the kings) through a network of officials appointed by them and by local *zamindars* – the landlords.
19. J. D. Derret, *Histories of India, Pakistan and Ceylon* (London: Oxford University Press, 1961), p. 21.
20. Fuller (ed.), *Caste Today*, p. 6.
21. See S. K. Purohit, *Ancient Indian Legal Philosophy*.
22. As Muller explains in the *Laws of Manu,* See P. Sen, *Penology: Old and New* (Delhi: Vikas, 1972).
23. S. Sengupta, *The Evolution of Ancient Indian Law* (Delhi: Deep and Deep Publications, 1950), p. 3.
24. As quoted in S. Roy, 'Customs and Customary Law in British India', *Tagore Law Lectures* (Calcutta: Sacred Books, 1908), p. 16.
25. S. K. Das, *Sahibs and Munshis* (New Delhi: Oxford University Press, 1978), p. 32.
26. Purohit, *Ancient Indian Legal Philosophy,* as well as R. Lavriere, 'Justice and Panditas: Some Ironies in Contemporary Readings of the Hindu Legal Past', *Journal of Asian Studies*, 48 (1989), pp. 757–69.
27. G. Raheja, 'India: Caste, Kinship, and Dominance Reconsidered', *Annual Review of Anthropological Studies*, 17 (1988), pp. 497–522.
28. Purohit, *Ancient Indian Legal Philosophy*, p. 7.

29. Ibid., 146.
30. N. K. Dutta, *Origin and Development of Criminal Justice in India* (Delhi: Deep and Deep Publishing, 1994), p. 24.
31. S. Suparkar, *Law of Procedure and Justice in Ancient India* (Bombay: Vikas, 1986), p. 78.
32. Das, *Sahibs and Munshis*, p. 34.
33. Dutta, *Origin and Development*, p. 26.
34. Ibid., p. 37.
35. Again, see the parallels with Georgian England in Hobsbawm, and Rude, *Captain Swing*.
36. Dutta, *Origin and Development*, p. 65.
37. Purohit, *Ancient Indian Legal Philosophy*, p. 12.
38. Ibid., p. 43.
39. *Warren Hastings Plan for the Administration of Justice extracted from the Proceedings of the Committee of Circuit, 15 Auguest 1771*. See also B. M. Gandhi, *Landmarks in Indian Legal and Constitutional History* (Lucknow: Eastern Book Company, 1998).
40. J. Majeed, *Ungoverned Imaginings: James Mill and the History of British India and Orientalism* (Oxford: Clarendon, 1992), p. 112.
41. Bhabha, *The Location of Culture*, p. 66.
42. I. Gilmour, *The Ruling Caste: Imperial Lives in the Victorian Raj* (Farrar: Straus Giroux 2006).
43. R. Dhavan, 'Motives and Opportunities: Reflecting on Legal Research in India', *Modern Law Review*, 5 (1987), pp. 105–15. The grant of Diwani and Nizamat jurisdictions by the EIC reflected the fact that it had no formal interest in the criminal justice system of India until the Cawnpur massacres in 1857.
44. the work of Patra, 'An Historical Introduction to the Indian Penal Code'. The Code substantially expanded the arena of activity juridicially defined as crime. Section XIV of the Indian Penal Code defined and prescribed punishments for 'offences affecting the public health, safety, convenience, decency and morals'.
45. E. Stokes, *The English Utilitarians and India* (London: Routledge, 1959).
46. Roy, *Indian Traffic*.
47. C. Dickens, *Works of Charles Dickens: 1855–1857*' (London: InfoStrategist. com: 2005), see ch. 4, 'The Perils of Certain English Prisoners: Dicken's Defensive Fantasy of Imperial Stability, 1857'.
48. Skuy, 'Macauly and the Indian Penal Code'.
49. U. Baxi, *Law and Poverty: Critical Essays* (Bombay: Tripathi Press, 1988).
50. the original manuscript by R. Orme, 'Of the Laws and Justice of Indostan', *Historical Fragments of the Mogul Empire* (New Delhi: Associated Publishing House, 1974), pp. 280–1.
51. M. Galanter, *Competing Equalities: Law and the Backward Classes in India* (Oxford: Oxford University Press, 1984).
52. L. Rudolph and S. Rudolph, *The Modernity of Tradition: Political Developments in India* (Chicago, IL: Chicago University Press, 1969).
53. Chairman (and MP) of the East India Company (1802–18). C. Grant, 'Observations on the State of Society Among the Asiatic Subjects of Great Britain, Particularly with Respect to Morals', in M. Moir, and L. Zastoupil (eds), *The Great Indian Education*

Debate: Documents Relating to the Orientalist-Anglicist Controversy, 1781–1843 (London: Curzon Press, 1999).

54. Ibid., p. 43.
55. K. K. Raman, 'Utilitarianism and the Criminal Law in Colonial India: A Study of the Practical Limits of Utilitarian Jurisprudence', *Modern Asian Studies*, 20 (1994), pp. 739–91.
56. Das, *Sahibs and Munshis*, p. 89.
57. J. Majeed, *Ungoverned Imaginings*, p. 20.
58. Macaulay to the Commissioners in Council, *British Parliamentary Papers*, vol. 10, 1831–2, 313.
59. A. Nandy, *An Intimate Enemy: Loss and Recovery of Self under Colonialism* (Delhi: Pluto, 1988), p. 34.
60. Bentham, *Of Laws in General.*
61. Ibid., p. 153.
62. J. S. Mill, *The History of British India*, vol. 10, p. 75.
63. J. S. Mill, to the House of Lords October 1830 in *British Parliamentary Papers* vol. 10, 1831–2, p. 126.
64. Mill, *The History of British India*, vol. 10, p. 156.
65. Ibid., p. 45.
66. B. Cohn, 'The Language of Command and the Command of Language', *Subaltern Studies,* 111 (1985), pp. 276–329, p. 296.
67. Sen, 'Retribution in the Subaltern Mirror', p. 442.
68. R. Guha, *An Indian Historiography of India: A Nineteenth Century Agenda and its Implications* (Delhi: Mittal, 1988).
69. However, as K. K. Raman argues, in 'Utilitarianism and the Criminal Law', key utilitarian thinkers, in works describing the state of the law in British India, were concerned with local, rather than universal conceptions of criminality. Bentham urged earlier reformers to fit utilitarian judgments about the law to the frames of local society. See J. Bentham, *Of the Influence of Time and Place in Matters of Legislation* (1843). Available from http:// www. la. utexas. edu/research/poltheory/bentham/timeplace/index. html
70. Raman, 'Utilitarianism and the Criminal Law', p. 743. .
71. Skuy, 'Macaulay and the Indian Penal Code'.
72. Raman, 'Utilitarianism and the Criminal Law'.
73. Hay, 'War, Dearth and Theft in the Eighteenth Century', in his thesis on the retention of capital punishment statutes, the theatre of public punishments and discretion.
74. See Chapter 3.
75. Beattie, *Crime and Courts in England* and Langbein, 'Albion's Fatal Flaws'.
76. See Chapter 3.
77. Skuy, 'Macaulay and the Indian Penal Code'.
78. Raman, 'Utilitarianism and the Criminal Law', who suspects that before England initiated its own criminal law reforms, India's people were ruled by a criminal justice system that was no more primitive than that of the colonists.
79. Raman, *Utilitarianism and the Criminal Law.*
80. Although this is an addendum to Skuy's argument, it follows directly from the structural critique of due process in Chapter 2 of this volume.
81. In India, this contradiction had been evident from as early as the rule of Warren Hastings. See R. Singha, *A Despotism of Law*, p. 169.
82. Most notably in the myriad clauses of the Town Police Clauses Act of 1848.

83. Skuy, 'Macaulay and the Indian Penal Code', who notes Macaulay's critique of the degree of discretion in English law (which Macaulay justified in terms of the 'higher standard of morality' in England), the existence of a long tradition of respect for the law and accountability to the legal profession. But legalization aimed at the thugs and the dacoits, as reified with the Criminal Tribes Acts of 1871 in procedural practice, replicated that discretion without any of the supposed English safeguards.
84. D. A. Washbrook, 'Progress and Problems: South Asian Economic and Social History 1720–1860', *Modern Asian Studies*, 22 (1988), pp. 57–96, who, following Pashukanis and Balbus, notes a contradiction between traditional Hindu laws based on status rather than equality, and the introduction of an open market process, which required the free movement of goods. The preservation of customary and religious norms was a strong barrier to market freedom and consequently the new law of contract aimed to abolish them.
85. B. Cohn, 'Notes on the study of Indian Society and Culture' in N. Singer and B. Cohn (eds) *Structure and Change in Indian Society* (Chicago, IL: Chicago University Press, 1968), pp. 1–20.
86. Note the peculiar examples in Arnold, *Police, Power and Colonial Rule*, of The Vagrancy Act of 1869 and of the Workhouse system being introduced into Southern India, not to deal with the indigenous population but with the growing population of 'poor whites' in the Indian seaports who 'embarrassed' the colonial rulers.
87. Mukhopadhyay, *Behind the Mask*, p. 223.
88. S. Freitag, *Crime in the Social Order*.
89. This account differs markedly from Weiner, *Reconstructing the Criminal*, p. 50, who argues that one feature of the new system, as opposed to the Georgian and Hanoverian versions, was the decrease in discretion. This may have been true with the bulk of offences relating to higher social classes and to more serious charges, but for the street people and the 'dangerous' classes trapped by a web of enabling legislation, discretionary treatment by law enforcement personnel was the norm, given the vagueness of some of the definitions of culpability with which they were faced. In England, as Weiner notes, after the 1850s, the main rise in offence rates was not in the number of offences where discretion of enforcement officials was least but rather in the number of trivial offences and minor misdemeanours of which the lower classes were normally accused by the new patrolling police. See also Gatrell (ed.), *The Decline of Theft and Violence*.
90. E. Hobsbawm, *Primitive Rebels*, and E. P. Thompson, 'The Moral Economy of the English Crowd in the Eighteenth Century', *Past and Present*, 50 (1971), pp. 76–136.
91. Skuy, 'Macaulay and the Indian Penal Code'.
92. Ibid., p. 45.
93. J. S. Mill, *The History of British India*, on the British attempt to create a more governable colonial society through the use of the notions of madness and mental illness. Mill's account is a textual study of the records of mental illness in Victorian India. Mill argues that lunatics should be added to the women who were targeted under the Contagious Diseases Act of 1875, the tribal castes that were shepherded into labour settlements under the Criminal Tribes Act of 1871 – the thuggees, the dacoits and the criminal tribes who were transported to the Andaman Islands and men and women who were forcibly vaccinated or subjected to anti-epidemic measures. Mill claims that the construction of madness in colonial India was related to the refusal to work and often politically based. But like Skuy and Arnold, Mill argues that the general Benthamite disciplining project

in India owed more to improvisation and failures in practice and the end result was far from the notion of a 'carceral' society.

94. Tolen, 'Colonizing and Transforming the Criminal Tribesman', pp. 80–1.
95. Mukhopadhyay, *Behind the Mask*, p. 223. p. 190.
96. Laws applied in the courts before 1860 consisted of the Company Regulations, English common law, Hindu and Muslim law, and many bodies of customary laws. See Stokes, *The English Utilitarians,* as well as Derret, *Histories of India.*
97. The Irish Constabulary was perceived of as a paramilitary organization and the Metropolitan Police as based on the notion of the unarmed patrol constable, but this difference has been challenged. See Emsley, *Crime and Society in England.*
98. D. Anderson, and D. Killingray (eds) *Policing the Empire: Government, Authority and Control, 1830–1940* (Manchester: Manchester University Press, 1991) and Brogden, 'An Act to Colonise the Internal Lands of the Island'.
99. A. Gupta, *The Police in British India: 1861–1947* (New Delhi: Concept Publishing, 1979).
100. Anderson and Killingray (eds) *Policing the Empire.*
101. Tobias, *Crime and Industrial Society in the Nineteenth Century* (Oxford: Oxford University Press, 1967).
102. S. B. Cook, *Imperial Affinities: Nineteenth Century Analogies and Exchanges Between India and Ireland* (New Delhi: Sage, 1992).
103. J. A. Sharpe, *Crime in Early Modern England: 1550–1750* (London: Longman, 1984), p. 67.
104. Gupta, *The Police in British India*, p. 23.
105. Thief-takers were important as major form of policing in London in the 1750s. They straddled the margins of the conventional and criminal worlds, forming a type of entrepreneurial police force, dependent on fees and rewards. See Sharpe, *Crime in Early Modern England*, p. 76.
106. Ibid., p. 39.
107. M. Kasturi, 'Law and Crime in India: British Policy and the Female Infanticide Act of 1870', *The Indian Journal of Gender Studies*, 1 (1994), pp. 169–94. In a study of the implementation of the Infanticide Act_of 1870 in India, Kasturi argues that the surveillance process included not just a concern with an orthodox notion of crimes, but also included machinery to deal with other 'native' barbarity, and crimes of suttee and infanticide.
108. Strachey, quoted in the *British Parliamentary Papers* (1845), vol. 45, p. 67.
109. Gazetteer of India, *The Indian Empire* (1907), p. 385.
110. Ibid., p. 384.
111. Miller, *Cops Bobbies: Police Authority in New York and London.*
112. A. Saxena, *The Military System of India 1850–1900* (New Delhi: Oxford University Press, 1974), p. 234.
113. Brogden, 'An Act to Colonise the Internal Lands', p. 179.
114. Alavi, *The Sepoy and the Raj*, p. 34 and Chapter 8 of this book.
115. Gupta, *The Police in British India*, 74.
116. Sen, *Retribution in the Subaltern Mirror*, p. 441 discusses the importance of the re-emergence of rural customary law during the rebellious in 1857.
117. R. Storch, 'The Policeman as Domestic Missionary'.
118. Mukhopadhyay *Behind the Mask*, p. 36.

119. See the *Report of the Famine Commission*, 1880, 24 and Davis, *Late Victorian Holocausts*, p. 238.
120. See Arnold *Police, Power and Colonial Rule,* p. 234.
121. See Gupta, *The Police in British India*, p. 36.
122. Ibid., p. 23.
123. Ibid., p. 12.
124. See F. Galton, as quoted in Weiner, *Reconstructing the Criminal,* p. 78.
125. See D. Arnold, quoted in B. Harris, and W. Ernst (eds), *Race, Science and Medicine: 1700–1960* (London: Routledge, 1999).
126. Mukhopadhyay *Behind the Mask*, p. 34.
127. Harris and Ernst (eds), *Race, Science and Medicine*, p. 17.
128. Sen, *Retribution in the Subaltern Mirror*, p. 444.
129. In the third quarter of the nineteenth century, Bertillon had developed anthropometric measurements as a means of informing identification. The intent was to identify habitual criminals who moved from place to place and concealed their identities: 'only members of criminal tribes, and often convicted of certain definite crimes should be so measured'. See Dirks, *Caste of Mind*, p. 45.
130. Much of the practice of this early science cannot, in reality, be distinguished from the aims of the imperial rulers. For example, a key passage in H. Kuklick, *The Savage Within: The Social History of British Anthropology 1885–1945* (Cambridge: Cambridge University Press, 1991) notes an attempt in the late nineteenth century to form a 'colonial ethnology office' to supplement the imperial administration in India and elsewhere. He notes that 'Colonial anthropology was a congerie of formulae developed to meet the practice needs of a specific client, less like academic anthropology than like other technical enterprises sponsored by particular government agencies or industries. Colonial anthropology rationalised systematic policies of colonial officials that had long lasting consequences', p. 183.
131. See K. Hobson, 'Ethnographic Mapping and the Construction of the British Census in India' *the Indian Caste System and the British* see www. btinternet. com~britishempire/article/castesystem. 'The early Indian Censuses, therefore, present not merely as statistical accounts of early modern India, but also as documentation of the British encounter with its colonised other; as documentation of the coloniser's attempts to come to an understanding of its colonial subjects and integrate India – at least from an administrative perspective – within the British Empire'. Census of India Reports from 1871 to 1901 Adam Bowles. http://www.chaf.lib.latrobe.edu.au/dcd/census.htm (accessed 21 October 2008).
132. See Herbert Risley quoted in R. Inden, *Imagining India* (Oxford: Blackwell, 1990), p. 59.
133. See E. Thurston, *The Caste and Tribes of Southern India* (Madras: Government Office, 1907).
134. See Tobias, *Crime and Industrial Society,* on the supposed migration of the criminal classes in England.
135. See Pratt, *Governing the Dangerous*.
136. Quoted in Freitag, *Crime in the Social Order*, p. 54.
137. Arnold notes that it was perhaps no accident that Sir Francis Galton purportedly invented regression analysis when surveying, for the greater glory of science, the naked bodies of Hottentots women in southern Africa. See Arnold, *Police, Power and Colonial Rule,* and H. Kuklick, *The Savage Within*.
138. C. Sengoopta, *The Imprint of the Raj: How Fingerprinting Was Born in Colonial India* (Oxford: Macmillan, 2003).

139. W. J. Herschel, 'Personal Letter', *Nature* (25 November 1880). This history of fingerprints is of course disputed. For example, Dr Henry Faulds, a British physician working in Japan, in the same period, corresponded with Charles Darwin about the possibilities of a science of fingerprints.
140. Arnold, *Police, Power and Colonial Rule*, p. 57.
141. R. Mukherjee, 'Satan Let Loose Upon Earth: The Kanpur Massacres in India in the Revolt of 1857', *Past and Present*, 128 (1990), p. 92–117.
142. Amin, *Event, Metaphor, Memory: Chauri Chaura, 1922–1992* (California: California University Press, 1995).

7 Constructing the Sansi as a 'Criminal' Class

1. Ibbetson, *Report of the Criminal Tribes of the Punjab*, p. 362.
2. Ibid., 10. 2. For a detailed and typical account of the Sansi from the perspective of a contemporary senior police officer, see Kennedy, *The Criminal Classes in India*, pp. 244–57.
3. As Singha, notes, 'colonial regulations were formulated on the notion of individual responsibility for a particular offence. However, there were police instructions relating to 'bad-livelihood', 'vagrancy', and 'criminal tribes' which would draw upon an association between a wandering lifestyle, low social status, and criminality. These people could be apprehended and sentenced, for example, to hard labour, simply by belonging to those associations. See Singha, *A Despotism of Law*, p. 44.
4. Ibbetson, *Report of the Criminal Tribes*. 'Crime management in India from 1858 through the 1870s', serves as an excellent example of the development of criminal anthropological practice'. See A. Maunder and G. Moore *Victorian Crime, Madness, and Sensation* (Aldershot: Ashgate, 2004), p. 197.
5. Freitag, 'Crime in the Social Order', pp. 227–61.
6. More ubiquitous feeling of racial bestiality (as epitomized in the images of Shelly's Frankenstein) and of the criminal and 'dangerous' castes of India crept into the white European consciousness as documented in Roy's 1996 discursive essay on images of thuggee in the colonial imagination. See Roy, *Indian Traffic*, and, in particular, the novel by J. Masters, *The Deceivers* (New York: Carroll and Graf, 1988).
7. A senior official in the Madras police, Fredrick S. Mullaly published an early ethnographic text entitled *Notes on Criminal Classes of the Madras Presidency* (Madras: Government Press, 1892).
8. Ibid., 12.
9. Sleeman, *The Thugs and the Phansigars of India*.
10. A seven-volume work on castes and tribes, See E. Thurston, *The Castes and Tribes of Southern India* (Madras: Government Office, 1907) and see the detailed summary of the work of Mullaly and his co-patriot on classifying Indian and social groups in Dirks, *Castes of Mind*, pp. 181–8.
11. Ibbetson, *Report of the Criminal Tribes.*
12. Herbert Risley quoted in R. Inden, *Imagining India* (Oxford: Blackwell, 1990), p. 65.
13. Despite Freitag's reservations, in India. Parama Roy notes that in the determination of thuggee, the idea of hereditary criminality by collectives had been long-standing. Thus the dacoits in Bengal in 1772, were explained not as a response to the mercantile order and procedures of the East India Company, or indeed, to any other material circum-

stance, but as fulfilling a hereditary calling if not a genetic predisposition. See Roy, *Indian Traffic.*

14. See Ibbetson *Report of the Criminal Tribes.*
15. Quoted in Part II of V. Lal, *Criminality and Colonial Anthropology* Introduction to the reprint edition (Gurgaon, Haryana: Vintage Press, 1995), pp. i–xxvii, and R. Bahadur and M. P. Naidu, *The History of Railway Thieves, with Illustrations and Hints on Detection*, 4th edn (Madras: Higginbothams Limited, 1915).
16. See Cohn, 'The Language of Command and the Command of Language', p. 223.
17. See Yang (ed.), *Crime and Criminality in British India*, and on the martial races, see Alavi, *The Sepoy and the Raj.*
18. See A. Major, 'State and Criminal Tribes in Colonial Punjab: Surveillance, Control and Reclamation of the Dangerous Classes', *Modern Asian Studies*, 33 (1999), pp. 657–88.
19. See S. Strachey quoted in the *British Parliamentary Papers* 1845, 45, p. 97.
20. For a useful discussion of inherited criminal occupations, see Lal, *Criminality and Colonial Anthroplogy.*
21. See Yang, *Crime and Criminality.*
22. See Nigam, 'Disciplining and Policing the "Criminals by Birth"' and see also C. H. Patrick, 'The Criminal Tribes of India with Special Emphasis on the Mang Garudi: A Preliminary Report', *Man in India*, 48 (1968), pp. 244–57.
23. Vagrants, for example, could be arrested and held indefinitely on the basis of their character through a range of enabling legislation. In other cases, involving more frequent suspected offences, the suspect could be incarcerated for life without any charge being levied. See Singha, *A Despotism of Law*. Sir John Strachey had introduced Indoor Relief system of the English Poor Law to India in 1835–6. Sustenance was only available to those who accepted the structures confinement bin the Workhouse.
24. See Sleeman, *The Thugs and the Phansigars of India.*
25. See Warren Hastings in the *British Parliamentary Papers* vol. 23, 1831.
26. See the Reports relating to the administration of criminal justice in the central provinces for the year 1884, L/P and J/ 6/171/ 51.
27. See Yang (ed.), *Crime and Criminality.*
28. See Sleeman, *The Thugs and the Phansigars.*
29. See Lal, *Criminality and Colonial Anthropology.*
30. See M. Dash, *Thug: True Story of India's Murderous Cult* (London: Granta, 2005).
31. For the most effective critique and analysis of this important precedent in defining crime as a collective activity, see Singha, *A Despotism of Law*; Roy, *Indian Traffic* and Dash, *Thug.*
32. See Singha, *A Despotism of Law*, p. 78.
33. See Act XXIV of 1836; see Singha, *A Despotism of Law*, p. 23.
34. See W. H. Sleeman as quoted in R. Temple, *India in 1880* (London: Weidenfeld and Nicolas, 1881).
35. An approver was someone who, on providing information and identifying other thugs and their crimes to Sleeman's office, would be given life imprisonment instead of being hanged for the crimes he committed. See Dash, *Thug.*
36. Ibid., pp. 126–7.
37. Quoted in D. Arnold, Police Powers and the Demise of British Rule in India, 1930–1947', in D. Anderson and D. Killingray (eds) *Policing and the Decolonisation: Nationalism, Politics and the Police 1817–1965'* (Manchester University Press: Manchester, 1992), p. 90.

38. See Arnold, *Police, Power and Colonial Rule*.
39. See Regulation XX of The Suppression of Thuggee Act of 1843; see Singha, *A Despotism of Law*, p. 65.
40. In present-day criminal parlance, approvers would be regarded as 'grasses'. Sleeman comments on one approver (in his Report of 1839), Feringee, as possessing qualities of a higher nature: 'a tall and handsome young man, stoutly built and about twenty-five. From the start he talked frankly admitting that his family, though Brahmins, the priestly caste, had been Thugs for generations'. See Sleeman, *The Thugs and the Phansigars*.
41. C. Hervey, *Report of the Operations of the Thuggee and Dacoity Department in Native States from the Abolition of its Executive Agency in British Territory to the end of the year 1868* (Calcutta: Calcutta Publishing Press, 1872).
42. See Roy, *Indian Traffic*, p. 45.
43. See Lal *Criminality and Colonial Anthropology*.
44. See Freitag, 'Crime in the Social Order', p. 231.
45. See Yang (ed.), *Crime and Criminality*.
46. See Major, *State and Criminal Tribes in Colonial Punjab*. He claims that there was some truth in the assumptions. During the threatened rebellion of 1857, several of the 'hereditary thieving races' especially some of the Harnis and the Sansi, joined together to engage in violent crimes in Eastern Punjab.
47. See Yang, *Crime and Criminality*, p. 7.
48. Ibid., p. 19.
49. See Freitag, 'Crime in the Social Order'.
50. The *Criminal Tribes Act of* 1871 was enforced in the northern part of British India first. Later it was extended to Bengal (1876) and other areas, with the Madras Presidency being the last to enact it in 1911. Act 150 notified castes of 'hereditary criminals'.
51. Quoted in Major, *State and Criminal Tribes in Colonial Punjab*.
52. Ibid., p. 665. In the Central Provinces the Criminal Tribes Act of 1871 had identified several groups (the *Bauraihs, Sanorias, Aherias, Harbwahs* and *Mughya Doms)* as criminal. In Bihar and Bengal, the *Mughya Doms, Rajwars, Nutts, Ahers, Bedyas and the Shikarees* were notified under the same legislation. In Hyderabad and Madras Presidency, the *Banjaries, Buddhuks, Kunjars, Nuths and Sunorias* were notified. In the Madras Presidency, the *Lumbardis* and the *Koravers* were identified as the worst of the criminal tribes and notified under the Criminal Tribes Act of 1871. Also, see Radhakrishna, 'Surveillance and Settlements under the Criminal Tribes Act in Madras'.
53. See Chapter 4 on the English device of probationing former long-term inmates. Also see Pratt, *Governing the Dangerous*.
54. See Major, *State and Criminal Tribes in Colonial Punjab*.
55. Again notice the parallel discourse in Victorian England. See Mathur, *Kala-Pani*.
56. See Major, *State and Criminal Tribes in Colonial Punjab*.
57. Ibid., p. 680.
58. See Radhakrishna 'Dishonoured by History'.
59. See Arnold, *Police, Power and Colonial Rule*.
60. W. J. Hatch quoted in Ibid., p. 89.
61. Ibid., p. 90.
62. See, for example, Bengal. Police Department, Register of members of Raghunandan Panday's gang of Jessore declared under section 3 and registered under section 4 of the Criminal Tribes Act (III of 1911). [Calcutta, 1917]
63. See Yang (ed.), *Crime and Criminality*, p. 112.

64. See Arnold, *Police, Power and Colonial Rule*, p. 41.
65. Ibid., p. 43.
66. Radhakrishna 'Dishonoured by History'.
67. There is now considerable Human Rights documentation on the current experience of the Sansi as a product of this particular social history. Remarkably, when the Government of India finally revoked the Criminal Tribes Act of 1952, it replaced it with a Habitual Offenders Act of 1956, a bizarre approximation to the English Habitual Criminals Act of 1869.
68. See Report on the Census of the Punjab 17 February and Ibbetson, *Report of the Criminal Tribes*, p. 312.
69. Indeed, the Sansi had been subject to legal controls for many years – Regulation XXVI of 1793, Act XXX of 1836, of the Thuggee and Dacoity Act, and the Indian Penal Code of 1860, see S. Singh, *The Sansi of Punjab*. The 1836 Act '...rested on the proposition that criminal intention could be assessed not only from a specific criminal act but also from the characteristics of a collectivity', see Singha, *A Despotism of Law*, pp. 214–5.
70. B. S. Shashi and P. S. Varma, *A Socio-History of Ex-Criminal Communities* (Delhi: Sundeep Prakashan, 1991), pp. 98–9.
71. V. P. T. Vivian, *A Hand Book of the Criminal Tribes of the Punjab* (Lahore: Punjab Government Press, 1912), p. 23.
72. Ibid., p. 678.
73. Ibid., p. 369.
74. See Hervey, *Report of the Operations on the Thuggee*, p. 5.
75. The General Superintendent of the Operations of Suppression in the Thuggee and Dacoity Department. The Thuggee and Dacoity Department continued to exist until 1904, though its operations had long been confined to the suppression of organized robbery in native states.
76. See Harvey, *Report of the Operation on the Thuggee*, p. 34.
77. The effects of the newly imposed forest laws, which prevented the Sansi and other tribes from collecting bamboo and leaves (necessary for making items like mats and baskets for their own use and sale) and preventing them grazing their cattle in the forests. See *Hindustani Times* (27 November 2000). Loss of cattle during the famines was particularly crucial because they were the only means of transporting goods to their inland villages. Because of the increasing network of railways, these communities had to travel further to sell their wares. Loss of cattle meant loss of trading activity – a situation not dissimilar to the loss of customary rights in England after the Enclosure Acts.
78. See the original work on this theme by Marx, *Critique of the Gotha Programme* and on the Ruhr foresters, see Linebaugh, 'Karl Marx'. Writers within the Warwick School, especially Linebaugh, adopt this theme. Yang (ed.), *Crime and Criminality* makes a similar point in India relating to the British introduction of forest regulations that prohibited the harvesting of forest products in India.
79. The Punjab Laws Act 1872 http://www. punjablaws. gov. pk/laws/4. html
80. See Singh, *The Sansi of Punjab*, p. 245.
81. Ibid., p. 106, see especially chapter 6 on the ex-Criminal Tribes of Delhi State.
82. See S. Strachey, as quoted in the *Imperial Gazetteer of India: The Indian Empire* (New Delhi: Government Press, 1903), p. 399.
83. R. Singha *A Despotism of Law*, p. 44.
84. On fingerprinting, see Galton, *Inquiries into Human Faculty*. Fingerprinting created its own problems, however. The use of the individualizing device doubled the number of

known criminal in Madras within a year. Consequently, the police found it more convenient to fall back on collective categories such as castes and tribes. G. G. Joseph, *George Joseph: The Life and Times of a Kerala Christian Nationalist* (Delhi: Orient Longman, 2003).

85. See V. Raghavan, *Problems of Criminal Tribes* (Delhi: Mittal Publishing Press, 1949), p. 9.
86. See Ibbetson, *Report of the Criminal Tribes*, p. 630.
87. B. Bhukya, 'Dacoity and the Creation of a Surveillance Society in Hyderabad state' *Indian Economic & Social History Review*, 44:2 (2007), pp. 179–212, p. 170.
88. E. J. Gunthorpe, *Criminal Tribes Residing in or Frequenting the Bombay Presidency and the Central Provinces* (Delhi: Times of India Steam Press, 1882).
89. Ibid., p. 140.
90. See Report of the Criminal Tribes Enquiry Committee, 1947, p. 4.
91. Reinforced by The Criminal Tribes Settlement Act of 1880.
92. See how this development was almost identical to the proposal by Booth, the founder of the Salvation Army, of plans for industrial and agricultural settlements for the criminal classes in England. See Booth, *Life and Labour of the People in London*.
93. Ibid., p. 141.
94. See L/ P and J/6/164.
95. An article in the *Hindu Times* (27 November 2000) provides a cryptic summary of contemporary settlement practice. The British subsequently built special settlements for the 'criminal' tribes and castes, where they were chained, caned, and flogged while being surrounded by high walls under the provisions of the Criminal Tribes Act of 1871. In the name of the home-grown science of 'curocriminology', it was declared that the 'criminals' would be cured of their criminal propensities if they were given work and this understanding had an obvious corollary: the more they worked, the more formed they would be. They could thus be forced to work up to twenty hours a day in factories, plantations, mills, quarries and mines throughout the first decade of the twentieth century.
96. See Arnold, *Police, Power and Colonial Rule*.
97. Sir John Symington as Criminal Tribes Settlement Officer in 1918 quoted in R. Hunt, and J. Harrison, *The District Officer in India: 1930–1947* (London: Scholar Press, 1980), p. 144.
98. For a pious account of the practices of the Settlements, see C. M. Edwards, *The Criminal Tribes* (London: Society for the Propagation of the Gospel).
99. For a detailed account – as perceived by the Commissioner of the Salvation Army at a time when he was bidding for settlement control by his agency – on the reported corrupt relationship between the police and the criminal tribes in the early Settlements see F. Booth-Tucker, *Forty Years with the Salvation Army India and Ceylon* (London: Marshall Brothers, 1916) '*the police ...did not view our coming with favour, as the (tribespeople) had shared with them the proceeds of their thefts and robberies in order to secure immunity from punishment*.' p. 207.
100. Tolen 'Colonizing and Transforming the Criminal Tribesman', p. 94.
101. See Mathur, *Kala-Pani*.
102. Ibid., p. 43.
103. See Booth, *The Mukti-Fauj*, p. 56.
104. Stigma of Criminality of India's Denotified and Nomadic Tribes HR Features 9 July 2004.
105. Tolen, 'Colonizing and Transforming the Criminal Tribesman', p. 112.

106. Evangelist missions charged with administering the Settlements include the American Marathi mission (one of its settlement sustained 3,000 people), the American Episcopal Church, the Society for the Propagation the Gospel, and the Salvation Army (which, by 1930 controlled 35 Settlements).
107. See Freitag, 'Crime in the Social Order'.
108. See Booth, *The Mukti-Fauj*, p. 23.
109. Ibid., p. xii.
110. Quoted by Arnold, *Police, Power and Colonial Rule*. For an insider account of the Salvation Army's work with 'criminal' tribes, see the publication by the Salvation Army Commissioner, D. Smith, *His Story* (London: Salvation Army, 2000).
111. Booth-Tucker, *Criminocurology or the Indian Criminal and what to do with Him* (Simla: Royal Army Temperance Assoc. Press, 1916), p. 3.
112. Quoted in Cole, *Suspect Identities*, p. 95.
113. One police report actually acknowledged culpability on the part of the colonial state in this regard, writing of one tribe: 'if there is foundation for complaints of their thieving propensities, the blame cannot be said to rest entirely with them. Between lack of land and industrial opening on the one hand, and rigid restriction of movements on the other, the people have been driven into seeking a means of subsistence by crime'. H. K. Kaul and L. L. Tompkins, *Report on Questions Relating to the Administration of Criminal and Wandering Tribes in the Punjab* (Lahore: Superintendent, Government Printing, Punjab, 1914), p. 18.
114. Galton 'Fingerprints and their Registration as a Means of Personal Identification', p. 301–3.
115. T. Mahmud, 'Colonialism and Modern Construction', *University of Miami Law Review* 23 (1999), pp. 1219–96. See M. Radhakrishna, 'Colonial Construction of a criminal tribe', *Economic and Political Weekly* (8–15 July 2000), p. 2553 on the effects of the famine of 1877 in the Punjab in pushing the tries into criminality. The forest laws of the 1880s did not alow them to collect materials for trade or bamboo amd leaves which they had made into mats and brooms. Land wsa cordoned of so they could nto lonegr graze their cattle.
116. See Roy, *Indian Traffic*.
117. See Cannadine, *Ornamentalism*.
118. As in England for the 'criminal classes', as not just their inferiors but also their rational-legal, scientific subordinates.
119. See D. Hardiman, 'Usury, Dearth and Famine in Western India' in *Past and Present*, 13 (1996), pp. 113–56, p. 152, on the detail of the effects of the forest laws on the Sansi and other 'criminal' tribes.
120. Ibid., p. 134.
121. Ibid., 43 and see Capter 5 and 6 of this book.
122. See Arnold, *Police, Power and Colonial Rule,* who provides similar accounts for Madras, but resorts to the Warwick School approach in conceptualizing these actions as *social crime.*
123. See Punjab Administration Report (PAR) 1868–9, p. 62.
124. See *State Gazetteer of the Punjab Government* (Punjab: Government Press, 1896), p. 32.
125. See Punjab Famine Report (PFR) 1878–9, pp. 73–4.
126. Ibid., p. 98.
127. See K. Yadav, *The Revolt of 1857 in Haryana* (Delhi: Vikas, 1977), p. 28.

128. See W. R. Butler, *The Land of the Vedas: India* (New York: Nelson and Phillip, 1875), p. 414.
129. Christian Missions especially the Society for the Propagation of the Gospel had been established in 1861 for this purpose. See the work of M. Sherring, *The History of Protestant Mission in India* (London: Smith, Elder and Company, 1881).
130. For an analysis of the implications of episodic famines, the export of foods and the subsequent hunger, see the work of A. K. Sen, *Poverty and Famine: An Essay on Entitlement and Deprivation* (Oxford: Oxford University Press, 1981).
131. See Skuy, 'Macaulay and the Indian Penal Code'.
132. The Sansi and other criminal tribes still remain stigmatized in present day India. Note the headlines from recent Indian newspapers in Radhakrishna, 'Dishonoured by History'.

8 Imperial Reflections: A Compelling Insistence

1. W. Booth, *In Darkest England and the Way Out* (Toronto, ON: W. Bryce, 1890), p. 46.
2. B. Abrahart *The Cartographic Methods and Mishaps of Henry Mayhew in 1861* http://www.ahc2005.org/en/new_1/the_cartographic_methods_and_mishaps_of_henry_mayhew_in_1861/ (accessed 21 September 2008). See also J. Marriott, *The Other Empire: Metropolis, India and Progress in the Colonial Imagination* (Manchester: Manchester University Press, 2003), p. 118.
3. P. Pels 'The Rise and Fall of the Indian Aborigines: Orientalism, Anglicism, and the Emergence of and Ethnology of India, 1833–1869', in P. Pels and O. Salemink (eds) *Colonial Subjects: Essays on the Practical History of Anthropology* (Ann Arbor, MI: University of Michigan Press, 2000), pp. 82–116, p. 89.
4. C. A. Bayley, *Imperial Meridian: The British Empire and the World 1780–1830* (London: Longman, 1987).
5. Quoted in Marriott *The Other Empire, p103.*
6. Ibid., p. 131.
7. J. Mullens, *Revised Statistics of Missions in India and Ceylon Compiled at the Request of the Calcutta Missionary Conference* (Calcutta: Baptist Mission Press, 1852).
8. Hobson, *The Indian Caste System and The British.*
9. N. Peabody, 'Cents, Sense, Census: Human Inventories in Late Precolonial and Early Colonial India', *Comparative Studies in Society and History*, 43:4 (2001), pp. 819–50.
10. D. Chakrabarty, 'Modernity and Ethnicity in India' D. Bennet (ed.), *Multicultural States: Rethinking Difference and Identity* (London: Routledge, 1998), pp. 91–110, p. 102.
11. The word originates in the Portuguese word 'casta' which means race, breed, race or lineage. However, during the nineteenth century, for the British imbued it with racial concepts. The term 'caste' increasingly took on the connotations of the word race. It appeared to represent a static indigenous system of social ordering that allowed the ruling class or Brahmins, to maintain their power over the other classes. What the British failed to realize was that Hindus existed in a different cosmological frame than did the British.
12. A count made in Bombay in 1780 had simply used the category of socio-religious communities.
13. Tolen, 'Colonizing and Transforming the Criminal Tribesman', p. 81.
14. Cohn, 'Notes on the Study of Indian Society and Culture', p. 15.
15. Tolen, 'Colonizing and Transforming the Criminal Tribesman', pp. 82–3.

16. Marriott, *The Other Empire*, p. 202.
17. Hobson, *The Indian Caste System and The British.*
18. Dirks, *Castes of Mind*, p. 249.
19. N. B. Dirks, 'Colonial and Postcolonial Histories: Comparative Reflections on the Legacies of Empire', *Global Background Paper for the Human Development Report, Building Inclusive Societies* (United Nations 2004).
20. D. Washbrook, 'The Development of Caste Organization in South India 1880–1925', in C. J. Baker, and D. Washbrook, *South India: Political Institutions and Political Change 1880–1940* (Delhi: Macmillan, 1975), pp. 157–96, p. 180.
21. Ibid., p. 181.
22. R. B. Bhagat, 'Census and the Construction of Communalism in India', *Economic and Political Weekly* (24 November 2001).
23. D. Chakrabarty, and H. Bhabha, *Habitations of Modernity: Essays in the Wake of Subaltern Studies* (Chicago, IL: University of Chicago Press 2002), p. 87.
24. P. Van der Veer, 'Ayodhya and Somnath: Eternal Shrines, Contested Histories', *Social Research*, 59:1 (Spring 1992), pp. 90–6, p. 96.
25. G. Viswanathan, 'Contested Polities Ethnographic Politics and the Discourse of Origins', *Stanford Electronic Humanities Review,* 5:1 (1996), available at http://www. stanford. edu/group/SHR/5-1/text/viswanathan2. html

    For example, it led to extraordinary hostility between Hindu and Muslim and contributed to later oppositional practices. Until this period of post-colonialism, Muslim–Hindu relations had been relatively peaceful and largely unproblematic. Viswanathan quotes Edward Gait, the census commissioner of the 1901 report, 'The Moghals are converts, just as much as are the Chandals [a low-caste tribe of Bengal]. It is only a question of time and place. The Christian religion prides itself as much on converts from one race as on those from another, and except for the influence of Hindu ideas, it is not clear why Muslims should not do so too'. Also see Bhagat, 'Census and the Construction of Communalism in India'.
26. H. H. Risley, and E. A. Gait, *Census of India: 1901,* vol. 1 (Calcutta: Government Press, 1903). Risley claimed that Hinduism would eventually be replaced by Islamic and Christian consciousness. Prominent locals preached the sane message (e. g N. Mukherji in his pamphlet, U. N. Mukherji, *Hindus: A Dying Race* (Calcutta: np. 1909), who suggested that as Hinduism would eventually be extinct, it was time to combat the process by 'reconverting' Hindus from Mohammedans and Christianity).
27. Quoted in T. L. Alborn, 'Age and Empire in the Indian Census, 1871–1931', *Journal of Interdisciplinary History,* 30:1 (1999), pp. 61–89.
28. Ibid., p. 67.
29. Tolen, Colonizing and Transforming the Criminal Tribesman, p. 86.
30. Bhagat, 'Census and the Construction of Communalism in India'.
31. D. Quigley, *The Interpretation of Caste* (Oxford: Clarendon Press, 1993), pp. 124–25.
32. See G. Viswanathan, 'Contested Politics: Ethnographic Politics and the Discourse of Origins,' *Stanford Electronic Humanities Review*, 5: 1 (1996), available at http: www.stanford.edu/group/SHR/5-1/text/viswanathan2.html.
33. Hobson, *The Indian Caste System and The British*.
34. Tolen, 'Colonizing and Transforming the Criminal Tribesman'.
35. Durkheim, *The Rules of Sociological Method*.
36. The Criminal and Disorder Act_of 1994 is the most recent example of dealing with the underclass.
37. Freitag, 'Crime in the Social Order', pp. 227–61.

38. Singha, *A Despotism of Law*, p. 170.
39. See Skuy, 'Macaulay and the Indian Penal Code of 1860'.
40. G. C. Spivak, and Harasym, S. , *The Post-colonial Critic: Interviews, Strategies, Dialogues* (London: Routledge: 1990).
41. Jean Paul Sartre's Introduction to F. Fanon, *The Wretched of the Earth* (London: Grove Press, 1963).

WORKS CITED

Primary Sources

The Times, 1785–1900.

Hindu Times, India.

Records and Manuscripts Cited, British Library, Oriental and India Office Collection, London, UK

British Parliamentary Papers (House of Commons)

BPP 1812–13, vol. x, no. 3 (paper 282).

BPP 1831–32 vol. 10.

BPP 1837–38 vol. 40.

BPP 1845–48 vol. 45.

BPP 1861–62.

L/ P and J: India Office: Public and Judicial Department Records 1795–1950

L/P and J/6/1 Indian Jail Reports 1881.

L/ P and J/6/5 Criminal Justice Reports 1884.

L/ P and J/6/158.

L/ P and J/6/164. Reports Relating to the Administration of Criminal Justice in the Central Provinces for the Year 1884

L/P and J/6/167.

L/ P and J/6/168.

L/ P and J/6/169.

L/P and J/ 6/171.

L/ P and J/6/172.

Marine Department Records

L/MAR/C/902, vol. 1, ff. 25–6
available at http://www.bl.uk/reshelp/findhelpsubject/history/history/asiansinbritain/ayahsservantsandsailors/britishayahs.html

Records Cited, Archives of India

Session Papers 10 Dec. 1868–69 vol. I and II

Bengal (State and Public Institutions) The Criminal Tribes Act 111 of 1911(1915).

Census Report 1901.

Census of India Nicobar and Andaman Islands 1941 Government of India Publication no. 15.

Gazetteer of India *The Indian Empire* Vol. IV. (Oxford: 1907).

Gazetteer of India, *The Indian Empire* Vol. II (Oxford: 1908).

Government of India, legislative Department *The Criminal Tribes Act* of 1871, (Calcutta: Government Printing, 1908).

House of Commons Report from the Select Committee on Aborgines, 1837.

Imperial Gazetteer of India: The Indian Empire.

Indian Penal Code, 1860.

Punjab Administration Report, (PAR) 1868–1869, 62.

Punjab Administration Report, 1877–78, appendix XIII, pp. XXVIIIX.

Punjab Famine Report, (PFR) 1878–79.

Report of the Census of the Punjab, 1881.

Report of the Criminal Tribes Enquiry Committee, 1947.

Report of the Famine Commission, 1880, Part 1.

State Gazetteer of the Punjab, Government: Punjab, 1896.

Warren Hastings Plan for the Administration of Justice Extracted from the Proceedings of the Committee of Circuit, 15th August 1772.

Primary Sources

Abrahart, B. *The Cartographic Methods and Mishaps of Henry Mayhew in 1861* http://www.ahc2005.org/en/new_1/the_cartographic_methods_and_mishaps_of_henry_mayhew_in_1861

Bahadur, R. and M. P. Naidu, *The History of Raiway Thieves, with Illustrations and Hints on Detection,* 4th ed. (Madras: Higginbothmans Limited, 1915).

Berner, F., 'A New Division of the Earth,' *Journal Des Scavans*, 29 (1648).

Booth, C., *Life and Labour of the People in London* vol. 1, (London: Macmillan, 1889).

Booth, T., *The Mukti Fauj: the Salvation Army* (London: Salvation Army, 1922).

Booth, W., *In Darkest England and the Way Out* (Toronto, ON: W. Bryce, 1890).

Booth-Tucker, F., *Criminocurology or the Indian Criminal and what to do with Him* (Simla: Royal Army Temperance Assoc. Press, 1916).

—, *Forty Years with the Salvation Army India and Ceylon* (London: Marshall Brothers, 1916).

Butler, W. R., *The Land of the Vedas: India* (New York: Nelson and Phillip, 1875).

Combe, C. *Essays on Phrenology* (Philadelphia, PA: n. p. 1822).

Darwin, C., *On the Origins of Species* (London: n. p. 1859).

—, *The Descent of Man and Selection in Relation to Sex* (New York: Appleton, 1883).

Engels, F., *Conditions of the Working Class in England* (New York: Panther, 1887).

Galton, F., (1865) 'Hereditary Talent and Character' *Macmillan's Magazine*, 12 (1865), pp. 327–412.

—, *Inquiries into Human Faculty and its Development* (London: Macmillan, 1883).

—, 'Fingerprints and their Registration as a Means of Personal Identification', *Transaction of the Seventh International Congress of Hygiene and Demography,* 10 (1892), pp. 30–43.

Gobineau, J. A., *The Inequality of the Human Races: 1853–55* (London: Heinemann, 1915).

Goring, C., *The English Convict: A Statistical Study* (London: Cavendish Press, 1913).

Greenwood, J., *The Seven Curses of London* (London: Adamant Media Publishing, 1869).

Gunthorpe, E. J., *Notes on Criminal Tribes Residing in or Frequenting the Bombay Presidency and the Central Provinces* (Delhi: Times of India Steam Press, 1882).

Hervey, C., *Report of the Operations of the Thuggee and Dacoity Department in Native States from the Abolition of its Executive Agency in British Territory to the end of the year 1868.* (Calcutta: Calcutta Publishing Press, 1872).

Hervey, M., *Report of the Operations on the Thuggee and Dacoity Department During 1859–1860 vol. 566* (London: Marston and Company, 1861).

Hughes, R. M., *The Laws Relating to Lascars and Asiatic Seamen Employed in the British Merchant Services or Brought to the UK in Foreign Vessels Smith* (London: Elder and Company, 1855).

Ibbetson, D. C., *Report of the Criminal Tribes of the Punjab* (New Delhi: Mittal, 1881).

Imperial Gazetteer of India, *The Indian Empire II* (Oxford: Oxford University Press, 1908).

Kaul, H. K., and Tompkins, L. L., *Report on Questions relating to the Administration of Criminal and Wandering Tribes in the Punjab* (Lahore: Superintendent Government Printing, Punjab, 1914).

Kennedy, M., *The Criminal Classes in India* (Delhi: Mittal Publications, 1908).

Kipling, R., *Under the Deodars* (New York: United States Book Company 1891).

Knox, R., *The Races of Man* (London: Renshaw, 1850).

MacLeod, J. M., G. W. Anderson and F. Millet, 'Notes on the Indian Penal Code by the Indian Law Commissioners' *Miscellaneous Works of Lord Macaulay* ed. Lady Trevelyan, 5 vols (New York: Harper, 1880).

Mayhew, H., *London Labour and the London Poor: A Cyclopaedia of the Conditions and Earnings of Those that will Work and those that Cannot* (London: Griffen, Bohn and Wiley, 1861).

—, and Binney, J., *The Criminal Prisons of London and Scenes of Prison Life* (London: Smith, Elder and Company, 1862).

Mill, J. S., *The History of British India*, 6 vols (London: Baldwin, Cradock and Joy, 1840).

Mullaly, F. S., *Notes on Criminal Classes of the Madras Presidency* (Madras; Government Press, 1892).

Pearson, K., *The Life, Letters, and Labour of Francis Galton*, 3 vols (Cambridge: Cambridge University Press, 1914).

Pegg, J., *The Asiatics Cry to England* (London: Ward and Company, 1844).

Prichard, J. C., *The Natural History of Man* (London: Bailiere, 1843).

Risley, H. H., and E. A. Gait, *Census of India: 1901,* vol. 1 (Calcutta: Government Press, 1903).

Rowe, R., *Life in the London Streets* (1881), available at http://www.victorianlondon.org/publications/lifein.htm

Roy, S., 'Customs and Customary Law in British India' *Tagore Law Lectures* (Calcutta: Sacred Books, 1908).

Sala, G. A., *Gaslight and Daylight with Some London Scenes they Shine Upon* (London: Chatto and Windus, 1872).

Salter, J., *The Asiatics in England* (London: Seeley, Jackson and Halliday, 1872).

—, *The East is West: Work among the Asiatics and Africans in London* (London: Patridge, 1886).

Select Committee on the Police, *Report From the Select Committee on the Police of the Metropolis* Parliamentary Papers, (600) vol. XXII. (1834).

Sherring, M., *The History of Protestant Mission in India* (London: Smith, Elder and Company, 1881).

Sleeman, J., *Thug, or a Million Murders* (London: Marston and Company, 1920).

Sleeman, W. H., *The Thugs and the Phansigars of India* (Delhi: Deep and Deep 1839).

Strachey, S., *The Imperial Gazetteer of India: The Indian Empire* (London: n.p. 1903).

The Amritsar Massacre, 1919 (London: Stationery Office, 1920).

Thornton, E., *Thugs: Illustrations of their History and Practice of the Thugs* (London: n.p. 1837).

Thurston, E., *The Castes and Tribes of Southern India* (Madras: Government Office, 1907).

Vivian, V. P. T., *A Handbook of the Criminal Tribes of the Punjab* (Lahore: Punjab Government Press, 1912).

Secondary Sources

Ackroyd, P., *London: The Biography* (Chatto and Windus: London. 2000).

Alavi, S., *The Sepoy and the Raj: Tradition and Transition in Northern India 1770–1830* (Oxford: Oxford University: Oxford, 1997).

Alborn, T. L., 'Age and Empire in the Indian Census 1871–1931', *Journal of Interdisciplinary History* 30:1, (1999), pp. 61–89.

Ali, A., *The Mews of Mewat* (Delhi: Oxford University Press, 1970).

Althusser, L., *Politics and History* (London: New Left Books, 1972).

Amin, S. *Event, Metaphor, Memory: Chauri Chaura, 1922–1992* (California: California University Press, 1995).

Anderson, D. and D. Killingray (eds), *Policing the Empire: Government, Authority and Control, 1830–1940* (Manchester: Manchester University Press, 1991).

Arnold, D., *Police, Power and Colonial Rule: Madras, 1859–1947* (Delhi: Oxford University Press, 1986).

—, 'Police Powers and the Demise of British Rule in India, 1930–1947', in D. Anderson. and D. Killingray (eds), *Policing and the Decolonisation: Nationalism, Politics and the Police 1817–1965',* (Manchester University Press: Manchester, 1992).

Ashworth, A., *The Criminal Process: An Evaluative Process* (Oxford: Oxford University Press, 1994).

Augstein, H. F., 'Clio Medica: The Wellcome Series in the History of Medicine: James Cowles Prichard and Apos', *Anthropology*, 48, (1993), pp. 57–104.

Bailey, V., 'The Fabrication of Deviance: Dangerous Classes and 'Criminal Classes' in Victorian England', J. Rule and R. Malcomson *Protest and Survival: the Historical Explanation Essays for E. P. Thompson,* (London: Merlin Press, 1993).

Balachandran, G., 'South Asian Seafarers and their World's 1870–1930', in J. Bentley et al., *Seascapes: Maritime Histories, Local Cultures, and Trans Oceanic Exchanges* (Hawaii: University of Hawaii Press, 2007).

Balbus, I., *The Dialectics of Legal Repression* (New York: Transaction Books, 1977).

Baldwin, J., and McConville, M., *Courts, Prosecution and Conviction* (London: Routledge, 1981).

—, *Negotiated Justice,* (Oxford: Martin Robertson, 1977).

Ballhatchet, K., *Race, Sex and Class Under the Raj* (London: Weidenfeld and Nicolson, 1980).

Banerjee, T., *Background to Indian Criminal Law* (Calcutta: Calcutta University Press, 1963).

Bartrip, P. W. J., 'Public Opinion and the "Ticket of Leave" Scare' in Bailey, V. (ed.) *Police and Punishment in Nineteenth Century England* (London: Routledge, 1991).

Baxi, U., 'The Laws Emissary: the Place of Law in Subaltern Studies', *Journal of Subaltern Studies,* 7, (1993), pp. 247–64.

—, *Law and Poverty: Critical Essays* (Bombay: Tripathi Press, 1988).

Bayley, C. A., (ed.) *The Raj: India and the British, 1600–1947,* (London: National Portrait Gallery, 1991).

—, *Imperial Meridian: The British Empire and the World 1780–1830* (London: Longman, 1987).

Beattie, J. M., *Crime and the Courts in England: 1660–1800* (Oxford: Clarendon Press, 1986).

Beccaria, C., *Of Crimes and Punishments* (New York: John Wiley, 1963), available from *http://www.constitution.org/cb/crim_pun.htm.*

Beck, U., *Risk Society* (London: Sage, 1992).

Becker, H., *Outsiders: Studies in the Sociology of Deviance* (New York: Free Press, 1964).

—, *The Other Side: Perspectives on Deviance* (New York: Free Press, 1964).

Bentham, J., Of the Influence of Time and Place in Matters of Legislation (1843), available from *http://www.la.utexas.edu/research/poltheory/bentham/timeplace/index.html.*

—, *An Introduction to the Principles of Morals and Legislation* (1789; Oxford: Blackwell Press, 1948).

—, *Of Laws in General* (London: Athlone Press, 1970).

—, 'The Panopticon: or, the Inspection House (1787)' in M. Bozovic (ed.), *The Panopticon Writings* (London: Verso, 1995), available from *http://cartome.org/panopticon2.htm*

Bennett, P., 'The Negro Never Knew: Emily Dickinson and Racial Typology in the Nineteenth Century', *Legacy* 19:1 (2002), pp. 53–61.

Bhabha, H., *The Location of Culture* (London: Routledge, 1994).

—, *Habitations of Modernity: Essays in the Wake of Subaltern Studies* (Chicago, IL: University of Chicago Press, 2002),

Bhagat, R. B., 'Census and the Construction of Communalism in India', *Economic and Political Weekly* (24 November 2001).

Bhukya, B., 'Dacoity and the Creation of a Surveillance Society in Hyderabad state', *Indian Economic & Social History Review*, 44: 2 (2007), pp. 179–212.

Blumenbach, J. F., *The Anthropological Treatises of Johann Friedrick Blumenbach* (London Anthropological Society, 1865).

Brogden, M., *The Police, Autonomy and Consent* (London: Academic Press, 1982).

—, 'An Act to Colonise the Internal Lands of the Island: Empire and the Origins of Professional Police', *International Journal of Sociology and Law*, 15 (1987), pp. 179–208.

—, M, Jefferson, T. and Walklate, S. *Introducing Policework* (London: Unwin Hyman, 1988).

—, and Nijhar, P., *Community Policing: International Approaches and Models* (Cullompton: Willan Publishing, 2005).

Brown, M., 'Crime, Governance and the Company Raj: The Discovery of Thuggee', *The British Journal of Criminology*, 42 (2002), pp. 77–95.

Burton, A. (ed.), *After the Imperial Turn* (Durham, NC: Duke University Press, 2003).

Cain, M., 'Trends in the Sociology of Police Work' *International Journal of the Sociology of Law*, 7 (1979), pp. 143–67.

Callender, A., *How Shall We Govern India: A Controversy among British Administrators, 1800–1882* (London: Gowland Publishing, 1987).

Cannadine, D., *Ornamentalism: How the British Saw Their Empire* (Harmondsworth: Penguin, 2001).

Carson, P., 'An Imperial Dilemma: The Propogation of Christianity in Early Colonial India', *Journal of Imperial and Commonwealth History,* 18: 2 (1990), pp. 169–90.

Chakrabarty, D., *Rethinking Working Class History: Bengal 1890–1940* (Delhi: Oxford University Press, 1989).

—, 'Modernity and Ethnicity in India', in D. Bennet (ed.) *Multicultural States: Rethinking Difference and Identity* (London: Routledge, 1998), pp. 91–100.

Chandavarkar, R., 'The Making of the Working Class: E. P. Thompson and Indian History and Related Essays', in V. Chatruvedi (ed.) *Mapping Subaltern Studies and the Postcolonial (*London: Verso, 1999).

Charlesworth, L., 'Why is it a Crime to be Poor' *Liverpool Law Review*, 21 (1999), pp. 149–67.

Chatterjee, I. and R. M. Eaton, *Slavery and South Asian History* (Bloomington, IN: Indiana University Press, 2006).

Cloward, R and Piven, F., *Regulating the Poor: The Functions of Public Welfare* (London: Tavistock, 1972).

Cohn, B., 'Notes on the Study of Indian Society and Culture' in N. Singer and B. Cohn (eds), *Structure and Change in Indian Society* (Chicago, IL: Chicago University Press, 1968), pp. 1–20.

—, 'The Language of Command and the Command of Language', *Subaltern Studies*, 111 (1985), pp. 276–329.

Cole, S., A., *Suspect Identities: A History of Fingerprinting and Criminal Identification* (Harvard, MA: Harvard University Press, 2001).

Cook, S. B., *Imperial Affinities: Nineteenth Century Analogies and Exchanges Between India and Ireland* (New Delhi: Sage, 1992).

Cooper, F. and A. L. Stoler, *Tensions of Empire: Colonial Cultures in a Bourgeois World* (Berkeley, CA: University of California Press, 1997).

Coser, L., *The Functions of Social Conflict* (Glencoe: Free Press, 1956).

Crush, J., 'The Global Raiders: Nationalism, Globalisation and the South African Brain Drain', *Journal of International Affairs*, 56 (2002), pp. 147–72.

Curtis, L. P., *Anglo Saxons and Celts: A Study of the Anti-Irish Prejudice in Victorian England* (Bridgeport, NY: New York Press, 1968).

Darby, P., *The Three Faces of Imperialism* (New Haven, CT: Yale University Press, 1987)

Das, S. K., *Sahibs and Munshis* (Delhi: Oxford University Press, 1978).

Dash, M., *Thug: True Story of India's Murderous Cult* (London: Granta, 2005).

Davies, D., *Classes and Police in Manchester 1829–1880* (London: Routledge, 1990)

Davis, J., 'The London Garrotting Panic of 1862: A Moral Panic and the Creation of a Criminal Class in Mid Victorian London' in V. A. C. Gatrell, B. Lenman and G. Parker (eds) *Crime and the Law: The Social History of Crime in Western Europe Since 1500* (London: Europe, 1980), pp. 190–213.

—, 'From Rookeries to Community: Race, Poverty and Policing in London, 1850–1985,' *History Workshop Journal,* 27 (1991), pp. 62–79.

—, 'Race and Poverty: The Underclass and the Making of Victorian England' (Paper given at the conference on *Underworld, Overworld or One World*, University of Cambridge, 1996).

Davis, M., *Late Victorian Holocausts: El Nino Famines and the Making of the Third World* (London: Verso, 2001).

Dayton, R., 'Science and the European Empires', *Journal of Imperial and Commonwealth History*, 13 (1995), pp. 134–45.

Derret, J. D., *Histories of India, Pakistan and Ceylon* (London; Oxford University Press, 1961).

De Quincey. T. and R. Morrison, *On Murder* (Oxford: Oxford University Press, 2006).

Desmond, A., *Huxley: From Devil's Discipline to Evolution's High Priest* (Reading: Addison Wesley, 1997).

Devlin, P., *The Criminal Prosecution in England* (London: Routledge, 1960).

Dhavan, R., 'Motives and Opportunities: Reflecting on Legal Research in India', *Modern Law Review,* 5 (1987), pp. 105–15.

Dickens, C., *Works of Charles Dickens : 1855–1857'* (London: InfoStrategist.com: 2005).

—, *Mystery of Edwin Drood,* ed. A. J. Cox (Harmondsworth: Penguin Press, 1974).

Dirks, N. B., 'Castes of Mind' *Representations,* 37 (1992), pp. 56–78.

—, *Castes of Mind: Colonialism and the Making of Modern India* (Princeton, NJ: Princeton University Press, 2001).

—, 'Colonial and Postcolonial Histories: Comparative Reflections on the Legacies of Empire', *Global background for the Human Development Report, Building Inclusive Societies* (United Nations: 2004).

Doyle, A. C., *The Adventures of Sherlock Holmes* (Wordsworth Editions, 2001).

Dumont, L., *Homo Hierarchicus: The Caste System and Its Implications* (Delhi: Vikas, 1970).

Durkheim, E., *The Rules of Sociological Method* (New York: Free Press, 1966).

Dutta, N. K., *Origin and Development of Criminal Justice in India* (Delhi: Deep and Deep Publishing, 1994).

Edwards, C. M., *The Criminal Tribes* (London: Society for the Propogation of the Gospel 1922).

Emsley, C., *Crime and Society in England: 1750–1900* (London: Longman, 1987).

—, *Hard Men: The English and Violence since 1750* (London: Hambledon, 2005).

—, *Crime, Police, and Penal Policy: European Experiences 1750–1940* (Oxford and New York: Oxford University Press, 2007).

Erickson, K., 'Notes on the Sociology of Deviance', *Social Problems*, 9 (1962), pp. 307–14.

Erickson, R., and P. Baranek, *The Ordering of Justice: A Study of Accused Persons as Dependants in the Criminal Process* (Toronto, ON: University of Toronto Press, 1982).

Etherington, N., *Theories of Imperialism: War, Conquest and Capital* (London: Croom Helm Routledge, 1984).

Fanon, F., *Black Skin, White Masks* (London: Pluto, 1986).

Ferri, E., *The Positive School of Criminology* (Chicago, IL: Charles Kerr Press, 1917.

Fine, B., Kinsey, R., Lea, J., Picciotto, S. and Young, J. (eds.) *Capitalism and the Rule of Law* (London: Routledge, 1979).

Finn, M. C., 'The Authority of the Laws', in P. Mandler (ed.), *Liberty and Authority in Victorian Britain* (Oxford: Oxford University Press, 2006).

Fisch, J., *Cheap Lives and Dear Limbs: The British Transformation of the Bengal Criminal Law 1769–1817* (Steiner: Wiesbaden, 1983).

Fisher, M. H., *Counterflows to Colonialism: Indian Travellers and Setllers in Britain 1600–1857* (Delhi: Permanent Press, 2004).

—, 'Working Across the Seas: Indian Maritime Labourers in India, Britian, and In Between, 1600–1857', *International Review of Social History*, 51 (2006), pp. 21–46.

Fitzpatrick, P., 'Racism and the Innocence of Law', *Journal of Law and Society,* 14 (1987), pp. 119–32.

—, 'Custom as Imperialism' in J. M. Abu-Nasr, U. Spellenburg, and U. Wanitzek (eds) *Law, Society and National Identity in Africa* (Hamburg: Helmet Buske Verlag, 1990).

—, *The Mythology of Modern Law* (London: Routledge, 1992).

—, *Modernism and The Grounds of Law* (Cambridge: Cambridge University Press, 2001).

Fitzpatrick, P. and E. Darian-Smith, 'Laws of the Postcolonial: An Insistent Introduction', E. Darian-Smith and P. Fitzpatrick (eds) *Laws of the Postcolonial* (Ann Arbor, MI: Michigan University Press, 1999).

Foucault, M., *Discipline and Punish: the Birth of the Prison* (London: Penguin, 1978).

—, 'Governmentality', *Ideology and Consciousness*, 6 (1986), pp. 521–43.

Fraser, S., *The Evolution of the Welfare System* (London: Macmillan, 1986).

Freitag, S., 'Collective Crime and Authority in North Indian' in Yang, A. (ed) *Crime and Criminality in British India (*Arizona: University of Arizona Press, 1985).

—, 'Crime in the Social Order of Colonial North India' *Modern Asian Studies,* 25 (1991), pp. 227–61.

Fryer, P., *Black People in the British Empire* (London: Pluto Press, 1989).

Fuller, C. J. (ed.) *Caste Today* (Delhi: Oxford University Press, 1996).

Gainer, B., *The Alien Invasion: The Origins of the Aliens Act 1905* (London: Heinemann, 1972).

Galanter, M., *Competing Equalities: Law and the Backward Classes in India* (Oxford: Oxford University Press, 1984).

Gandhi, B. M., *Landmarks in Indian Legal and Constitutional History* (Lucknow: Eastern Book Company, 1998).

Gandhi, L., *Postcolonial Theory: A Critical Introduction* (Edinburgh: Edinburgh University Press, 1998).

Garfinkel, H., 'Conditions of Successful Degradation Ceremonies', *American Journal of Sociology*, 61 (1956), pp. 420–44.

Garland, D., *Punishment and Welfare: A History of Penal Strategies* (Aldershot: Gower, 1985).

—, *Punishment and Modern Society* (Oxford: Oxford University Press, 1991).

Gatrell, V. A.C. (ed.), *The Decline of Theft and Violence* (London: Routledge, 1980).

—, 'Crime, Authority and the Policeman's State', in F. M. L. Thompson (ed.), *The Cambridge Social History of England 1750–1950* (Cambridge: Cambridge University Press, 1990).

—, *The Hanging Tree: Execution and the English People 1770–1868* (Oxford: Oxford University Press, 1994).

—, Radzinowicz, L. and Hood, R., *The Emergence of Penal Policy in Victorian and Edwardian England* (Oxford: Clarendon Press, 1990).

—, Lenman, B., Parker, G. (eds) 'The Decline of Theft and Violence in Victorian and Edwardian England' *Crime and the Law: The Social History of Crime in Western Europe since 1500* (London: Europa, 1980).

George, D., *London Life in the Eighteenth Century* (Harmondsworth: Penguin, 1966)

Gilman, S., *Difference and Pathology: Stereotypes of Sexuality, Race and Madness* (New York: Cornell University Press, 1985).

Gilmour, I., *Riot, Rising and Revolution* (London: Pimlico Press, 1992).

—, *The Ruling Caste: Imperial Lives in the Victorian Raj* (Farrar Straus Giroux, 2006).

Gilroy, P., *The Black Atlantic: Modernity and Double Consciousness* (London: Verso Press, 1993).

Gilling, D., *Crime Prevention: Theory, Policy and Politics* (London: Routledge, 1997).

Ginzburg, C., *Clues, Myths and the Historical Method* (Baltimore, MD: John Hopkins Press, 1989).

Goffman, E., *Asylums* (Harmondsworth: Penguin, 1968).

Goldberg, D., *Racist Culture: Philosophy and the Politics of Meaning* (London: Blackwell, 1993).

Gordon, S. N., 'Scarf and Sword: Thugs, Marauders and State Formation in Eighteenth Century Malwa', *Indian Economic and Social History Review*, 4 (1969), pp. 403–29.

Grant, C., 'Observations on the State of Society Among the Asiatic Subjects of Great Britain Particularly with Respect to Morals', in M. Moir and L. Zastoupil (eds), *The Great Indian Education Debate: Documents Relating to the Orientalist Anglicist Controversy, 1781–1843* (London: Curzon Press, 1999).

Graves, J. L., *The Emperor's New Clothes: Biological Theories of Race at the Millennium* (New Brunswick, NJ: Rutgers University Press, 2001).

Guha, R., 'On Some Aspects of the Historiography of Colonial India' in Spivak, G. and Guha, R. *Selected Subaltern Studies* (New York: Oxford University Press, 1982).

—, Elementary Aspects of Peasant Insurgency in Colonial India (Oxford: Oxford University Press, 1983).

—, *'Chandra's Death' Subaltern Studies V: Writings on South Asian History and Society* (Delhi: Oxford University Press, 1987).

—, *An Indian Historiography of India: A Nineteenth Century Agenda and its Implications* (Calcutta: Mittal, 1988).

—, *The Police in British India 1861–1947* (New Delhi: Concept Publishing, 1979).

Gupta, A., *The Police in British India: 1861–1947* (New Delhi: Concept Publishing, 1979).

Gusfield, J., *Symbolic Crusade* (Illinios: University of Illinois Press, 1969).

Hardiman, D., 'Usury, Dearth and Famine in Western India', *Past and Present,* 13 (1996), pp. 113–56.

Hardt, M. and Negri, A., *Empire* (Cambridge: Cambridge University Press, 2000).

Harrison, B., *Drink and Victorians* (Oxford: Oxford University Press, 1971).

Harris, B., and W. Ernst (eds), *Race, Science and Medicine: 1700–1960* (London: Routledge, 1999).

Hay, D., 'Property, Authority and the Criminal Law', in D. Hay, P. Linebaugh, J. Rule, E. P. Thompson and C. Winslow (eds) *Albion's Fatal Tree: Crime and Society in Eighteenth Century England* (London: Allen Press, 1975).

—, 'War, Dearth and Theft in the Eighteenth Century: The Record of the English Courts' *Past and Present*, 95 (1982), pp. 117–60.

—, 'Prosecution and Power: Malicious Prosecution in English courts 1750–1850' in Hay, D. and Snyder, J. (eds.) *Policing and Prosecution in England: 1750–1850* (Oxford: Oxford University Press, 1989).

Hay, D., Linebaugh, P., Rule, J., Thompson, E.P. (eds) *Albion's Fatal Tree: Crime and Society in Nineteenth Century England* (London: Allen Press, 1975).

Hennock, E. P., 'The Measurement of Urban Poverty', *Economic History Review*, 40 (1987), pp. 208–27.

Himmelfarb, G., *The Idea of Poverty* (London: Faber and Faber, 1984).

Hobsbawm, E. J., 'Social Criminality' *Bulletin of the Society for the Study of Labour History,* 25 (1972), pp. 56–9.

—, *Primitive Rebels* (Manchester: Manchester University Press, 1974).

— and G. Rude, *Captain Swing* (London: Penguin, 1973).

—, *The Age of Empire: 1875–1914* (London: Vintage, 1989).

Hobson, K., 'Ethnographic Mapping and the Construction of the British Census in India' in the *Indian Caste System and the British*', available from *www.btinternet.com~britishempire/article/castesystem*.

Hoffemister, J. and F. Hamburg, 'G. W. F. Hegel', *Hegel's Einleitung in die Geschichte der Philosophie* (Hamburg: Felix Meiner, 1959).

Holdaway, S., *The British Police* (London: Routledge, 1979).

Holmes, C., *John Bulls Island: Immigration and the British Society: 1871–1971* (London: Routledge, 1988).

Howe, L., 'The Deserving and the Undeserving', *Journal of Social Policy*, 14 (1985), pp. 49–72.

Hughes, R., *The Fatal Shore* (New York: Knopf, 1987).

Hunt, R., and Harrison, J., *The District Officer in India: 1930–1947* (London: Scholar Press, 1980).

Huttenback, R. A., 'No Strangers within the Gates: Attitudes and Policies Towards the NonWhite Residents of the British Empire of Settlement', *Journal of Imperial and Commonwealth History*, 1 (1973), pp. 271–302.

Hyam, R., *Empire and Sexuality: the British Experience* (Manchester: Manchester University Press, 1990).

Ignatieff, M., *A Just Measure of Pain: The Penitentiary in the Industrial Revolution: 1750–1850* (New York: New York Press, 1978).

Inden, R., 'Orientalist Constructions of India', *Modern Asian Studies*, 20 (1986), pp. 436–65.

—, *Imagining India* (Oxford: Blackwell, 1990).

Innes, J. and J. Styles, 'The Crime Wave: Recent Writing on Crime and Criminal Justice in Eighteenth Century England', *Journal of British Studies*, 25 (1986), pp. 380–435.

—, 'The Crime Wave: Recent Writings on Crime and Criminal Justice in Eighteenth Century England' in Wilson A. (ed) *Rethinking Social History: English Society 1570–1920* (Manchester: Manchester University Press, 1993).

Jackson, L. A., 'The Medical Origins of Criminology', *MetaScience* 16:2 (2007), pp. 281–84.

Jan Mohamed, A. R., *Manichean Aesthetics: the Politics of Literature in Colonial Africa* (Amherst, MA: Massachusetts University Press, 1983).

Jassal, S. T., 'Caste and the Colonial State: Mallahs in the Census' in *Contributions to Indian Sociology*, 35 (2001), pp. 319–54.

Jefferson, T., *Interpretating Policework* (London: Unwin Hyman, 1987).

Jenkinson, J., 'The Glasgow Racial Disturbances of 1919', Lunn, K. (ed) *Race and Labour in Twentieth Century England* (London: Routledge, 1985).

John, M., *The Deceivers* (New York: Carroll and Graf, 1988).

Jones, I., *Immigration and Social Policy in England* (London: Sage, 1977).

Jones-Steadman, G., *Outcast London: A Study in the Relationship between Classes in Victorian Society* (Harmondsworth: Penguin, 1984).

Joseph, G. G., *George Joseph: The Life and Times of a Kerala Christian Nationalist* (Delhi: Orient Longman, 2003).

Kasturi, M., 'Law and Crime in India: British Policy and the Female Infanticide Act of 1870', *The Indian Journal of Gender Studies*, 1 (1994), pp. 169–94.

Keith, M., 'From Punishment to Discipline: Racism, Racialisation and Policing of Social Control' in Cross, M. and Keith, M. (eds.) *Racism, The City and the State* (London: Routledge, 1993).

King, P. J. R., 'Decision Makers and Decision Making in English Criminal Law: 1750–1800' *Historical Journal,* 27 (1984), pp. 27–41.

Kirkby, D. E. and Coleborne, C., *Law, History and Colonialism* (Manchester: Manchester University Press, 2001).

Kitsuse, J., 'Social Reactions to Deviant Behaviour: Problems of Theory and Method', *Social Problems,* 7 (1962), pp. 112–25.

Kuklick, H., *The Savage Within: The Social History of British Anthropology 1885–1945* (Cambridge: Cambridge University Press, 1991).

Lal, V., *Criminality and Colonial Anthropology* Introduction to the reprint edition (Gurgaon, Haryana: Vintage Press, 1995).

Land, I., 'Cutoms of the Sea: Flogging, Empire and the "True British Seamen", 1770–1870', *Interventions: the Journal of Postcolonial Studies,* 3:2 (2001), pp. 169–85.

Langbein, J., 'Albion's fatal flaws' *Past and Present,* 98 (1983), pp. 96–120.

Laplanche, J. and J. Pontalis, *The Language of Psychoanalysis* (London: Karnac Books, 1988).

Lavriere, R., 'Justice and Panditas: Some Ironies in Contemporary Readings of the Hindu Legal Past', *Journal of Asian Studies,* 48 (1989), pp. 757–69.

Law, I. and Henfry, J., *A History of Race and Racism in Liverpool 1650–1950* (Liverpool: MCRC, 1981).

Le Mercier Du Quesney, F., *The Longs of 'Longville'* 1964, August 25, 2006, http://jamaicafamilysearch.com/samples/freed2.htm..

Lea, J. A., 'Some Structural Aspects of Police Deviance' in C. Shearing (ed.), *Organizational Aspects of Police Deviance* (Toronto, ON: Butterworths, 1981).

Lea, J. and Young, J., *What Is To Be Done About Law and Order* (London: Pluto Press, 1984).

Lemert, E., *Social Pathology* (New York: McGraw Hill, 1951).

—, *Human Deviance: Social Problems, and Social Control* (Englewood Cliffs, NJ: Prentice Hall, 1972).

Leng, R., R. Taylor and M. Wasik, *Crime and Disorder Act 1998* (London: Blackstone Press, 1998).

Leopold, J., 'The Aryan Race Theory in India', *Indian Economic and Social History,* 7 (1970), pp. 271–97.

Leps, M., *Apprehending the Criminal* (London: Routledge, 1994).

Lindeborg, R. H., 'The Asiatics and the Boundaries of Victorian Englishness', *Journal of Victorian Studies,* 3 (1994), pp. 381–404.

Linebaugh, P., 'The Tyburn Riots Against the Surgeons' in Hay, D., P. Linebaugh, J. Rule and E. P. Thompson (eds) *Albion's Fatal Tree: Crime and Society in Nineteenth Century England* (London: Allen Press, 1975).

—, 'Karl Marx: the Theft of Wood and Working Class Composition', *Crime and Social Justice,* 7 (Autumn–Winter 1976).

—, *The London Hanged: Crime and Civil Society in the Eighteenth Century* (London: Allen Unwin, 1991).

—, and Rediker, M., *The Many Headed Hydra: The Hidden History of the Revolutionary Atlantic* (London: Verso, 2000).

Llewellyn, J. R., *A Fatal Friendship: the Nawabs, the British and the City of Lucknow* (Oxford: Oxford University Press, 1992).

Lombroso, C., *The Criminal Man* (New York: Putnam, 1911).

Lombroso, C. and Ferrero, G., *Criminal Man According to the Classification of Cesare Lombroso (*Montclair: Patterson Smith, 1972).

London, J., *The People of the Abyss* (1903; Chicago, IL: Chicago Review Press, 1995).

Long, E., *The History of Jamaica: Reflections on its Situations, Settlements and Inhabitants, Laws and Government* (Montreal, QC: Queen University Press, 2003).

Longmate, N., *The Workhouse Temple* (London: South Press, 1974).

Maguire, M., Morgan, R., Reiner, R. (eds.) *The Oxford Handbook on Criminology* (Oxford: Oxford University Press, 1997).

Mahmud, T., 'Colonialism and Modern Constructions', *University of Miami Law Review* 23 (1999), pp. 1219–96.

Majeed, J., *Ungoverned Imaginings: James Mill and the History of British India and Orientalism* (Oxford: Clarendon, 1992).

Major, A., 'State and Criminal Tribes in Colonial Punjab: Surveillance, Control and Reclamation of the 'Dangerous Classes', *Modern Asian Studies*, 33 (1999), pp. 657–88.

Malik, K., *The Meaning of Race: Race, History and Culture in Western Society* (Basingstoke: Palgrave Press, 1996).

Mani, L., 'Contentious Traditions: The Debate on Sati in Colonial India' in *Cultural Critique,* 23 (1987), pp. 25–45.

Mannheim, H., *Comparative Criminology* (Boston, MA: Houghton, 1965).

G. Mariscal, 'The Role of Spain in Contemporary Race Theory', *Arizona Journal of Hispanic Cultural Studies,* 2 (1998), pp. 7–22.

Marriott, J., *The Other Empire: Metropolis, India and Progress in the Colonial Imagination* (Manchester: Manchester University Press, 2003).

—, and M. Matsmurra, *The Metropolitan Poor,* 6 vols (London: Pickering and Chatto, 1999).

Marshall, D., *English People in the Eighteenth Century* (London: Longmans, 1956).

Marshall, P. J., *The Making and the Unmaking of Empires: Britain, India and America, 1750–1783* (Oxford: Oxford University Press, 2005).

Marshall, T., *The New Racism* (London: Routledge, 1981).

Marx, K., *Critique of the Gotha Programme* (Peking: Foreign Languages Press, 1972).

Masters, J., *The Deceivers* (New York: Carroll and Graf, 1988).

Mathur, L., *Kala-Pani: History of the Andaman and Nicobar Islands with a Study of India's Freedom Struggle* (Delhi: Eastern Books, 1987).

Matza, D., *Becoming Deviant* (London: Prentice Hall, 1969).

Maunder, A. and Moore, G., *Victorian Crime, Madness and Sensation* (Aldershot: Ashgate, 2004).

May, R. and Cohen, R., 'The Interaction between Race and Colonialism: a Case Study of the Liverpool Riots of 1919', *Race and Class,* XV1 (1974), pp. 34–56.

McBarnet, D., 'Arrest: The Legal Context of Policing' in S. Holdaway (ed), *The British Police* (London: Routledge, 1979), pp. 24–40.

—, *Conviction* (London: Routledge, 1981).

McConville, M. and Baldwin, J., *Negotiated Justice* (Oxford: Martin Robertson, 1977).

—, *Courts, Prosecution and Conviction* (Oxford: Clarendon, 1981).

—, 'Sentencing Problems Raised by Guilty Pleas: An Analysis of Negotiated Pleas in the Birmingham Crown Court', *Modern Law Review*, 41 (1978), pp. 544–58.

McConville, M., Sanders, A. and Leng, R., *The Case for the Prosecution* (London: Routledge, 1991).

McConville, S., *A History of Prison Administration 1750–1877* (London: Routledge, 1981).

McLaughlin, E and Muncie, E., *Controlling Crime* (Milton Keynes: Open University Press, 1996).

H. Melville., *Redburn: His First Voyage* (London: Penguin, 1976).

Mendelsohn, O., 'The Pathology of the Indian Legal System', *Modern Asian Studies*, 15 (1981), pp. 822–63.

Merton, R., *Social Theory and Social Structure* (New York; Free Press, 1968).

Merry, S. E. 'Law and Colonialism', *Law and Society Review*, 25: 4 (1991), pp. 890–917.

Metcalf, T. R., *Imperial Connections: India in the Indian Ocean, 1860–1920* (London: University of California Press, 2007).

Mill, J. S., *Madness, Cannabis, and Colonialism* (New York: St Martins Press, 2000).

Miller, W., *Cops Bobbies: Police Authority in New York and London 1830–1870* (Ohio: Ohio University Press, 1999).

Moir, M. and Zastoupil, L. (eds.) *The Great Indian Education Debate: Documents Relating to the OrientalistAnglicist Controversy 1781–1843* (London: Curzon Press, 1999).

Moir, M., Peers, D. and Zastoupil, L., *J. S. Mill's Encounter with India* (Toronto: University of Toronto Press, 1999).

Moore, S. F., 'Treating Law as Knowledge: Telling Colonial Officers What to Say to Africans About Running Their Own Native Courts', *Law and Society Review*, 26 (1992), pp. 115–27.

Morris, L., *The Dangerous Classes* (London: Routledge, 1994).

Morris, M., 'Metamorphoses', *New Formations,* 10 (1990), pp. 110–23.

Morrison, W., *Theoretical Criminology: From Modernity to PostModernism* (London: Cavendish, 1995).

Mukhopadhyay, A., *Behind the Mask: The Cultural Definitions of the Legal Subject in Colonial Bengal 1715–1911* (Oxford: Oxford University Press, 2004).

Mukerjee, S. N., *Sir William Jones: A Study in the Eighteenth Century Attitudes to India* (Cambridge: Cambridge University Press, 1968).

Mukherjee, R., 'Satan Let Loose Upon Earth: the Kanpur Massacres in India in the Revolt of 1857', *Past and Present*, 128 (1990), pp. 92–117.

Mullens, J., *Revised Statistics of Missions in India and Ceylon complied at the Request of the Calcutta Missionary Conference* (Calcutta: Baptist Mission Press, 1852).

Myers, N., *Reconstructing the Black Past: Black in Britain 1780–1830* (Abingdon: Routledge, 2004).

Nandy, A., *An Intimate Enemy: Loss and Recovery of Self under Colonialism* (Delhi: Pluto, 1988).

Neal, E., *Sectarian Violence: The Liverpool Experience 1819–1914* (Manchester: Manchester University Press, 1988).

Nigam, S., 'Disciplining and Policing the "Criminals by Birth": The Making of a Colonial Stereotype' *The Indian Economic and Social History Review*, 27 (1990), pp. 131–64.

—, 'Disciplining and Policing the 'Criminals by Birth: the Development of a Disciplinary System, 1871–1900', *The Indian Economic and Social History Review*, 27 (1990), pp. 257–87.

Oday, A., 'Varieties of Anti-Irish Behaviour, 1845–1922' Panayi, P. (ed) *Racial Violence in England in the Nineteenth and Twentieth Centuries* (Leicester: Leicester University Press, 1996).

Oddie, G., *Popular Religion, Elites and Reform: Hookswinging and Its Prohibition in Colonial India, 1800–1894* (Delhi: Manohar, 1995).

Oppenheim, J., *Shattered Nerves: Doctors, Patients, and Depression in Victorian England* (Oxford: Oxford University Press, 1991).

Orme, R., 'Of the Laws and Justice of Indostan', *The Historical Fragments of the Mogul Empire* (New York: Associated Publishing House, 1974).

Panayi, P., *Racial Violence in England: 1840–1950* (Leicester: Leicester University Press, 1993).

—, *Immigration, Ethnicity and Racism in England: 1815–1945* (Manchester: Manchester University Press, 1994).

Pashukanis, E., *Law and Marxism: A General Theory* (London: Villiers Publishing, 1978).

—, 'The General Theory of Law and Marxism' Beirne, P. and Sharlet, R. (eds.) *Pashukanis: Selected Writings on Marxism and Law* (New York: Academic Press, 1980).

Patra, A. C., 'An Historical Introduction to the Indian Penal Code' *Journal of the Indian Law Institute*, 3 (1961), pp. 120–43.

Patrick, C. H., 'The Criminal Tribes of India With Special Emphasis on the Mang Garudi: A Preliminary Report', *Man In India*, 48 (1968), pp. 244–57.

Pavlich, G., *The Accusations of Criminal Identity* (2006), http://www.mcgill.ca/files/legal-theory-workshop/Pavlich-Accusations-Criminal-Identity.pdf

Peabody, N., 'Cents, Sense, Census: Human Inventories in late Precolonial and Early Colonial India', *Comparative Studies in Society and History*, 43:4 (2000), pp. 819–50.

Pels, P. 'The Rise and fall of the Indian Abrogines: Orientalism, Anglicism and the Emergence of the Ethnology of India, 1833–1869', in P. Pels and O. Salemick (eds), *Colonial Subjects: Essays on the Practical History of Anthropology* (Ann Arbor, MI: Michighan University Press, 2000).

Perkin, H., *The Origins of Modern British Society: 1780–1880* (London: Routledge, 1969).

Petrow, S., *Policing Morals: The Metropolitan Police and the Home Office 1870–1914* (London: Clarendon Press, 1994).

Petrunik, M. W., *Models of Dangerousness* (Ottawa: University of Ottawa, 1994).

Phillips, D., 'A New Engine of Power and Authority: the Institutions of Law Enforcement in England, 1780–1830' V. A. C. Gatrell, *Crime and the Law: The Social History of Crime in Western Europe since 1500* (London: Routledge, 1980).

Phillips, W., 'The Wild Tribes of London' Marriot J. and Matsumara, M. *The Metropolitan Poor: Semifactual Accounts 1795–1910* (London: Pickering and Chatto, 1999).

Phillips, D. and D. Storch, 'Whigs and Coopers: the Grey Ministry's National Police Scheme, 1832' *Historical Research*, 67 (1994), pp. 75–99.

Phillipson, C., *The Three Criminal Law Reformers: Beccaria, Bentham and Romilly* (Jersey, 1972).

Pinney, C., 'Colonial Anthropology in the "Laboratory of Mankind', C. A. Bayley (ed.) *The Raj: India and the British, 1600–1947* (London: National Portrait Gallery, 1991).

Piven, F. and Cloward, R., *Regulating the Poor: The Functions of Public Welfare* (London: Tavistock, 1972).

Prashad, V., 'Native Dirt/Imperial Ordure: The Cholera of 1832 and the Morbid Resolutions of Modernity' *Journal of Historical Sociology*, 7 (1994), pp. 243–60.

Pratt, J., *Governing the Dangerous: Dangerousness, Law and Social Change* (Sydney: The Federation Press, 1997).

Purohit, S. K., *Ancient Indian Legal Philosophy: Its Relevance to Contemporary Jurisprudential Thought* (New Delhi: Deep and Deep Publications, 1994).

Quigley, D., *The Interpretation of Caste* (Oxford: Clarendon Press, 1993).

Quinney, R., *The Social Reality of Crime* (Boston, MA: Little Brown and Company, 1970).

—, *Critique of Legal Order: Crime Control in Capitalist Society* (Boston, MA: Little Brown and Company, 1973).

Radhakrishna, M., 'Surveillance and Settlements under the Criminal Tribes Act in Madras' *The Indian Economic and Social History Review*, 29 (1992), pp. 171–98.

—, 'Colonial Construction of a criminal tribe', *Economic and Political Weekly* (8–15 July 2000), p. 25–53

—, 'Dishonoured by History', *Hindu* (16 July 2000). Available from http://www.hinduonnet.com/folio/fo0007/00070240.htm

Radhakrishnan, R., 'Ethnicity in an Age of Transition' *Transition*, 54 (1991), pp. 103–10.

Radzinowicz, L., 'A History of Criminal Law and Administration from 1750', in J. S. Cockburn (ed.), *Crime in England 1550–1800* (Manchester: Manchester University Press, 1977).

—, and Hood, R., *The Emergence of Penal Policy in Victorian and Edwardian England* (Oxford: Clarendon Press, 1990).

Raghavan, V., *Problems of Criminal Tribes* (Delhi: Mittal Publishing Press, 1949).

Raheja, G., 'India: Caste, Kinship, and Dominance Reconsidered', *Annual Review of Anthropological Studies*, 17 (1988), pp. 497–522.

—, 'The Illusion of Consent: Language, Caste and Colonial Rule in India' in Pels, P., and Salemink, O. (eds.) *Colonial Subjects: Essays on the Practical History of Anthropology* (Michigan: University of Michigan Press, 1999).

Rajan, R. S., 'Representing Sati: Continuities and Discontinuities', in Goodwin, S. and Bronfen, E. (eds) *Death and Representation* (Baltimore, MD: Johns Hopkins, 1993).

Rajula, S., *Essays on the Indian Penal Code* (New Delhi: Vikas, 1962).

Raman, K. K., 'Utilitarianism and the Criminal Law in Colonial India: A Study of the Practical Limits of Utilitarian Jurisprudence', *Modern Asian Studies*, 20 (1994), pp. 739–91.

Rankin, G. G., 'The Indian Penal Code', *Law Quarterly Review*, 60 (1944), pp. 37–50.

Reiner, R., *The Politics of the Police* (Brighton: Wheatsheaf, 1985).

—, *The Politics of the Police* (Oxford: Oxford University Press, 1989).

Robert, D., 'How Cruel was the Victorian Poor Law', *Journal of Historical Journal*, 6 (1963), pp. 97–107.

Roberts, J. D., 'Public and Private in Early Nineteenth Century London', *Social History*, 13 (1988), pp. 273–94.

Rock, P. and Macintosh, M. (eds.) *Deviance and Social Control* (London: Routledge, 1974).

Rowbotham, J. and K. Stevenson (eds), *Criminal Conversation: Victorian Crimes, Social Panic and Moral Outrage* (Ohio: Ohio University Press, 2005)

Roy, P., *Indian Traffic: Identities in Question in Colonial and Postcolonial India* (California: California University Press, 1996).

Rude, G., *The Crowd in History: A Study of Popular Disturbances in France and England* (New York: John Wiley, 1964).

Rudolph, L., and S. Rudolph, *The Modernity of Tradition: Political Developments in India* (Chicago, IL: University of Chicago Press, 1969).

Rushby, K., *Children of Kali: Through India in Search of Bandits, the Thug Cult and the British Raj* (India: Penguin, 2003).

Sagarin, E., *Deviance and Deviants: An Introduction to Devalued People* (New York: Praeger, 1975).

Said, E., *Orientalism* (New York: Vintage, 1979).

—, *Culture and Imperialism* (London: Chatto and Windus, 1993).

Sangar, S., *Crime and Punishment in Mughal India* (Delhi: Vikas, 1967).

Sarkar, S., 'Orientalism Revisited: Saidian Frameworks in the Writing of Modern Indian History', *Oxford Literary Review*, 16 (1994), pp. 205–24.

Saxena, A., *The Military System of India 1850–1900* (New Delhi: Oxford University Press, 1974).

—, *Law and Order in India* (Delhi: Abhinav Publishing, 1987).

Sayce, A. H. *The Races of the Old Testament* (London: Adamant Press, 2005).

Scobie, E., *Black Britannia: A History of Blacks in England* (Chicago: Chicago University Press, 1972).

Scott Clarke, S and Levy, A., 'Survivors of Our Hell' *Guardian* June 23, 2001.

Seagel, R., *The Black Diaspora* (London: Faber and Faber, 1996).

Semmel, B., *J. S. Mill and the Pursuit of Virtue* (New York: Yale University Press, 1984).

Sen, A. K., *Poverty and Famine: An Essay on Entitlement and Deprivation* (Oxford: Oxford University Press, 1981.

Sen, P., *Penology: Old and New* (Delhi: Vikas, 1972).

Sen, S., *Colonialism and Convict Society in the Andaman Islands* (Delhi: Oxford University Press, 2000).

—, 'Retribution in the Subaltern Mirror: Popular Reckoning of Justice in and Figure of the Qazi in Medieval and Precolonial Bengal', *Journal of Postcolonial Studies* 8 (2005), pp. 439–58.

Sengoopta, C., *The Imprint of the Raj: How Fingerprinting was Born in Colonial India* (Oxford: Oxford University Press, 2003).

Sengupta, S., *The Evolution of Ancient Indian Law* (New Delhi: Deep and Deep Publications, 1950).

Shashi, B. S. and P. S. Varma, *A SocioLegal History of ExCriminal Communities* (Delhi: Sundeep Prakashan, 1991).

Sharpe, J. A., *Crime in Early Modern England: 1550–1750* (London: Longman, 1984).

—, *Judicial Punishment in England* (London: Faber and Faber, 1990).

Shearing, C., *Organisational Aspects of Police Deviance* (Toronto: Butterworhs, 1981).

Shyllon, F. O., *Black People in Britian* (Oxford: Oxford University Press, 1977).

Simhadri, V. C., *Ex-Criminal Tribes of India* (Delhi: National Publishing House, 1979).

Singh, S., *The Sansis of Punjab* (Delhi: Munshiram Manoharlal, 1965).

Singha, R., 'Providential Circumstances: The Thuggee Campaign of the 1830s and Legal Innovation', *Modern Asian Studies*, 27 (1993), pp. 24–49.

—, *A Despotism of Law: Crime and Justice in Early Colonial India* (Delhi: Oxford University Press, 1998).

Skuy, D., 'Macaulay and the Indian Penal Code of 1860: The Myth of the Inherent Superiority and Modernity of the English Legal System Compared to India's legal System in the Nineteenth Century', *Modern Asian Studies*, 32 (1998), pp. 513–57.

Smith, D., *His Story* (London: Salvation Army, 2000).

Smith, J. M., 'Eugenics and Utopia' *Daedalus*, 94 (1965), pp. 487–505.

Smith, I., 'Race, Crime and Statistics' in R. Morgan, et al. (eds), *The Oxford Handbook of Criminology (*Oxford: Oxford University Press, 1997).

Spitzer, S., 'Towards a Marxian Theory of Crime' in *Social Problems*, 22 (1975), pp. 369–401.

Spivak, G. and S. Harasym, *The Post-colonial Critic: Interviews, Strategies, Dialogues*. (London: Routledge: 1990)

Sponaza, L., *Italian Immigrants in Nineteenth Century England: Realities and Images* (Leicester: Leicester University Press, 1988).

Srinivas, M. N., *Caste in Modern India and Other Essays* (Bombay: Deep and Deep Publishing, 1962).

Stevenson, S., 'The "Habitual Criminal" in Nineteenth Century England: Some Observations on the Figures' in *Urban History Yearbook*, 13 (1986), pp. 37–66.

Stokes, E., *The English Utilitarians and India* (London: Routledge, 1959).

—, *The Peasant Armed: The Indian Revolt of 1857* (Oxford: Oxford University Press, 1986).

Storch, R., 'The Plague of the Blue Locusts: Police, Reform and Popular Resistance', *International Review of Social History*, 20 (1975), pp. 61–90.

—, 'The Policeman as Domestic Missionary: Urban Discipline and Popular Culture in North England 1850–80', *Journal of Sociological History*, 9 (1976), pp. 481–509.

Styles, J., 'Problem of Criminal Investigation in Eighteenth Century England' in *Transactions of the Royal Historical Society*, 33 (1983), pp. 127–49.

Styles, J. and Innes, J., 'The Crime Wave: Recent Writing on Crime and Criminal Justice in Eighteenth century England' in *Journal of British Studies,* 25 (1986), pp. 115–34.

Suparkar, S., *Law of Procedure and Justice in Ancient India* (Bombay: Vikas, 1986).

Sutherland, E. and Cressey, D., *Criminology*, 8th edn (Philadelphia, PA: Lippincott, 1970).

Swift, R. and Gilley, S. (eds.) The *Irish in England: The Local Dimension* (Dublin: Four Courts Press, 1999).

Taylor, I. Walton, P and Young, J., *Critical Criminology* (London: Routledge, 1975)

Theodore M., *The Rise of Statistical Thinking*, 18201900. (Princeton: Princeton University Press, 1986).

—, 'Statistical and Social Facts from Quetelet to Durkheim' in *Sociological Perspectives*, 38 (1995), pp. 15–26.

Thomas, R. R. (ed.), *Dreams of Authority: Freud and the Fiction of the Unconscious* (Ithaca, NY: Cornell University Press, 1990).

Thome, S., 'The Conversion of the Englishman and the Conversion of the World Inseparable: Missionary Imperialism and the Language of Class in Early Industrial Britain', in F.

Cooper and L. Stoler, *The Tensions of Empire: Colonial Cultures in a Bourgeoise World* (California: University of California Press, 1997).

Thompson, E. P., *The Making of the English Working Class* (Harmondsworth: Penguin, 1968).

—, 'The Moral Economy of the English Crowd in the Eighteenth Century', *Past and Present,* 50 (1971), pp. 76–136.

—, *Whigs and Hunters: The Origins of the Black Act* (London: Allen Lane, 1975).

—, 'Eighteenth Century English Society: Class Struggle Without Class', *Social History*, 3 (1978), pp. 133–65.

Thompson, F. M. L. (ed.) *The Cambridge Social History of England 1750–1950* (Cambridge: Cambridge University Press, 1990).

Thornton, A. P., *Doctrines of Imperialism* (New York: Wiley and Sons, 1965).

Timmons, M., *Conduct and Character* (Oxford: Oxford University Press, 1987).

Tobias, S., *Crime and Industrial Society in the Nineteenth Century* (Oxford: Oxford University Press, 1967).

Tolen, R. J. 'Colonising and Civilising the Criminal Tribesmen: the Salvation Army in British India', *American Ethnologist*, 18:1 (1991), pp. 106–25.

—, 'Colonising and Transforming the Criminal Tribesman: The Salvation Army in British India', J. Terry and J. Urla (eds) *Deviant Bodies: Critical Perspectives on Difference in Science and Popular Culture* (Bloomington, IN: Indian University Press, 1995).

Upadhayaya, G. P., *The Origin, Scope and Mission of the Arya Samaj (*Allahabad: Allahabad University Press, 1976).

Van De Veer P., 'Ayodhya and Somnath: Eternal Shrines, Contested Histories', *Social Research*, 59:1 (Spring 1992), pp. 90–6.

Visram, R., *The Ayahs, Lascars and the Princes* (London: Pluto, 1986).

—, *Asians in England: 400 Years of History* (London: Pluto, 2002).

Viswanath, L. S., 'Efforts of Colonists to Suppress Female Infanticide: Use of Sacred Texts, Generation of Knowledge' in *Economic and Political Weekly*, 33 (1998), pp. 12–24.

Viswanathan, G., 'Contested Politics: Ethnographic Politics and the Discourse of Origins', *Stanford Electronic Humanities Review*, 5:1 (1996), available at http://www.stanford.edu/group/SHR/5-1/text/viswanathan2.html

Walkowitz, J. R., *Prostitution and Victorian London* (London: Cambridge University Press, 1980).

Ward, A., *Our Bones are Scattered: The Cawnpore Massacres and the Indian Mutiny of 1857* (New York: John Murray, 1996).

Washbrook, D., 'The Development of Caste Organisation in South India 180–1925', in C. J. Baker and D. Washbrook (eds), *South India: Political Institutions and Political Change 1880–1940* (Delhi: Macmillan, 1975), pp. 157–96.

Washbrook, D., 'Progress and Problems: South Asian Economic and Social History 1720–1860', *Modern Asian Studies*, 22. (1988), pp. 57–96.

Webb, S. B., *English Poor Law Policy* (London: Frank Cass, 1963).

Weinberger, B., 'The Police and the Public in Mid Nineteenth Century Warwickshire' Bailey, V. (ed) *Policing and Punishment in Nineteenth Century England* (London: Cross Helm, 1981).

Weiner, M., *Reconstructing the Criminal: Culture, Law and Policy* (Cambridge: Cambridge University Press, 1991).

Weisser, M., *Crime and Punishment in Early Modern Europe* (Manchester: Manchester University Press, 1979).

Wilson, A., *Rethinking Social History in English Society* (Manchester: Manchester University Press, 1993).

William, B., 'The not so Rascally Lascar' P& D no 143 (Aug 1990).

Wohl, A. S., *Racism and Anti-Irish Prejudice in Victorian England* (1990), available at http://www.victorianweb.org/history/race/Racism.html

Yadav, K., *The Revolt of 1857 in Haryana* (Delhi: Vikas, 1977).

Yang, A., *Crime and Criminality in British India* (Tucson, AZ: University of Arizona Press, 1985).

Yin, R., *Case Study Research: Design and Methods* (London: Sage, 1994).

Young, R. J., *Colonial Desire: Hybridity in Theory, Culture and Race* (London: Routledge, 1995).

Zastoupil, L., *John Stuart Mill and India* (California: Stanford University Press, 1994).

INDEX

For Product Safety Concerns and Information please contact our EU representative GPSR@taylorandfrancis.com
Taylor & Francis Verlag GmbH, Kaufingerstraße 24, 80331 München, Germany

www.ingramcontent.com/pod-product-compliance
Ingram Content Group UK Ltd.
Pitfield, Milton Keynes, MK11 3LW, UK
UKHW022130190926
475702UK00013B/1735
9781138665125